MISS D & ME

LIFE WITH THE INVINCIBLE
BETTE DAVIS

KATHRYN SERMAK

WITH DANELLE MORTON

hachette
BOOKS

NEW YORK   BOSTON

Hachette Books
Hachette Book Group
1290 Avenue of the Americas
New York, NY 10104
hachettebooks.com
twitter.com/hachettebooks

First trade paperback edition: September 2018

Hachette Books is a division of Hachette Book Group, Inc.
The Hachette Books name and logo are trademarks of Hachette Book Group, Inc.

The publisher is not responsible for websites (or their content) that are not owned by the publisher.

The Hachette Speakers Bureau provides a wide range of authors for speaking events. To find out more, go to www.hachettespeakersbureau.com or call (866) 376-6591.

ISBN: 978-0-316-50786-8

Printed in the United States of America

LSC-C

10 9 8 7 6 5 4 3 2 1

Pr Me

"Delightful... *Miss D & Me* details the sweet and deepening bond between the much-feared actress and a timid, young Kathryn Sermak—a pairing set against a steady drumbeat of menace."   —New York *Daily News*

"Endearing... Inspired by a fateful road trip the two women embarked upon through France in 1985, the book—based on Sermak's extensive archive of datebooks, photographs, and audio cassettes—offers an intimate glimpse into the last 10 years of the screen icon's life, until her passing in 1989 with Sermak by her side."   —*The Hollywood Reporter*

"Deeply personal, strangely enthralling."
                                   —*New York Times Book Review*

"Poignant with touches of humor, *Miss D & Me* is a fitting fade-out for an actress who made it look easy to stay tough."
                                            —Associated Press

"When Kathryn Sermak was hired as Bette Davis's personal assistant in 1979, she was a 22-year-old ingenue who had no idea who the great movie star was. For the next ten years she would help the woman she regarded as her mentor and, subsequently, friend, through her twilight years that brought illness and a devastating betrayal by her daughter, B.D. Hyman, in a brutal memoir about her mother. Davis's heartbreak is also keenly felt by Sermak in her deeply _____ *Miss D & Me*. The _____ ters emerges as a loyal, kind, and vulnerable person, emotionally maimed by a child she adored."

—*Daily Mail* (named a Best Book of the Year)

"America loved Bette Davis for the great star she was. I had the privilege of being her friend. Kathryn Sermak's book is a beautifully insightful look at the real Bette Davis."

—George Hamilton

"*Miss D & Me* is a fascinating look at the life of this indomitable star and her young assistant, Kathryn, during the last ten years of Miss Davis's life. I highly recommend it."

—Ann-Margret

"Kathryn Sermak has given us a well written and vivid account of her long association with one of the most remarkable women of the past century: Bette Davis. I read it and was enthralled."

—Olivia de Havilland

"We should all hope that we have a Kathryn Sermak in our lives whose love and devotion overcame any odds she might have encountered in her remarkable journey with Miss D. This book is homage to both ladies and a wonderful read."

—Stefanie Powers

"None of us knew or loved Bette Davis during her later years more than Kathryn Sermak. This is a wonderful book about one of the greatest women I ever knew—and one of the greatest actresses who gave us all so very, very much. You'll enjoy this read and realize what a truly great woman Bette Davis was—and an inspiration to women of all ages." —Robert Wagner

For Miss D.

*This is our book, our story, our "blood,
sweat, tears," and laughter.
Times change, but the wisdom you've
shared with me is everlasting.
I am forever grateful for your love and the
tutelage you gave me.
This book is also for your fans, to whom
you bequeathed lessons on a well-lived life.
Love,
Kath*

CONTENTS

CONTENTS

MISS D & ME

THE
AMERICAN
COLLEGE
DICTIONARY

Darling B. D.
May this
dictionary
stand you in
"good stead"
while writing.
The Legend

M aughan

PREFACE

"Don't Be Afraid to Face Your Fears; They Won't Go Away Until You Do."

I LOOKED OUT of the window of my apartment on the Rue Robert Fleury to confirm that the car and driver were waiting for me in the street below. Miss Davis' plane was scheduled to land at the Charles de Gaulle airport in three hours, and it had been my practice as her personal assistant to arrive two hours before the plane landed to ensure that all arrangements were in place. I saw the chauffeur, Patrick, well dressed in his pressed black suit and tie, standing next to the gleaming black Mercedes. The driver was new to me, recommended by the U.S. Embassy, which assured me that he was trustworthy, discreet, and skilled at evading the paparazzi. The date of Miss D's arrival had been the top item in *Celebrity News*, a weekly bulletin that announced prominent people visiting Paris and their agendas. Patrick had to get us past customs and out of Charles de Gaulle, to the Orly airport on the other side of Paris, and onto our flight to Biarritz. Given the state of

Miss D's health, I wanted to make sure that no one got any photos of us as we made our way to Orly.

As the car glided down the Peripherique, I took out my datebook to triple check the preparations for our stay in Biarritz and the return to Paris. I'd met two weeks earlier with the manager at the Hotel du Palais in Biarritz, a resort town on the Atlantic near the French border with Spain, and had spoken with him again yesterday to reconfirm the details.

Miss D and I would stay ten days at the Hotel du Palais, where we would work on her second memoir *This 'N That*. I had reserved her an ocean-view suite with a large terrace facing the Bay of Biscay, while I would be across the hall in a junior suite. Her rooms would be decorated with gardenias, if available. If not, daisies were Miss D's second choice. A bottle of Pouilly Fuisse would be chilling in an ice bucket with a bottle of club soda when we arrived. Since her stroke two years ago, Miss D could only drink wine spritzers. I had met also with the head chambermaid to ensure that the same maids attended to the suite morning and evening, arriving precisely at 9:00 a.m. to clean, and returning at 8:00 p.m. to turn down the beds and place a sheet over the top blanket making a proper coverture. The head chambermaid assured me that there would be enough hangers in the closets to hold the clothes I would unpack from Miss D's multiple suitcases.

Satisfied that everything was arranged, I closed my datebook and settled back into my seat as Paris rushed past the window. I pictured Miss D, easy to do as we had seen each other in New York a few months before. In my six years as her full-time, live-in assistant (a position I'd just recently left, though I was still part of her intimate inner circle) I'd rarely seen her so rattled.

*   *   *

The storm had been brewing for several weeks. I had flown back to New York for her birthday in April and to attend a meeting with Miss D's lawyer, Harold Schiff. Harold had discovered that Bede (her nickname for her daughter, Barbara Hyman) had written a tell-all memoir in the style of *Mommie Dearest*, scheduled to be published that Mother's Day. Miss D's agent, Robbie Lantz, had joined us in her suite at the Lombardy Hotel to discuss how to handle Bede's upcoming public betrayal of her mother. The timing could not have been worse. Miss D had just started working again after a 1983 stroke that nearly killed her. We did not tell her about the book before she flew to London to work on the film *Murder with Mirrors*, fearing that if she knew she might suffer a setback or worse. We told her only after the movie had wrapped. She was deeply wounded, but she seemed to have bounced back. That afternoon in the Lombardy she was very much in charge.

With Harold and Robbie seated on the beige sofa in the large living room of the suite, Miss D was smoking and pacing. I stood at the edge of the room, ready to act if anyone needed anything. Miss D wore a crisp navy blue dress with a flared skirt, nipped in at the waist, and with a stiff, angled collar that accentuated her neckline. She had three of these stylish tailored dresses in different colors, all made of sturdy poplin that did not wrinkle when she sat.

She rarely sat! Miss D thought more clearly when she paced. That afternoon she was quietly seething, her eyes ablaze with energy. She took firm, quick steps and turned decisively on her heel, with the same pace she had that summer in 1979 when she hired me. Since her stroke, those steps had become more tentative and her turn was not as quick. At the Lombardy that day her vigor had returned and she stepped and turned crisply back and forth across the room.

"I cannot believe she is doing this to me!" Miss D said. "How could she?"

She paused at the credenza and consulted a list of questions on a yellow legal pad, taking the pad with her as she finally sat in a chair opposite the sofa.

"How do we know for sure it's a *wretched* book?" Miss D asked Harold.

"My sources tried to get me a copy, but the publisher has it securely locked up. Those allowed to read it are only permitted to do so in their offices. Rumor has it that she paints a very unflattering portrait of you," Harold said.

"Well, find a way to read it and then tell me," Miss D said.

"Bette . . . I'm told the same thing," Robbie said in his gentle voice with a slight German accent. "Word has it that it is a scathing book and a ferocious attack on you. We must discuss what your response to the press will be."

"This is just horrible. Bede has no idea what the press will do to her," Miss D said. "She told me she wrote this book so we would have a better understanding of one another. I'm now utterly confused by who she is and her way of life."

"I'm sure Mrs. Hyman will be doing interviews, but from what I've heard, many of the networks are standing by you," Robbie said. "I've had many requests. Mike Wallace at *60 Minutes* said he will re-air your interview where Bede spoke glowingly about you."

"Kath, make a note," Miss D said, looking at me. "I wish to call and thank him."

I could see her mounting distress as she stood, lit a cigarette, and walked across the room to the window. She put out that half-finished cigarette and lit another. She made a long exhale as she looked out at Manhattan, and then took another thoughtful drag. We all sat in silence as she sorted her thoughts. Then Miss D turned toward us.

"She's expecting me to lash out and have a fight," she said. "Oh, yes she is. Well, I will not dignify her by giving a response to her so-called book. No, I will not! I will say nothing and give no interviews in reply!"

There was a certain tone when Miss D had decided, a voice of dark refusal that contained all the sorrow of this betrayal as well as her firm resolve. Anyone who knew her well understood that when she spoke in this way there would be no further discussion.

Since then Bede's book had become the biggest entertainment media event in the weeks leading up to Mother's Day. In it she described a traumatic childhood and a drunk, neglectful mother. For all the strength Miss D had displayed at the Lombardy, her voice was barely audible when she and I spoke by phone after I returned to Paris. Miss D was a fighter, a champion, and a bon vivant—and *always* a survivor. But after she read Bede's book, Miss D described waking up to feelings of dread and told me she never wanted to see anybody again.

Yet somehow she had made it onto this plane for our long-planned French adventure: working on the book by the beach, and then a four-day road trip from Biarritz to Paris where she could see my new place. I was shifting in my shoes as the Concorde came into view, eager to see her after such a long time. No matter what state she was in when she boarded the plane, I knew her mood would be improved by a visit to the ocean. I was so happy to help her get away, and eager and proud to show her off to my friends in Paris.

The Concorde pulled up to the gate and I was escorted into the first-class cabin. I scanned the faces but at first simply did not recognize the small, slumped figure next to the window. After the stroke, she had lost so much weight that the designer Nolan Miller agreed to alter her clothes, but she had lost even more weight since I last saw her. Now her suit hung loose at the sleeves, swallowing up her small hands. When I reached to help her to her feet, I felt how fragile she was. I hugged her and she lit up for a moment. I caught a brief glimpse of the old sparkle in those Bette Davis eyes. Then it too was gone. She leaned heavily on me as we made our way from her seat and up the aisle where she paused to thank the crew.

Although the airline had insisted we have a wheelchair standing by, I knew Miss D would never allow herself to be seen in one. I placed her makeup case and the small duffle bag she'd brought on the plane in the seat of the wheelchair for the chauffeur to push through customs while I offered my arm to Miss D. I escorted her to the golf cart that waited for us at the gate. Normally when we sped through the airport in one of these she stopped to greet her fans. This time we drove straight through customs, then took a back route to the Mercedes, so that fewer people had a chance to recognize her. Looking at her next to me, I was certain no one would. I began to comprehend what a monumental task it would be to get her back to being the Miss D I had known so well.

Once we were through customs, Patrick drove us across town to Orly airport to board the plane to Biarritz, without incident and without any words spoken between us. I knew she was happy to see me, but there was something more than depression in her eyes as she stared out the airplane window. She seemed furious and, because she would not speak, it was unclear to me if she was angry with me or at how much had been taken from her or both.

When Miss D hired me in 1979 I was twenty-two, just out of college, and she was seventy-one. For our first five years together she was strong, sharp, and powerful. Since then everything was harder for her as she endured loss after loss. The public humiliation by her beloved daughter was the hardest of all. It seemed to have sapped all her strength. Just before Bede's book was published, I had left her employ to move to Paris to be with a man I loved, and although she encouraged this, it was another loss.

Independence was Miss D's dominant quality, and for better or for worse preserving it was what had guided her private and public life. She lived to a high standard, a life deliberately chosen, one conducted with a strict set of rules. Only a woman in full command of her world had the ability to live her life this way. If she slipped into dependency it would infuriate her, and I feared that this was what had created the chilly silence now separating us.

Upon our arrival at Hotel du Palais, the porters carried our luggage to our suites and the bellman opened the curtains revealing a breathtaking view of the sea. Miss D sat on the

chaise lounge silently. When the staff departed, I tried to improve her mood.

"Shall we go for a swim?" I asked brightly. "Or lunch? The
Hippocampe has tables overlooking the water."

Miss D said nothing.

"Would you like to take a walk around the hotel?"

She looked out the window to avoid my gaze. I took the fact
that she was staring at the sea as a clue.

"How about a walk on the beach then? The weather is
beautiful today and the afternoon sun is perfect."

No response.

"Fine then. Fine!" I said brusquely. For the past three
hours I had tolerated her shutting me out, but I was at my
limit. "If you want to sulk in this room you do not need my
company. I'm going for a walk around the hotel."

I grabbed my purse and left, but paused in the hallway. I
couldn't leave her. What if someone tried to enter the room?
She didn't speak the language well. And if something happened to her physically—if she fell or had another stroke—
I would never forgive myself for walking out on her. I found
myself frozen outside her suite, listening at the door like a
tabloid reporter. Still, I couldn't return without some proof of
my walk. I dashed down to the lobby and collected menus
from the restaurants so I'd have something to give her. I re-
entered the suite to find that she had not moved an inch in
the half hour since I left. I decided to act as if nothing was
wrong, hoping this might brighten the atmosphere.

"Well it is a glorious day outside and the water is a lovely
deep and sparkling blue," I said. "I'm sure you'll love it out
there! Shall we order lunch? Would you like to take it on the
terrace? I brought some menus from the restaurants."

I offered her the menus but she was unwilling to lift a hand to receive them.

I paused, but ultimately could not hide my exasperation. "Is this how it's going to be?" I said. "You said you wanted to come to France, to the seaside to work on the book and to take a drive through the countryside back to Paris. Well, you're here, it's beautiful, and you won't even speak to me. Is this the way you want it?"

The question dropped between us.

"Nothing is the way I want it anymore," she said softly. "Nothing is. I'm definitely alone in this world. Yes I am. Yes I am. Why didn't I die in that hospital? So I never, ever had to go through this horrible, horrible thing."

I took a seat next to the chaise lounge, silently letting her know I was ready to listen. In her face I saw the devastation. We all start as fragile creatures on this earth, and heartbreak can make one regress quickly. My strong and proud mentor Miss D was suddenly a wisp, a feather struggling not to be blown away by the harsh wind of her daughter's betrayal.

"A woman who wrote to Bede sent me a copy of her letter. It ends with her saying that she pities me. She asked Bede why she couldn't have told the world her grievances after her mother was gone. She described me as old, old and lonely." She paused to gather herself. "That's how my daughter has made people see me. That's how my fans see me now. She said I beat her children when they visited us in California.

"That's ridiculous! I was there and I know that did not happen," I said. "I don't think there is any possibility that I will ever get over this. I just don't think it's possible."

She started to cry, just a little at first, as if she did not want to give in to it. I had only seen her cry one other time, when her sister died and she could not leave the movie set of *The Watcher in the Woods* to attend the funeral. This was different. She placed her hands over her face. Her small controlled sobs gave way to a wailing so deep that she frightened me. These tears came from a deeper place, where a sword had been thrust into her heart.

I tried to get her to eat dinner but she was not interested in food. I ordered her caramel custard, one of her favorites, but she would not look at it. Finally before bed, I got her to take her medicine with some Ensure Plus, now a diet staple. We had scarcely spoken further.

When I closed the door to my room for the night, I considered that this time maybe I could not bring her back. Her battle to recover after the stroke had been fueled by pride, a test of her will, and she had not been defeated. This time the enemy was attacking her heart directly and she was weakened by the stroke.

As angry as she had made me when she arrived, alone in my room I desperately wanted to help her. I had experienced betrayal by a lover, but never by a child. Her daughter's treason was being played out for the whole world to see. With all the skills I had acquired over the years to help her with the difficulties life presented, this time I was fresh out of ideas.

When I rose the next morning I decided to try a new tack to pull her up from the darkness. She was a Yankee, New England born and bred, who had always found those who wallowed in their defeats distasteful. "The cure for any ailment is hard work," she'd often told me. I needed to resurrect that Yankee. I would be efficient, decisive, and make plans for the day to rekindle her habit of looking to the future and moving swiftly to set each crisis behind her. When I entered her room and moved the curtains open, she no longer seemed angry with me. I was not angry with her either, so the silence between us had a different quality. I knew it was best to leave her alone. I retired to my suite to review the galleys of her book, ready to try again the next day.

On the morning of the second day, I saw a glimmer of my Miss D returning when she agreed we would have lunch on the terrace. With a wine spritzer in one hand and her cigarette in the other, she took a short step back to the living. She was suddenly somewhat chatty.

"Kath, look at this gorgeous view of the ocean. Do you know Napoleon III built this hotel for his stunning wife, Eugénie? This was their villa. A love nest. Beware of a woman's wiles. Look at Wallis Simpson. Yes, and she and King Edward lived in Biarritz for a while after he resigned the throne and was exiled from England. They even came to this hotel. If the villa could talk, what stories lay inside the Palais."

She ate well and after lunch agreed to take a walk. We stood on the balcony that swept around the back of the hotel, facing the sea. She turned her face up to take in the sun and pulled in deep breaths of the sea air. Seeing her this way gave me hope that I was not the only one trying to breathe life into her, that my prayers for her strength to return might have been heard.

"Kath, look at that table," she said, pointing to a place where the curve of the balcony jutted out the furthest to the sea. "That's where we should work on the book tomorrow."

The Yankee was back.

From then on we started being ourselves again. The next morning we worked on her memoir for a few hours at the table on the balcony. In those decades before computers, the work was hands on. I used scissors and tape and wrote her changes on legal pads. When Miss D decided that a passage was in the wrong place, I cut it out of the galley and taped it where she thought it fit better.

We rented one of the beach bungalows so we could work by the ocean the next day. The air was bright and the sun seemed to rebuild Miss D, very chic in her classic white pants, red-and-white-striped shirt, hat, and sunglasses. There she came back into full voice. She read the book aloud to me so we could correct errors in tone, while I wrote out her changes and pasted them into the manuscript. Each day she grew stronger, and we worked longer hours.

A few days into this regimen, Miss D started to swim in the ocean and her appetite increased. We began dressing for cocktails and eating in the restaurants. We did not speak of the state she was in when she arrived in Paris, except for one evening after dinner when Miss D simply said, "Kath, we're going to get through this."

As her strength returned we began to explore the town. It was a place I knew well from my summer there in 1977, two years before she hired me, when I worked for the Vivianos as an au pair to their two children. I had stayed in touch with them over the years. Mario and Bernadette were among the first people I contacted when I returned in 1985 to live in Paris, where they lived most of the year. I knew they were in Biarritz for the summer, and thought if Miss D were up for it we might drop by.

Miss D was in a good mood the day we toured the town. We explored the shops we found along cobblestone streets and visited Angela, who, like José Eber, was a famous hairdresser and friend who had a salon across from the hotel. We stopped for lunch at a small café that was only a short drive from the Vivianos'.

"Let's go visit Bernadette and Mario," I said as we were finishing up lunch. I'd stayed with them when I came to Biarritz to make the arrangements for our stay at the Hotel du Palais, but we'd never decided when Miss D would meet them. That moment seemed as good a time as any. "They live just up the street."

"Don't we have to phone first?" Miss D asked.

"No it is not like that here," I said. "People pop over anytime." This was not her way of doing things, but her shrug of assent gave me further hope that she was, indeed, coming back to the "when in France" mood that had led to this trip.

I drove us to the Avenue du Docteur Claisse, a beautiful street with a canopy of trees. I opened the gate and we entered the garden, rich with the scent of roses and lilacs. As I rang the doorbell Miss D took a long deep inhale.

"Kath, smell that," she said. "This woman has a green thumb."

Bernadette answered the door in her apron, surprised and pleased to see me. When she saw Bette Davis standing behind me, without thinking she shut the door in our faces and fled. I could hear her running to the downstairs powder room. As we exchanged amused glances, Mario re-opened the door, rescuing the moment.

"Miss Davis, what an honor it is to have you here," he said. "Please, please, come in."

As we sat down in the living room, Bernadette returned with some lipstick on and without her apron. Bernadette was awestruck seeing Miss D in person, as she had loved her

movies since she was a little girl. I stood and walked toward
the kitchen to get us something to drink.

"Kathryn, whatever are you doing?" Miss D said, watching
me opening the refrigerator. She turned to the Vivianos. "I
must apologize. I have no idea what has gotten into her."

"No, no, this is Kati's home too," Mario interrupted.

"Yes," said Bernadette. "She is family!"

I could see discomfort on Miss D's face, as if seeing my casual familiarity with the Vivianos required her to become the
more regal Bette Davis. As close as I was to Miss D, we were
still fairly formal and proper in public, as she had tutored me
to be. In her mind, I was being rude to our hosts. But there
was more, too—if I was reading her correctly, she was actually a bit jealous. She did not quite like the idea that I was
more comfortable with this family than I was with her. Imagine that! Miss D jealous over me!

As we sat on the patio, I began to appreciate why Miss D
might see the Vivianos as her rivals. Miss D now needed me
more than she wanted to admit. My obvious joy in being with
the Vivianos may have made Miss D wonder if I already had
moved away from her in these few months. We soon would
be leaving on our adventure, a journey without a map, that
contrasted with all the other trips we'd taken where every
moment of the day had been planned well in advance. As we
sat with my friends, who were not yet her friends, I realized
that our four days on the road from Biarritz to Paris would reveal what we were to each other now that our old roles had
been altered by time and circumstances.

When at last our work on the book was done and we were departing for Paris, the staff acted as if the queen were leaving

the palace. In some sense this was true. As Miss D had built back her strength, her charm had come back too, and many members of the staff would be able to recount for decades the little kindnesses she demonstrated to them at each interaction. A large retinue accompanied us to the front of the hotel where our car rental, a black BMW sedan, waited for us. The porters had placed our luggage in the trunk. The staff had fashioned "Biarritz Bandanas" for us, ribbons braided into colorful crowns, which we wore to the car. The manager wanted a photograph with Miss D, as did many others. She accommodated everyone. Her public spirit, at least, was truly back.

This trip would be different, different for both of us. We did not have a chauffeur navigating us to Paris in a limousine and she had told me not to make my usual thorough arrangements. After all we had been through in the last seven years, and in the hotel in the last ten days, this road trip was to be improvisation that she hoped would bring us both joy.

"Kath, bad beginnings always make for good endings," she said as we took our places in the car.

We wheeled out of the hotel drive and headed north, not knowing or caring where we would end up that night.

CHAPTER 1

I HAVE A HUNCH ABOUT YOU
June 8, 1979

"Instincts Exist for a Reason—Follow Them"

THE DOORMAN CLOSED the brass gate of the small elevator with a white-gloved hand. He wore a dark green blazer and a captain's hat, an outfit more suited to a New York City doorman than one in West Hollywood. From the moment I stepped out of my car underneath the green and white awning, and then onto the thick green carpet at the Colonial House, it felt as though I was stepping into another era. At my side was Mr. Wes Carlson, impeccably dressed in a light gray double-breasted suit with European lapels and a tufted white silk pocket square. He had found me through June Art, an employment agency that catered to the stars. In my simple beige dress from The Highlander Boutique in San Bernardino and new shoes to match, I felt underdressed, but eager for what awaited me on the fourth floor.

The day before, Mr. Carlson had called to ask if I was interested in the position of Girl Friday to Bette Davis while she shot a film in London. I was not sure what a Girl Friday was, but I knew I could be whatever-day-of-the-week girl I had to be if it meant a summer in Europe before starting graduate school that fall. The next morning I drove to Mr. Carlson's office in Beverly Hills so he could assess my qualifications. After we'd spoken for a few minutes, he asked me to wait in the lobby. Apparently he had called Miss Davis to say he had a candidate for her to consider.

"Miss Davis will see you now," Mr. Carlson said when he returned. "Please follow me in your car. It's not far."

In truth, when Mr. Carlson said that the prospective job was with Bette Davis, I had had to hide the fact that I had no idea who she was. Maybe I had blocked her out. My parents recalled that at age seven I ran screaming from the television room when *Whatever Happened to Baby Jane?* was playing. Scenes from that movie, like Bette Davis' "Baby Jane" serving up her sister's pet parakeet on a platter, would have been horrifying to any young girl, but particularly to me and my brother and sisters. My parents were devout Catholics who tried to keep their children from being corrupted by the world. Although my father had studied film at USC, he detested what he saw as the moral excesses of Hollywood. I grew up seventy miles to the east of Los Angeles but it might as well have been thousands of miles away. From the time I was a teenager I wanted a much bigger world than the one my father had built for us in San Bernardino. Hollywood had nothing whatever to do with my plans.

The night before my interview with Miss Davis, I borrowed my friend Helen Ann's cherished copy of *The Lonely Life*, Miss Davis' autobiography. I had intended to skim it, but found I could not put it down. She wrote as though she were standing before you with her hands on her hips saying, "This is who I am. Take it or leave it." She wrote about how she'd always been a perfectionist, and how even as a kid she'd be driven into a frenzy by a wrinkled dress or a bow not fluffed perfectly, "a passion unheard of in a child so young," as she wrote. At the circus as a young girl, she watched the animals walking into the ring and noticed that the seam in the carpet they stepped on was crooked, after which she was unable to enjoy the show.

It was an attitude I'd seen firsthand for much of my own life. My father also noticed details others didn't and was un-yielding in the quality of work he required. He was once so enraged by the poor job I did cleaning out the silverware drawer that he pulled the drawer out and threw all the cutlery onto the floor, demanding that I do it again. So I knew how to present myself to someone like that, and felt confident I knew how to meet those standards. When I woke up that morning I was certain that this job was mine and I would soon be back in Europe.

When the elevator reached the fourth floor, Mr. Carlson pulled back the brass gate, then opened the elevator door and there stood Miss Bette Davis, a mere five feet two inches, but with the presence of someone much larger in her steep red leather heels.

"Miss Davis, I'd like you to meet Catherine Sermak."

Miss Davis extended her hand for me to shake. She seized mine firmly, gradually increasing her grip as she held it. She left an imprint on my fingers.

"How do you do?" she said in her honey-and-gravel voice. "Please come in."

We walked through the living room and into an enclosed

terrace where Miss Davis sat in a throne-like high-back wicker chair. Her crown was a matching beige baseball cap. At seventy-one years old, she looked more vibrant than most do in their forties. She gestured for me to sit opposite her on the red velvet settee. Mr. Carlson remained standing. Miss Davis nodded and he began to read from an index card.

"University of California at Santa Barbara...studied with Jane Goodall and Carl Rogers...work-study program in Spain...recently graduated from the University of Southern California...fluent in Spanish and French...recommended by Princess Shams Pahlavi, sister of the Shah of Iran, for whom she worked...passport is current."

As he read off my qualifications my eyes darted around, taking in her awards and signed photos of her with people like John F. Kennedy and Anwar Sadat displayed on the walls of the room next to the lanai. From where I sat, I saw two Oscars and an Emmy, and a library case filled with awards and certificates from her ten Academy Award nominations. When my gaze traveled back into the porch, I locked eyes with Miss Davis, who had been scrutinizing me the whole time. When Mr. Carlson finished, he excused himself. Silence settled over the room.

Miss Davis selected a cigarette from the engraved silver box that rested on the table next to her chair and chose a strike-anywhere match that stood upright in a silver cup. She struck the match on the underside of the table and brought it to the tip of her cigarette, an unhurried graceful sequence of actions that felt like they took an eternity. Her eyes never left mine. Finally she spoke.

"What sign are you, Catherine?"

"Libra."

"Oh, that's good. Very good. I'm an Aries," she said.

Miss Davis took a drag on her cigarette as she continued to examine me.

"Catherine, can you cook a three-minute egg?"

"Yes, Miss Davis. Yes, I can cook an egg."

"That's good, because I have one every morning."

She paused, smiled, and then leaned forward a little, slightly more intensely. "And what do you know about the film industry?"

"Nothing," I said. "I don't know anything about it, I'm afraid."

She sat back with a pleased confidence. "No, that's good. I will teach you everything you need to know."

Working for Princess Pahlavi had taught me not to offer anything unless asked. I was replaying in my head all the things I could and should have said, but remembering Princess Pahlavi I remained silent.

After a moment's pause, she rose from her chair.

"You're hired, Catherine," Miss Davis said. "I have a hunch about you."

Mr. Carlson walked me back to my car.

"Your life will change after today in ways you cannot know now," he said. "Plan to be ready in three weeks."

I knew what it was like to work for a princess. What would it be like to work for a queen?

I couldn't stop smiling as I climbed into my car because fate and luck were bringing me back to Europe, the only place I really wanted to be. In college I had used every opportunity I found to get as far away from San Bernardino as possible. I spent summers in Hawaii. Senior year, 1977, I took a fall semester in Spain and stayed on. By July I was living in the southwestern part of France in Biarritz, serving as the au pair for the Vivianos, who had a summer house there and hired me to watch their two children and teach them to surf. I was too smitten with France to return to collect my diploma from USC. When the summer was over, I got a job in Neuilly-sur-Seine, a wealthy suburb of Paris, as the au pair for the grandchildren of Madame Sandrini, a famous French ballet dancer.

Madame Sandrini and her daughter had the top two floors at 11 Rue Perronet. Every day when she and I walked to the *boucherie* or patisserie to pick up treats for the children, I admired her regal posture, her flawless coiffure, and the fine quality of her clothes. In public she always wore couture. The French designer Givenchy was her close friend and a frequent guest. After a few months caring for her grandchildren, Madame grew to like me and volunteered to help me with my French studies. In her big living room with floor-to-ceiling windows overlooking the Rue Perronet, I would sit on her plush white carpet with my homework from my French class at the Institut Catholique spread out on the marble coffee table while she reclined next to me on the sofa. She was a gentle tutor, as she did not speak English well. Madame Sandrini would indicate if I had misspoken with a facial reaction and eye contact, one of many lessons I received when I lived in Europe about how to communicate without words—lessons that would later prove invaluable to me with Miss Davis. When Madame Sandrini noticed my interest in fashion she started taking me along when she visited her designer friends' ateliers to choose her wardrobe for the next season. In the grand showrooms we would sit as the models paraded past. When Madame Sandrini observed that my California clothing was too thin for the colder months, she gave me one of her short black mink jackets, which I treasured like gold.

My plan for my life at the age of twenty-one was to spend more time in Europe and come home to start graduate school at USC in clinical psychology in the fall. My parents loved the idea of me getting a master's degree and were proud of me. I was too. I imagined my future with a Beverly Hills practice, my select clientele and my equally accomplished husband and children, of course. But when I entered France I fell in love with the country, the people, the food, and the freedom. I had spent the last year studying in Spain, where the revolution was taking place, students were shot, and Juan Carlos was just made King—the Franco regime was over and Spain was fifty years behind the United States. When I arrived in Paris at the Musee d'Orsay train station, however... it was magical. The way people spoke was music in my ears. The colors and *la joie d'vivre* were vibrant and everywhere, and the gloom of the revolution was behind me. I felt a strong desire like no other I'd ever felt before, and I knew I had to pursue whatever this was—a calling? After a few months, I decided to postpone graduate school, career, family—everything American.

In April 1978 my father called to tell me that my grandmother had just passed. I could hear the pain in his voice and I told him I'd be home for her funeral. I had been away for close to two years and it was as if I could hear my grandmother saying, "Catherine, your parents need you now. It's time to go. You've been away long enough." I knew then that I would not soon be returning to Europe. I did not have the money to come back to Paris. I was sad to be trading the splendor of Madame Sandrini's for the tedium of San Bernardino, where I would be under the thumb of my father once again.

My father, Cas Sermak, was a first generation Polish immigrant, and was happiest when he was working. His high standards made a strong impression on the town of San Bernardino, where he was a community leader and a devout and generous member of the Catholic church. My mother was the brains of the business who booked the appointments, handled the finances and generally managed the "business." My father prided himself that his handshake was as secure a promise as any signature on a written contract. He had the same high standards for his children, whom he kept constantly busy. Why hire gardeners, painters, cleaners, or shop clerks when he had five able bodies to help him in his home and his business? We always felt the power of his watchful crystal blue eyes as he worked in our home at the top of Quail Canyon, a lush cut in the hillside surrounded by orange trees and bright California poppies in the spring. The house was on an acre of land that offered a panoramic view of the city far away to the north through the sliding glass doors in the living room. His pride was his garden of fruit trees—plum, persimmon, apricot, several types of citrus—as well as the beds of roses and the arbors hung with grapes. His gardens also reflected his faith. He erected an enormous bronze cross in the backyard and two life-sized angels that he and my mother bought from a monastery, all positioned to keep watch over our home and our family.

He kept his four daughters—the Sermak girls—on a tight rein. My curfew was 10:00 p.m., not midnight like our peers'. Young men interested in dating one of us had to pick us up at home. As a suitor pulled into the driveway, my father would open the front door to greet him—accompanied by his five German shepherds. It was a wonder that any of us ever got a second date. As the only professional photographer in San Bernardino back then, he took the yearly photos for all the public and private schools as well as for weddings and any other big family or civic celebrations. He knew everyone and was well liked and respected. We went to a Catholic school where the nuns kept us in line, but he had that wired too—if one of the Sermak girls stepped out of line, he was likely to know about it before we got home.

Each family wittingly or unwittingly assigns roles for its members to play. My oldest sister, Pam, was the popular vice president of student affairs in our school, and the first to receive a scholarship to the University of Southern California. Coleen had a natural talent for drawing and was a great seamstress and cook. My younger brother, Cas, was an outdoorsman who loved to ski, surf, and fish. Judy—ten years younger than I—was the glue that, as we got older, kept us all together. I was the tomboy who loved sports, particularly surfing. I was also the rebel and the black sheep, strong and confident and not easy to control. I suspected my year away in Europe had only intensified those traits. My suspicions proved to be correct. Every minute I was home since I had returned from France I was in conflict with my father.

Within days of being home that magical feeling of France had faded in the arid California winter. Now that I was back among the flip-flops and t-shirts, my family and friends wouldn't stop teasing me about my new accent: part French, part Spanish, part pidgin English, a mash-up of all the languages I had been trying to master in my years away. I was not taking this very well. After living independently, I did not want to be in San Bernardino defending my "fake" accent and chafing under my parents' rules. Since I didn't have a job, my parents put me to work tending the register in the gift shop of his photography studio. I was an indifferent employee, never jumping up to help a customer as she browsed the decanters, frames, scrapbooks, and hundreds of Hummel figurines my father impulsively collected and sold. I did not care if customers bought anything or not—I was thinking about Paris, about Spain, and about how I could get back to Europe before school started.

Thankfully I had an ally in this. Ever since I'd returned from Europe, I found myself spending more time with Helen Ann, the mother of a boy I'd dated for a while. She was close to my mother in age and an independent woman of means, a daughter of San Francisco high society, who had raised her children on her own. She painted murals for the wealthy, as well as oils, and she used her eye for design to renovate homes and sell them at a profit. I admired her independence, and was grateful for the refuge she provided me that summer as I sought to escape my father's demands.

Helen Ann was as indifferent to graduate school as I had become, and she agreed that life held bigger adventures to be explored by the young. She helped me write letters to all the European consulates in Los Angeles, and to high-quality employment agencies, emphasizing my international experience and my language skills. She allowed me to use her phone number as the one where I could be contacted. A few weeks after we sent off the letters, one of the agencies called to interview me for the job with the Princess. Princess Shams Pahlavi, the older sister to the Shah of Iran, was in exile with her family in the United States, frightened that they might be executed by the revolutionaries who had taken power in their native country. In their secure compound in Beverly Hills, the grandeur of their royal ways continued, and I would be a part of her retinue of servants.

My father was very upset when I was hired and left home to live in Beverly Hills to serve as a personal Spanish tutor for the Princess. After six months the Pahlavis left for Acapulco. Despite receiving an offer to go with them, I remained behind, feeling that graduate school was inevitable but with my eyes still open for another foreign adventure.

Now that my restlessness had led me to Miss Davis, I knew my father would be furious I'd taken a job without consulting him first. To him, Bette Davis was likely much worse than the Princess. She was a personification of what he saw as the immoral, un-Christian world of Hollywood. I feared he'd forbid me to take the job. Now that I'd tasted freedom, I knew that being told I could not do something—especially *this* something—was a thing of the past. Still, I steered my car toward Helen Ann's instead of home after my Colonial House meeting.

As I anticipated, Helen Ann was ecstatic that I'd been offered the position.

"This is perfect! It's the perfect job!" she said. "You need to work, become worldly. You can't learn that from books. You get to be a fly on the wall with Bette Davis! This woman can teach you like no other, mark my words."

The next day Helen Ann and I went through my clothes so she could advise me what to bring and what I would need to add. Helen Ann called her mother and they had a lively talk about my wardrobe. A few days later a large box containing another wide, flat box from I. Magnin, an elegant store that was the Saks Fifth Avenue of the West, arrived. I took the top off a pale gray-and-black-edged box and carefully separated the tissue paper to reveal the most beautiful garment I'd ever seen: a little black cocktail dress, accessorized with elbow-length satin gloves. It was cradled on a bed of cashmere sweaters, with a St. John knit skirt and a white cotton shirt tucked under those.

Just sliding on the cool and smooth gloves filled me with anticipation for the trip ahead, one where I'd be able to travel in a way that I had not before. Not with a backpack and book, but staying in the grand hotels where one had to have a dress like the one I held in my hands.

The other topic of discussion between Helen Ann and her high-society mother, also named Helen, was what exactly I would do as a Girl Friday. Helen traveled in the circles where ladies had personal servants, and even though Girl Friday sounded like something out of a newsroom, Helen convinced Helen Ann that I would need to improve my household skills.

With her mother's guidance, Helen Ann taught me how women who wore the kinds of clothes I found in the I. Magnin box packed and unpacked their suitcases. She also asked Helen Ann to teach me how to iron. I told her I already knew how to iron. "We're not talking about everyday ironing," she said. "You cannot leave a single wrinkle. You've got a taskmaster to please! Now, go fetch me that lovely white cotton shirt Mother sent you." When I returned, she was setting up an ironing board with the iron, a bottle of water with a perforated top, and a can of spray starch. I handed the shirt to Helen Ann who held it up to me.

"This is beautiful fabric. Touch that Egyptian cotton. The

long strong fibers make it very soft," Helen Ann said. She ran her fingers along the flat fell seams on the sleeve and along the fine hand stitching at the cuff. "Look at the construction. The seams are perfect. All of Miss Davis' clothes will be this quality."

I smoothed the shirt out on the board, a bit annoyed by the fuss over this garment. It was a shirt, after all, and while a better one than those that hung in my closet, it was still just a white shirt as far as I was concerned.

"The clothes must be damp if you are going to get the best result," she said, handing me the water bottle.

"Don't worry. It will take some practice to get this right," she said. "Start with the cuffs and the collar. If you do the sleeves first they will wrinkle when you iron the cuffs."

As I smoothed out the shirt on the ironing board and sprinkled it with water, I thought back to the women who served Princess Pahlavi. Aside from the Secret Service and FBI, who guarded the Princess' compound round the clock, she had eighteen servants. There were two ladies-in-waiting whose sole job it was to dress and undress her. Princess Pahlavi would stand, her arms straight out at her sides, while the servants pulled on her clothes, buttoning, zipping, moving in the same choreography day after day. They could never go to bed before the Princess, sometimes waiting up until 4:00 a.m. so that they could undress her. And if the Princess was entertaining dignitaries or secretaries of state, it would take hours of preparation to ready her. There was one girl whose only job was to curl and paint the Princess' eyelashes. Another inventoried her jewels—a much-coveted position which they offered me, but I politely declined—I did not want to be the one they blamed if a thousand-year-old jewel went missing. So

I, with my language skills and my bachelor of science in psychology, would dress Miss Davis and iron her clothes? I was confused; would I also be inventorying her jewels, or painting on her eyelashes, in addition to cooking her egg?

Three weeks later, on a Friday the thirteenth, Miss Davis again greeted me in the hallway of the fourth floor. My father drove me up to the Colonial House, with reluctant acceptance despite overwhelming disapproval, to meet the woman who was taking his daughter away from home for four months. But he didn't stay long. After a polite but perfunctory greeting to Miss Davis, he turned away and was gone.

"Come along," she said, and gently guiding my elbow, she escorted me to the room where I would be sleeping and advised me that dinner was in an hour.

An hour later I sat at the round pinewood dining room table with its large lazy Susan center. The only place was laid out for me. Although Miss Davis had prepared a delicious Cornish hen, I was the only one eating. Miss Davis sat nearby, smoking, watching me eat. My tutorial on being a Girl Friday had begun.

"Catherine, we will be leaving tomorrow morning at 10:00 a.m., and I would like your suitcases to be in the hallway an hour before departure," she said. "As we travel there may be press, and fans may stop to speak with me. Say absolutely nothing and stick close by. People will come to you and ask you questions. You say nothing to them. I have a certain way of doing things, Catherine, and you will have to learn as you go."

"Yes, Miss Davis."

"Well, good night my dear. See you early tomorrow. Set your alarm."

The next morning at the appointed hour I carried my two pieces of luggage out to the foyer to join the seven pieces traveling with Miss Davis. I had never seen such an assortment of traveling cases: a tackle box of a makeup case, two hat boxes, four suitcases, each adorned with a ridiculous enormous red ribbon. I thought, *This woman has utterly lost it.* But when we entered the limo and I saw the luggage stacked up in the station wagon that would follow us, I had to admit those bows looked great.

At the airport, a golf cart with a driver and an escort from the airlines were waiting for us when we pulled up at the terminal entrance. Miss Davis and I sat on the rear bench seat. As the golf cart maneuvered through the crowd, I was alarmed by the stir we caused. People would stop what they were doing, pivoting on their heels away from their children, just to watch us pass. From all corners, and from inside the shops along the way, people were calling out: "Bette!" "Miss Davis!" "We love you!" I remained mute, amazed that so many people adored this woman they knew only from the screen and who was still a mystery to me.

In New York the destination was the Lombardy Hotel, Miss Davis' home-away-from-home. When we arrived in her suite the first task was to unpack the "New York" suitcases. I saw that it impressed Miss Davis, as she quietly observed, that I knew to hang the outfits together, never a skirt or a blouse on its own, with the shoes directly below and jewelry nearby. Last to be unpacked were the lingerie bags made out of the most beautiful burgundy and red silk material I'd ever touched. Each undergarment, slip, and pair of stockings lived in its own perfect silk cocoon, embroidered with Miss Davis' initials.

Afterwards, Miss Davis told me to write down the many appointments she would keep in the days ahead. She had to see her dentist and her attorney and close friend, Harold Schiff. Besides accompanying her to these meetings, my responsibilities included placing her breakfast order with room service (scrambled eggs moist, hash brown potatoes, and buttered toast with jam). At the end of the day, I was to turn off the phones, put the DO NOT DISTURB sign on the door to the suite, and lock the door behind me.

"And Catherine, I'd like to speak with you about your handshake." She stood and moved closer. "You can tell a worthwhile person by the firmness of their handshake and, as you will be representing me, I would like yours to be a bit firmer. Stand up, Catherine."

I stood, and extended my hand. She took it in hers.

"Firmer, Catherine, confident," she said.

I squeezed her hand with force.

"Ouch!" She snatched her hand away and waved it around as if trying to restore blood to the fingers.

"Not *desperate*, Catherine. *Confident. In charge.* Again."

She extended her hand and I grasped hers more solidly.

"Much better. Much. We'll practice again."

I walked across the hallway to my room feeling exhausted by the last twenty-four hours, and a little at odds over the constant instruction. I could not tell if Miss Davis resented having me there, or if this was what she always required of a traveling companion. Perhaps having someone young like me was new to her and she was trying to figure out what to tell me to do. The woman she had traveled with before, she told me, was her hairdresser and forty years my senior. I offered a different set of skills. Or was I just paranoid in thinking she was annoyed by me? I supposed I would find out before we left for London.

Over lunch in her room the next afternoon, I chose the wrong fork for salad. Very matter-of-factly, Miss Davis pointed out the proper one to use instead. I picked up the correct one and began cutting up my lettuce into bite-sized pieces. When I looked up I saw Miss Davis staring in horror.

"Catherine, what are you *doing*?" she asked.

"Eating my salad?" I said tentatively, suddenly unsure.

"Don't you ever cut your salad again, ever, if you're going to be with *me*. It's simply bad manners."

I felt the gap formed by the fifty years difference in our ages. Among my friends, cutting up our salads *was* good manners. We were all young women watching our weight, and taking small bites and chewing carefully was part of the folk wisdom we followed as if it had been handed down from experts. Doing something so commonplace and finding it was a faux pas unnerved me. Even my handshake had required training! I did not know what to make of Miss Davis. Suddenly I could not eat. I sat with my hands in my lap.

"Why don't you go for a walk, Catherine?" suggested Miss Davis after a pause. I did not have to be asked twice.

I came back quickly from my walk, entering the suite so quietly that she did not hear me come in. She was staring out the living room window of the two-bedroom suite, pacing and smoking as she talked to Mr. Schiff on the phone. They were talking about me.

"Harold, she's not working out. You need to find someone at least thirty-five years old. She hardly knows *anything*. She seems much too young."

I stood very still.

"Yes, I was impressed, too, that she worked for the Princess, but I thought that she was *well-trained*...No, she never *traveled* with the Princess...She chats with the waiters and the maids! She just does not understand protocol."

She was going to fire me before we even left New York and I'd be back in San Bernardino. My father's satisfaction at this would be worse than losing the chance to go to England.

"...Yes...Yes...Oh Harold...Oh all right. All right... I'll give her a few days off."

She hung up and turned around and saw me standing there. She knew I had overheard her conversation, but apparently it didn't matter enough to her for her to scold me for eavesdropping.

"Catherine, why don't you go visit that aunt of yours you said lives in DC," she said. "It's historical and a place every American should have a chance to see, so take this opportunity." Again, I didn't need to be asked twice.

The days in DC were not a vacation, as I spent my entire visit worrying that when I returned I would be fired. I kept defending myself against this certainty, rehearsing speeches to her. I wanted to say: *I'm smart. I'll learn. I can do anything I set my mind to.* She'd probably think that I was undignified, along with believing me to be grossly inexperienced. When I returned, though, I felt a shift in Miss Davis' demeanor. She welcomed me and almost seemed to be excited to see me. Something had changed, without any effort on my part.

"I have to admit, I had second thoughts about you, Catherine," Miss Davis began. "But something tells me you're special. I actually missed you while you were gone, and that's why I want you to stay. I said before I had a hunch about you. I have always trusted my hunches."

CHAPTER 2

ON THE SET IN LONDON
August–October 1979

"Discretion Is the Better Part of Loyalty"

IN THE LOUNGE while we waited to board the Concorde to London, I saw Miss Davis in a different context than I had before. During the weeks we spent in New York we glided through the city in a limo, cut off from the public, or entertained guests in her suite. That world was quiet and protected, with doors opened for us and people always prepared to greet us. While golf-carting through JFK, again among her adoring fans, I paid more attention to the way Miss Davis carried herself, how her posture and self-possession increased her stature. She was composed and undistracted. She missed little and reacted to less. Seated in a leather chair in the lounge, she silently chain-smoked Philip Morris cigarettes. In her black knit two-piece dress, black felt hat with a black veil, and large square sunglasses, she implied that she was traveling incognito despite being recognized everywhere we went. In the seat next to her, I felt sheltered within the protection of the border she maintained between herself and the world. People around us stared at her and I could see them struggle internally about whether to approach, but no one did.

I was excited, my mind racing, as I tried to come off as a grownup who had everything under control. I knew and she knew that I did not. In New York it was obvious that my resume, while truthful, had given Miss Davis an exaggerated idea of my experience. One would not think that someone who was multilingual and had traveled as much as I had was so young. She may have believed that when I traveled through Europe I had done so as part of the Princess' entourage instead of with a backpack.

During our time in New York, Miss Davis never directly instructed me about my duties, as opposed to my handshake, eating habits, and other personal conduct. She carried on about her business and tested me periodically to see if I was paying attention. I watched her arrange for a car and driver several times before she handed me the phone number and told me to do it for her. Although she had sent me on more and more complex errands when we were in New York, she did not yet trust me enough to allow me to handle the airline tickets for the flight to London. I found that insulting. I had navigated my way through Europe alone under much more improvisational circumstances. She ought to give me credit for that. Sometimes the rebel in me wanted to scream at all of the rules and the assumptions that supported them. Most of these rules were news to me, and that was a constant source of annoyance to Miss Davis.

But my sassiness was all internal. I remembered Helen Ann's advice that I soak up every detail, the moments when I was frustrated as well as when I was excited, and to write all of it down. I started to jot notes in my datebook describing the Concorde, a supersonic jet like no other, which stood just outside the wall of windows. The Concorde had an elegant tapered nose and the sleek lines of a fighter jet, not the bulky form of a commercial jetliner. It carried only a hundred passengers and was capable of flying at Mach 2, nearly 1,500 miles an hour. We would be in London in less than three and a half hours. Amazing!

Helen Ann was right. I needed to count my blessings. I was out of San Bernardino and traveling with a world-renowned actress who, I now knew, had been awarded two Academy Awards, and had reputedly given the statuette its nickname, "Oscar." Miss Davis claimed that it reminded her of "the derriere of my husband [Harmon Oscar Nelson]!" In her heyday, she made so much money for her studio that a Hollywood wit once dubbed her "The Fifth Warner Brother." Even if being under the control of a lady the same age as my grandmother sometimes made me cranky, I was learning something or experiencing something new every minute. I resolved—over and over again—to soak it all up.

It felt as though we were in London almost as soon as we finished dinner on the Concorde. A publicist from the Disney Studios greeted us at the gate, and he and our driver Brian escorted us through customs and to the Grosvenor House Hotel in Mayfair, a posh part of the city. When the publicist offered Miss Davis a thick envelope from the studio, she waved a hand to indicate that she wanted him to hand it to me. I grabbed it as if I had been given a prize, but then recognized I should remain subdued, following the lead of Miss Davis. Her gesture involved me in her business and I saw it as a little step forward.

Her suite in the Grosvenor House overlooked Hyde Park. After the man from Disney departed, she handed me some ten-pound notes and instructed me to pick up a few items from the store and a few rolls of fifty-pence coins from the front desk for us to use for tips. When I returned to her suite, the luggage had arrived, stacked in a corner of the room, resplendent with those big red bows. The room seemed subtly different, with the coziness of home rather than the impersonal formality of a big hotel. I noticed one of the smaller cases was open on a chair and halfway unpacked. The end tables and bureaus now displayed her family pictures and some knickknacks from home. The change in the room was more than that though. Had she re-arranged the furniture? I didn't have a strong enough memory of the room to decide.

Miss Davis sat in a high-backed chair, smoking.

"Sit down, Catherine," she said. "We must review the contents of this envelope, as it will be your responsibility."

The envelope was on the sofa. I opened it and pulled out a thick stack of papers in many colors and letters on various official stationery.

"Here is the contact information for the director and first assistant director. That's who you will be dealing with. Every night after filming you'll get a call sheet like this that sets the schedule for the next day, and also new pages of the script in different colors to tell them apart. Two copies of the script revisions: one for me and one for you so we can run my lines. It's your responsibility to make sure that the new pages are switched out for the old. These blue pages are my personal schedule. Make sure that I am aware of every appointment at the beginning of the day. We're not filming yet, but there are many meetings ahead and a press conference."

I looked down at the pages in my hands, confused but unable to form a question.

"That's all for now, Catherine," she said, standing. I stood too. "You may take breakfast in your room tomorrow. Get some rest. I know I will. The first appointment is not until late in the afternoon. I will call you when I need you. Good night."

I saw from the schedule that the next day's appointment was with the director of *The Watcher in the Woods*, John Hough, who was coming to meet with Miss Davis. I curled up in bed, tired but too stimulated to sleep, to read the script. Miss Davis was playing Mrs. Aylwood, an elderly woman who rents a house to a young American family. Decades before that moment in the film, Mrs. Aylwood's ten-year-old daughter, Karen, disappeared into the woods, gone forever. This memory haunts Mrs. Aylwood, who is certain that her daughter will return, a mania that transforms into a fixation on the young family's own ten-year-old daughter. Although Mrs. Aylwood did not have many scenes, every one of them was a creepy turning point in the plot, especially the flashback to the moment some forty years before when her daughter disappears.

The next afternoon Miss Davis called me into her suite an hour before Mr. Hough's appointment. She had me order some assorted sandwiches and tea service for two from room service. I watched her pace and smoke, deep in her thoughts, leaving me not much to do after the refreshments were delivered. The phone rang announcing Mr. Hough's arrival.

"Catherine, make note the director's name is pronounced like 'Huff.' You want to show respect in proper pronunciation of his name."

When I greeted him at the door, Mr. Hough brushed right past me.

"Oh, Miss Davis," he exclaimed as he took long, quick strides into the room. I guessed he was about forty, a tall man with thick dark shoulder-length hair and a charming British accent. His arms were open as if he had an urge to hug Miss Davis, but you could see from the look on her face that he better not try.

"Miss Davis, you look spectacular! As if you've just come back from a week at the spa." He beamed.

"Oh how kind of you to say that," she said with a coquettish smile and a fetching turn of her head. I could not believe that Miss Davis, more than thirty years older than he, was flirting with Mr. Hough, and that he appeared receptive to her charms.

"This is my assistant, Catherine Sermak," she said.

I walked over to shake his hand.

"Pleased to meet you, Mr. Hough," I said, squeezing his hand confidently but not forcefully, as Miss Davis had taught me. "Would you like some tea?"

"Yes, that would be lovely," he said.

"Please, sit down," Miss Davis said, indicating the sofa. They took their places while I attended to the tea.

"No really, I think you look marvelous," Mr. Hough said. "And I agree it's right that we should give it a try. Who says you can't play both roles? The young Mrs. Aylwood as well as the old."

"I'm so glad you agree," Miss Davis said, as I brought over the tray with the tea service and started to position the cups.

"That will be all, Catherine," Miss Davis said.

I turned to go to my room.

"Yes, so we'll give it a go," I heard Mr. Hough say as I closed the door behind me. I was grinning when I got out into the hallway at the notion that Miss Davis was going to take direction from a man she so clearly had wrapped completely around her finger.

We stayed a few more days in London and then drove through Ascot near Pinewood Studios, which is thirty miles and a bit south of London. The drive from London to Ascot was a journey into the green, lush countryside, unlike the dry and spare beauty of Southern California. Our destination was the Berystede Hotel, which looked like a little castle, but of much smaller proportions. The suite I shared with Miss Davis was a round room in a tower. Again she sent me to the front desk to get fifty-pence coins. When I returned, she had another task.

"Oh good you're back," she said. "Help me re-arrange this furniture. Gawd, look at this. If the hotel designers would just *live* in these suites they would not choose such impractical arrangements. You can't set your drink on the table, it's so far away. Grab that chair and put it here, no *there*. Good. Let's put the coffee table right here.... Angles make it warm and cozy."

I moved the coffee table closer to the sofa. Miss Davis scrutinized the new arrangement from the doorway.

"All end tables must be to the *right* of the chair, Catherine," she said. "Most people are right handed, so you don't want to make them reach across the body. On that end table is where you place the cigarettes. The ashtray goes like so. Always make a pyramid, a triangle: ashtray closest, cigarettes, then matches." I was dumbstruck by her specificity...and then realized it all *did* make sense.

She opened the bag that contained the pictures of her family and Nerack, a small porcelain cat that her daughter Bede promised would bring good luck. When the knickknacks and photographs were positioned satisfactorily, Miss Davis sat in the high-backed Queen Anne and smiled at the new arrangement.

"What time does the call sheet say we need to be there, Catherine?"

"It says 8:00 a.m., Miss Davis," I said.

"Yes, 8. Call Brian and tell him to bring the car around at 5:45 a.m. We will be down by 6," she said.

She walked to the closet and picked up a navy blue and white duffle bag made of heavy canvas with thick leather handles and gave it to me. The "CD" embroidered into the fabric, I saw when I discovered the label inside, stood for Christian Dior.

"We take this bag with us to the set every day," Miss Davis said. "It has everything we would need in an emergency, and the scripts. Don't forget it. Catherine, do you remember what I like to have for breakfast?"

"Yes, Miss Davis," I said. "You like an egg."

"Yes, I like a three-minute egg," Miss Davis said. "In fact I'd like one right now. Please make one. Knock on my bedroom door when the egg is ready."

I walked to the table where she'd placed the electric kettle, percolator, and timer alongside the eggs and butter I brought from the shop. I realized there was no way I could make an egg: not a burner to warm the water or a pot in which to cook it. I wasn't sure what to do, and I was annoyed that she had devised another test for me to fail. I knocked on her door.

"Miss Davis, I'm afraid there is no way I can make an egg here. There is no kitchen."

She opened the door and regarded me with a slight hint of a smile. It was a nice change in her instructional demeanor.

"Let me show you, my dear," she said.

She filled the kettle about halfway. When it boiled, she turned it off and used a spoon to carefully place two eggs inside it, setting a timer for three minutes. The timer sounded. She poured the hot water into the sink and ran cold water inside the kettle, then poured it out. Miss Davis took two cups from the tea service and placed a dab of butter at the bottom of each. One by one, she cracked the eggs open and spooned their contents onto the butter. After a sprinkling of the salt and pepper from the shakers she'd brought from Los Angeles, we sat with our eggs at the dining table.

I understood her better while all of this was underway. She didn't want to leave anything to chance. Although I had said at my initial interview that I knew how to cook an egg, considering all my mistakes in the last few weeks, she was no longer sure I could do anything I'd promised. She could have demonstrated for me this unique way she devised to make an egg without a hotel kitchenette, but she instead chose to let me flounder a bit to remind me how little I knew. Still, she seemed more amused now than annoyed. The best response, I suspected, was a compliment. I would lose ground if I filled the air with complaints or apologies.

"So you've never had a three-minute egg?" she asked.

"This is delicious, Miss Davis," I said.

"Thank you," she said. "I want one of these every morning before we leave for the set." I had guessed right.

"Tomorrow on the set I will introduce you to a few people, the ones you will be dealing with on my behalf. No mingling with the crew. Through me, you will be giving orders to people much older than you and you need to gain their respect. Do you have any questions?"

"No, Miss Davis."

The next morning I was up two hours before we were scheduled to leave so that I could make sure that all was as she liked it before we saw each other. I also practiced making my own three-minute egg. Miss Davis came out of her room exactly at 5:30, dressed in Brooks Brothers pants and shirt, carrying her large dark sunglasses and a light brown straw hat. Her face was free of makeup except her red lipstick. We did not speak. As she ate her egg, I gathered up the items we were taking with us to the set. Apparently my egg passed muster.

On our way to the car, we were assaulted by paparazzi.

"Hello Bette! Give us a twirl, love!"

Miss Davis kept her head down and walked quickly to the car with me trailing behind.

There was some fan mail in the duffle bag, and I knew it was my responsibility to sort it out while she was on the set. I had looked through some of the letters the night before and knew that she had to have some system for how she responded. There were requests for autographs, requests for appearances, and direct pleas that Miss Davis send money to support a fan who had fallen on hard times.

"Miss Davis, I wanted to speak with you about how to handle fan mail," I said.

She turned her head toward me in a cocked angle of incredulity and tilted it toward Brian, the driver, indicating that he might be listening. Not a word passed her lips during the entire journey. Soon we drove up in front of the romantic Tudor façade of Pinewood Studios. Brian pulled up in front of the sound stage where *The Watcher in the Woods* was being shot. As he exited to come round to open her door, Miss Davis shifted up from her seat to look at me directly.

"You must always be aware that *everyone* in this business talks," she said. "Anything you say in the car you should assume we might find the next day in the tabloids. So you say nothing."

"Yes, Miss Davis."

I was chagrined, but I got the feeling that I was more upset than she. She exited the car and stood for a moment taking stock of her new surroundings. I gathered the bag from the car and we strode toward the cavernous sound stage, already bustling this early in the morning, with gaffers taping down electrical cords and the crewmembers adjusting the lights and testing the sound. Miss Davis seemed to grow taller from the moment we entered this place where she had unquestioned command. We walked to the set of one of the interiors and she turned to face the lights. She scanned them from top to bottom, then up to the top and across.

"A yellow legal pad and a pen, Catherine," she said. I fished those items out of the duffle bag and handed them to her. She made a few notes, walked along the tracks that had been laid out for the camera. After making a few more notes, the first assistant director appeared, surprised to see Miss Davis already on the set. They were not expecting her for another hour. After assessing the situation she asked him to take us to her trailer. I could see Miss Davis' appearance on the set caused quite a commotion.

The stars' trailers were assembled in a rough grouping on a muddy patch of ground outside the sound stage. Her trailer had two rooms, one of which had a tall director's chair in front of a large mirror with lights clamped at its sides. The other room was a lounging area. The whole place was crammed with flower arrangements.

"Catherine, take all the cards from the arrangements," she said. "On the back of the cards describe each arrangement and who sent it. Then when you write a thank-you note, you can make it personal. 'Thank you for those spectacular red roses....' or 'The scent of the lilies brightened my trailer for days.' Make everyone who sent something feel that they were uniquely generous."

As I was taking my notes, there was a knock on the door. I opened it and saw a tall slender woman about a decade older than I.

"Catherine, who is it?" Miss Davis asked.

"Jill Carpenter," the woman said.

"Jill! Yes, yes! Come in."

Miss Davis greeted her makeup artist with a hearty handshake and sat in the makeup chair next to the palettes of colors, jars of foundations and contouring creams, and brushes and pencils that Jill had set up on a table next to the makeup chair before we arrived. Jill turned on the lights, illuminating every wrinkle in Miss Davis' face. I watched Jill artfully contour Miss Davis' nose with shades of brown, defining stronger cheekbones and a sharper jawline. After she created that base of shadows, she applied a tint of white covered by layers of foundation that disguised her wrinkles. Then she set to work on the finer points of Miss Davis' eyes and brows. At the end of this silent hour in the chair Miss Davis looked twenty years younger.

"Very good, Jill," she said as she scrutinized her face in a hand mirror. "You are truly an artist when it comes to matters of the face. Remarkable."

After Jill departed, the wardrobe assistant arrived. Miss Davis was expected on the set in thirty minutes. The wardrobe assistant helped Miss Davis into a dress that seemed suited for a much younger woman. Then it occurred to me this was Miss Davis' screen test for the flashback of Mrs. Aylwood the younger, the moment that would decide if she could play a woman half her age.

"Come, Catherine," she said as she exited the trailer.

The sun was up and the studio grounds were even more crowded, but nonetheless a path parted before Miss Davis. She walked briskly toward the sound stage, cigarette in one hand and legal pad and pen in the other.

I took my position at the canvas director's chair emblazoned with MISS BETTE DAVIS. Mr. Hough and Miss Davis huddled in the middle of the set. From her hand gestures I saw she was recommending adjustments in the lights. She walked over to the fireplace and I assumed that she was suggesting that part of her scene be played there. They walked along the camera tracks with her pointing here and there. At the end of their discussion Mr. Hough addressed the crew.

"Let's have a run through."

It took twenty minutes to make all the changes Miss Davis had suggested. As these preparations were underway, she stood with her head angled down, I assumed gathering her focus.

"ACTION!"

Miss Davis lifted her head and became the young Mrs. Aylwood. Two takes of the scene and we were done. I thought we would go quickly back to the hotel. I did not realize it would take nearly as long to remove the makeup as it had to apply it. When at last we were back at the hotel, the afternoon papers were arrayed on the coffee table in the suite, among them a tabloid with a front-page photo of Miss Davis snapped when we were on our way to the studio. The headline: BETTE DAVIS DOESN'T GIVE A DAMN HOW SHE LOOKS!

That really stung! That simply was not true.

"Oh Miss Davis, look!" I said, holding up the front page of the tabloid for her to see. "Should I phone the man from Disney's press department? We need to speak to them about this."

"No," she said.

"But it's so unfair," I said.

"Those men have a job to do, Catherine," she said with not a hint of rancor in her voice. "They have families to feed. No need to make a fuss. Remember that it is always the best food that the birds pick at."

The next day we returned to Pinewood to view the makeup test in the screening room. Miss Davis sat in the center row, center seat in the small theater. Jill and I were seated behind her. The projector was so close we could hear the clacking of the film as it moved through the sprockets. Then there was Miss Davis' face huge on the screen, filling it completely. The thought of having my face magnified to that size terrified me, but when I looked over at Miss Davis I could see how carefully she was studying the image. Her face was her fortune, and she was giving it a hard look. She displayed no emotions.

In real life she looked too young for seventy-one, but even with all that makeup, she looked too old for thirty-five. I was anxious about what would happen when she met up with Mr. Hough. If she insisted on playing this part and he disagreed, there might be a fight. I suppose everyone feared that. When we exited the screening room we found Mr. Hough waiting outside the door. They regarded each other, each trying to read the other's mind.

"Miss Davis, I don't think you've made it," he said.

She took a long drag of her cigarette, all the time looking Mr. Hough directly in the eye. He didn't flinch although he looked like he wanted to.

"You're goddamned right," she said.

And that was that.

On the ride back to the Berystede, I wanted to know every thought she was having. Here was something she had worked so hard to have, and she had let it go without a fight. Had she really let it go? Was the woman in the seat next to me taking an inventory of herself, of her dreams and of her capacities, now that she was past the age of seventy? Already I had an instinct to protect this woman who needed no protection, and certainly none from me.

For the next six weeks her schedule at the studio was intermittent. As she only had a few scenes, there were stretches of time as long as a week where we were free to do as we pleased. If we only had a few days between scenes, she spent hours in the garden of the Berystede where she pruned the geraniums or picked blueberries for our meals. During longer breaks she happily filled our days with adventures. We took a three-day trip to the country to retrieve a grandfather clock that was important to Bede and her husband, Jeremy. After a visit with his parents, we arranged to have it shipped back to their farm in Pennsylvania. On the way home we stopped at the White Cliffs of Dover.

We were at the Berystede much more often than any other

place in England, and to me it was my least favorite of the
places we stayed. Yes, it was lovely. The number of weddings held there every weekend was proof of how picturesque
its grounds were and the competence of the wonderful staff.
Their vigilance was clear in the constant fire drills we endured. One of the staff told me that a hundred years earlier
a fire had burned the Berystede nearly to the ground, which
created this habit of frequent emergency preparations.

One evening close to midnight I was awakened by the
sound of the fire alarm. I threw on some clothes and rushed
out to the sitting room where Miss Davis was running toward
me to roust me from my room.

"It's not a drill this time!" she said, grabbing her mink
coat.

We opened the doors to the balcony, a perch from which
it was possible to get over to the roof. The grounds below us
were filling up with guests in their robes and slippers. We
stood for a moment contemplating the route we should take
over the rooftop when Miss Davis grabbed my arm.

"Catherine, you must go back in!" she said, her eyes fran-
tic. "Quick! Grab my cigarettes!"

I rushed back into the room and retrieved a carton from
the duffle bag. I marveled that she would direct me back into
the burning building not to get her passport, or her treasured
family photographs, but her cigarettes.

We stood on the balcony for half an hour before we recognized that this was, indeed, a drill, not a real fire as Miss
Davis had feared. Then we, among all the other annoyed
guests, made our way, grumbling, back to our rooms, unable
to sleep the rest of the night.

This was one of the many reasons that I was in a much

better mood every time we left the Berystede. I yearned for London. Within walking distance of the Grosvenor House was the British Museum, the National Gallery, and St. James' Palace, plus the huge luxurious department store Harrods that stood just on the other side of Hyde Park. The English countryside seemed as dull as the food, boiled clean of flavor, and I was losing so much weight that I felt gaunt. I missed the lush sauces of French food.

When Miss Davis said she was too exhausted to get dressed up for Sunday brunch with Roy Moseley, I agreed without enthusiasm to take her place, dreading another drab English meal.

As I entered the dining room, my spirits lifted when I saw that the Sunday brunch buffet had choices I liked. Across the big dining room I saw Mr. Moseley, who rose and scrutinized me carefully as I approached the table. I suspected he recognized me for the Southern California girl that I was and immediately downgraded his expectations about my intelligence. The meal started off in a lively way as he described how he adored Miss Davis from a very young age and schemed for a long while to get to meet her. Once he did they had become close but evidently not close enough for her to put forth the effort to dine with him. He entertained me with great stories of Laurence Olivier and Vivien Leigh, two people I had known no more about than I had about Miss Davis a few months earlier. Now that I was a bit more familiar with her world, however, I was able to laugh sincerely at his insightful anecdotes about the world of acting. Yet I had the sense that for all the frothy conversation, he was driving toward something.

"So you are enjoying England then?" he asked. "I'm sure

with all the demands of the job you haven't been able to see much of the sights."

"Oh I have!" I said. "Miss Davis has been very generous with her driver Brian on the days when she does not need the car. I've seen the Tower of London, Windsor Castle, the changing of the guards at Buckingham Palace. My favorite was Carnaby Street. I am so grateful to Miss Davis for arranging for me to see the sights."

"So there are days when Bette is not needed on the set?" he said. "How big is her part in this film?"

My skin tensed at this question. It was not my place to answer this, not my information to distribute. If I had learned one thing from my Catholic school upbringing, it was not to promote gossip. And Miss Davis clearly valued her privacy. Yet I could not be rude.

"I'm afraid I do not know how to answer you, Mr. Moseley," I said. "This is my first time working on a movie and it is impossible for me to gauge whose part is big and whose part is small."

"Ah, of course," he said. "And what do you and Bette do in the evenings? Do you dine together?"

If this were Miss Davis' true friend, he would not need to ask. Something felt wrong about his questions. I suddenly felt invaded.

"Well I confess I'm just a homebody," I said. "I spend a lot of evenings in my room."

"In your room!" he said. "A beautiful young woman like you should not be spending her evenings alone."

Mr. Moseley clearly was launching an invasion. It was time for me to go.

"Mr. Moseley, it's been a pleasure to meet you," I said, as

I took a glance at my watch. "I'm afraid I must be on my way as I have some tasks to complete for Miss Davis."

I stood up, as did he. We shook hands.

"*Enchanté* and please give my regards to Bette," he said.

"I certainly will."

Miss Davis told me to come straight back to the suite when the meal was complete, and I did, but I went into my room and sat on my bed, hiding out. If I told the truth about our meal I might cause a rupture in their friendship. I did not want to be responsible for that. I was trying to figure out how to describe my brunch with Mr. Moseley when there was a knock on my door that could only be Miss Davis.

"And how was your brunch?"

"The buffet was delicious," I said.

"What did you and Mr. Moseley talk about?" she asked.

"He has wonderful stories."

"Catherine, do not waste my time." She clearly could sense something was bothering me.

"Well it was uncomfortable at the very end," I confessed. "He asked all these questions about how we spent our time together, how big your part was and what we did in the evenings."

"And what did you say?"

"I said nothing."

"Excellent, Catherine," she said and walked to the end table that held the phone.

"Operator, get me Roy Moseley."

She paced back and forth with a tight grip on the phone. I heard a small voice as Mr. Moseley answered.

"How dare you!" Miss Davis said. "How dare you probe my assistant for information about me! Don't you ever!"

She slammed the phone down. She was incensed.

"Now, that's the end of it," she said. She turned to me and her pause made me know another lesson was coming. "You must always be honest with me, Catherine. Always ask me anything you need to know. You will make mistakes. Make a hundred I don't mind. Just don't make the same mistake twice and you'll do just fine." Clearly another big step forward in our relationship—she now seemed to remember that she knew from the outset that I had a lot to learn, and she had promised to teach me.

We found out later that Mr. Moseley checked out of the hotel in the dead of night. Mr. Moseley liked to gossip, something I saw in the way he directed his questions to uncover intimate information about how Miss Davis and I spent our days. He liked to entertain her with the little bits he gathered at meals like the one he had with me, and she always wanted to know what was going on. She did not, however, want the same skill used in gathering information about her from someone else. His line of questioning with me had made Miss Davis suspicious that he was trying to manipulate me into disclosing something private to him that he could share with others. I saw firsthand the price one paid for running afoul of Miss Davis' standards for personal discretion and loyalty.

Miss Davis' work on the film continued, as did my education. Because her role was relatively brief, the lessons I had learned the first few days on the set had become ingrained by the time her work was done—it had been a short dip in the moviemaking pool for me, but a constructive one. Her remaining days on the set passed without mistakes on my part.

The last big occasion before we returned to California

was dinner at the home of the famed writer Roald Dahl and
his wife, the renowned actress Patricia Neal. They lived in
the village of Great Missenden, nearly an hour north of the
Berystede, in a home they named the Gipsy House. As we
walked down a long, paved path, its yellow front door swung
open and there stood Dahl, a man who seemed bigger than
the doorframe, beaming at us and eager to show us around his
world. Once inside, my eyes were confused sorting through
the layers of objects lining the walls: the collection of big
Norwegian smoking pipes, multiple paintings on every wall,
and primitive masks. Mr. Dahl was keen to tell me the stories
behind the objects that we saw, and there were many. It was
the kind of house that had grown organically from the inter-
ests of its inhabitants, and felt lived in and loved.

He invited us out to the garden to see his writing studio.
As we walked out the front door he told me how Gipsy House
got its name. He pointed to a bright blue wagon on tall wheels
with a short set of stairs leading up to its front door. It looked
like something out of Hansel and Gretel.

"That's Danny's gipsy caravan," he said.

"Oh, of course," said Miss Davis.

Who is Danny? I thought. *One of his children?*

We entered the small cottage where he wrote in a big arm-
chair with a green board positioned across the arms. It was
cozy, crammed with knickknacks, and filthy too, dusty and
dense. I bet he would not let anyone clean it. I felt honored to
be in this private space. Mr. Dahl was delighted by the look
on my face as I admired his hideaway.

"So you have no idea who Danny is?" he asked me.

"No, I'm sorry I do not," I said a bit sheepishly.

"You've never read my books! Let me give you some," he

said, plucking a few volumes from the shelves and signing each one before he handed it to me, beaming his lop-sided smile. Soon I was holding copies of *James and the Giant Peach, Charlie and the Chocolate Factory,* and *Danny the Champion of the World.* Danny and his father, I later discovered, lived in a gypsy caravan.

"Cocktails, shall we?" he said brightly. "Let's see if I can rouse Pat."

We were seated in the living room, cocktails in hand, when Patricia Neal made her entrance.

She was tall and long-limbed. Her pointed jaw and strong eyebrows amplified the heart shape of her face. Although she moved slowly, she cut a striking figure as she made her way toward me to shake hands. I remembered Miss Davis' instruction that you could understand much about a person from the strength of her handshake. Mrs. Dahl's was faint, and her hand was chilly. Her speech was slow and deliberate, much like the way she moved across the room and the care with which she sat down in her chair. Mr. Dahl quickly brought her a martini, and then another, while Miss Davis sipped her scotch and water. As the drinks accumulated on that side of the room, the hosts separated from the guests, taking off on a separate trajectory toward dinner. By the end of their second drink they were laughing and talking much more loudly than Miss Davis. I had said very little so far that evening and believed I would say even less as the night went on.

We adjourned from the parlor and took our places at the dining room table. Mr. Dahl, the chef, was busy in the kitchen. Atop the credenza I noticed three open bottles of French Bordeaux set out to breathe. Mr. Dahl brought out an appetizer and filled our glasses with wine. By the time we had finished the appetizer, he and Mrs. Dahl moved on to the second bottle. In the lull as Mr. Dahl served dinner, Mrs. Dahl seemed to finally notice me.

"How old are you, Catherine?" she asked.

"I'm twenty-three," I said.

"Oh to be twenty-three again!" she said. "Twenty-three is a perfect time to fall in love. Are you in love, Catherine?"

"I don't have a boyfriend at the moment," I said, relying on the candlelight to disguise how much I was blushing.

"Ah, but you will, you will," she said. "I met the love of my life when I was twenty-three."

"Really? Where did you two meet?" I asked.

"The love of my life was not him!" Mrs. Dahl said with a sarcastic laugh. "Him? Not him. No, no, no."

"Stop it!" Mr. Dahl said in a sharp voice. "Right now."

"Twenty-three. Twenty-three," Mrs. Dahl said, repeating the words slowly like an incantation. Every syllable made Mr. Dahl more furious.

Miss Davis started telling a story about someone they all knew in Los Angeles, and I was happy they all shifted to that. As incredible as the evening had been, it was slipping into dangerous territory and I wanted to be back at the Berystede, which was saying a lot.

After they finished discussing their mutual friend, Mr. Dahl brought out coffee for Miss Davis and me. He refilled his wine glass and Mrs. Dahl's.

"What did you study at university, Catherine?" he asked.

"I have a bachelor's degree in psychology," I replied.

"Really?" said Mrs. Dahl. "You're certainly getting to use your degree tonight. What do you think of us, Catherine? The aging movie star and the bitter author of children's books? Have you got us figured out?"

"Patricia!" Mr. Dahl shouted.

"We really must be going," Miss Davis said as she stood up from the table.

I took my cue to gather our things. "You know, I have an early call to be on the set tomorrow."

As we all walked outside, Miss Davis stopped and looked to acknowledge her hosts.

"It's always lovely seeing you both and what a treat it was to have dinner at your charming home. Thank you for a delicious meal. I hope to see you soon in New York or London."

The Dahls escorted us quickly to the car. Perhaps they were as happy to see us go as we were to leave, but I doubt they went right to bed after that. I heard them shouting at each other as Brian closed Miss Davis' door. When I got inside the car she grabbed my wrist with her gloved hand and whispered.

"I'm very sorry they embarrassed you that way. I think you behaved admirably. I'll explain everything when we are back in the suite."

During the brief drive back to the Berystede I composed myself as well as I could. I do not know why I was on the edge of tears. I didn't want to provoke their conflict, yet I ended up in the middle of it nonetheless. I was grateful that Miss Davis assured me I behaved well, but I was confused.

In our suite, Miss Davis sat in her chair and I took my place on the sofa.

"I am so sorry for the outbursts, Catherine, none of which was your fault," Miss Davis explained. "Patricia Neal was a stunning ingénue. When she was twenty-three she started an affair with Gary Cooper, who was married and twenty years older than she. This affair lasted until Gary Cooper's wife forced him to break it off. After him, she married Roald Dahl, but her heart remained with Gary."

"Oh, *they* met when she was twenty-three," I said, trying to see myself falling for a man two decades my senior. When I lived in France I had had a flirtation with a man named Pierre who was a few years older than I, but twenty years seemed like too great of a distance.

"So Roald and Patricia quickly began having children," Miss Davis continued. "When she was pregnant with their fifth child she suffered a stroke. Roald nursed her back to health and he was very strict with her, *very* strict. She owes her recovery to him, but it has ruined their marriage. He expects and deserves her gratitude. No one thought she would work again, but she has, and has done so brilliantly. But to bring her back he controlled her completely and he is having a hard time releasing that. What they said about you this evening reveals everything."

"She wanted to be twenty-three again," I said.

"When everything was perfect. And now even a woman as young as you can see what they have become."

"So it was never about me."

"No," she said.

We said our good nights as soon as she finished her cigarette.

The next day we packed to leave and I distributed Miss Davis' gifts to the staff of the Berystede. I had been excited when, a week earlier in London, I had passed a costume shop that stacked in the front window plastic replicas of the yellow helmets British firemen wear. With Miss Davis' approval, and indeed her surprise and happiness at my suggestion, I bought a dozen in honor of our late-night fire (false) alarm. The day before we left the Berystede, I presented them to the manager with a note from Miss Davis.

The morning we departed for home, the staff assembled in the lobby to see us off. They stood smartly at attention in two lines—wearing their bright fire brigade helmets. As we walked down the corridor they'd made, Miss Davis paused to thank each of them individually. They followed us out to the car, where Brian stood beaming, door open for Miss Davis. As we took our seats the staff applauded and Miss Davis exited the car one last time to wave and blow them a kiss.

On the Concorde back to New York, the first leg of the journey to California, I compared how different I felt seated next to Miss Davis this time. I may not have fulfilled all the job requirements, but I had mastered the proper demeanor. That might be even more important than the fine points of cooking a three-minute egg. After four months, I actually felt comfortable sitting next to her. We had begun to settle into our respective roles. She was opening the world to me, explaining it, and I was an apt pupil eager to learn more. Yet I also understood that my job was over as soon as the plane touched down in Los Angeles. I'd be starting graduate school after that. Wouldn't my father be pleased?

CHAPTER 3

THE PYGMALION YEAR
October 26, 1979

"Standards Matter"

I SAT IN Miss Davis' Colonial House living room waiting for my friend Stephanie, who was on her way to drive me back to San Bernardino. I had my datebook open on my lap recording notes about our journey back from Europe: what we had eaten, the names of our drivers, the way Miss Davis ordered a drink on the flight from New York to Los Angeles. I held the menu from the Concorde back to New York to jot down the delicious choices offered on that flight. In the four months I'd been with Miss Davis, I learned that as her Girl Friday my domain was the details. Even though these were my last few minutes on this job, I hadn't dropped the habit of writing everything down. I enjoyed how comforting it was to live in Miss Davis' organized and deliberate way, and I was going to keep that habit going as long as I could. I was sad, too. Despite how tough Miss Davis had been on me these four months, I had learned a lot and in truth I wanted to learn more.

When we had arrived back at the Colonial House her housekeeper Lupe was there to greet us, ready to help Miss Davis unpack her suitcases and address the mountain of mail. There were flower arrangements everywhere welcoming her home, but it was no longer my job to note down who sent which one and the details for the thank-you cards. As I continued to write about our trip in my datebook, I heard her in her bedroom. She and Lupe were putting away her jewelry and other personal items and deciding what needed to be laundered and what should go to the drycleaner. Our days had been so intertwined while we were in England that it was odd now not to know exactly what she was up to, and not to know her schedule for the days ahead. When I thought back on the months we'd spent together, I tended to remember the dramatic moments, but as I looked through my datebook I realized it was the adventures and the great meals that stood out.

The datebook fell open to August and the arrangements I had made to go to the country to retrieve that grandfather clock for her daughter, Bede. Miss Davis was in high spirits when we set off, never so happy as when she was being useful, fulfilling someone's long-held wish. It was clear how much she enjoyed pleasing her daughter. Collecting the clock and arranging for it to be shipped was fun. On the way back to the Berystede, when we stopped for lunch at a restaurant the day we visited the White Cliffs of Dover, I remembered a moment when we didn't have that much to say. It was then I appreciated that the silence between us had become a comfortable one. Despite her ongoing frustrations with my ignorance about so many things, there was an ease about the way we were together, a relaxed feeling that I'd never experienced in my other jobs. I had had four months of this life and though I wanted nothing more than to stay, I resolved simply to be grateful that I had had this time with her.

The phone rang and Lupe announced that my friend was waiting for me downstairs in the lobby. Miss Davis came into the living room to say farewell.

"Thank you for everything, Catherine," Miss Davis said, extending her hand for me to shake. As we walked toward the foyer, she put her arm through mine and drew me close, a surprisingly affectionate gesture.

She opened the door to her apartment. The elevator door receded and Russell, the Colonial House doorman, came into the apartment to help me with my suitcases. I walked with him to the elevator, and looked back to wave goodbye to Miss Davis.

"I'll call you in a day or two," she said.

"Thank you, Miss Davis!"

As Russell drew the door closed she shouted, "And your handshake, Catherine, it is much improved!"

As the elevator door shut I was filled with joy. She would call me! Perhaps I could postpone graduate school yet again. Thank you, Miss Davis! Thank you, indeed.

"She'll never call you," my father said at dinner the day after I returned home. "You better start thinking about graduate school. Enough! Enough of this taking jobs on a whim, working for a princess."

Despite my certainty that she would call, I did my share of praying. The heavens answered my prayers because two days after I got home I received a call from Miss Davis, just as she had promised.

"Catherine, can you get up here right away?" she started off abruptly. "I start filming on Monday and Miss Shannon just told me that she is too ill to work. She pulled her back out. Can you come?" Miss Shannon was her hairdresser and close friend, and I felt guilty for not feeling bad about her condition.

"Why yes, Miss Davis."

"Great! You'll move in here. Bring enough clothes for a few weeks. You can stay in the guest room. We'll work out the details later. We'll have a script ready for you. We must cue right away. See you in two days."

When I told my parents my plans, my father's contempt was clear but he didn't argue or try to convince me to refuse to take the job. It was as if he'd washed his hands of me. The morning I was packing to move to the Colonial House he stood at the door to my bedroom watching, shaking his head at my folly.

"Where is it going to get you?" was all he said. That was a question I didn't feel I needed to answer precisely, but Miss Davis' words about "hunches" were shouting at me from inside.

That afternoon I entered the guest room at the Colonial House knowing that it was mine for as long as I held this job. Helen Ann reminded me to continue enjoying every minute while always assuming it might not work out. We knew Lupe and Miss Shannon lived elsewhere, and Miss Davis might decide it was too annoying to have a young person underfoot every day. I remembered how often she had sent me away when she needed some time to herself in England. But in California, we would be roommates. She did not have one of those Hollywood mansions where the assistant lived in a guesthouse on the property. We would hear everything each other did and said. Helen Ann and I agreed that if I got on her nerves she would fire me without thinking much about it. But I was ready to continue my education with Miss Davis for as long as it lasted.

My new room was larger than my childhood bedroom, with its own bathroom and a telephone. Although I'd stayed in this room the night before we left for New York, I hadn't really had the time to appreciate her New England style: the fine colonial furniture, the smooth cotton sheets and the comfy and welcoming bed that was now all mine. In her house each object was precious and everything had a professional or personal story behind it. One of her treasures was an 18th century Banjo Clock with a parchment-colored face that stood prominently at the end of the main hallway. The clock face was at the top of a column of well-polished wood with an etching of a New England sailing ship on the base. Miss Davis told me not to touch it and that she alone would wind it. A clockmaker came and fine-tuned it once a year. Her home was a living museum of the gifts she had received from the many people from around the world who had been touched by her and her work.

That evening at dinner she had described the week ahead. The next day we would run lines for her scenes in *White Mama* to prepare for a table reading, where the actors sit at a table reading their parts to get a feel for how they interact. The wardrobe woman was coming to the apartment for costume fittings. When I looked at the many tasks for the week that I had written in my datebook, it was clear that she really did need my help. I undressed and put on one of the lovely new nightgowns my mother bought for me before I left. I was so revved up I knew it would take forever for me to get to sleep. I took out the copies of the script she had given me and sat in bed preparing them for our session the next day: discarding the pages of the scenes she was not in, highlighting her lines one color and the lines of the character that came before her in another. I had learned to do this in England, but in *White Mama* her part was huge and the job of preparing the script was enormous. I didn't get to sleep until way past midnight.

That next morning I woke up to the smell of coffee brewing in the kitchen. I'd bought a new robe before I left San Bernardino so that I could be presentable in the morning if Miss Davis and I met up at the breakfast table. I opened the Dutch door that separated the kitchen from the rest of the apartment and used my Spanish to ask Lupe for a cup of coffee. Her face lit up and we started chatting about where I learned Spanish. I took my coffee, thanked her, and turned to go back to my room when I saw Miss Davis at the half doorway. The look on her face was alarming. She motioned for me to follow her into the living room.

"How dare you!" she said in a whisper that was as cutting as a shriek.

"I'm sorry?" I answered.

"Don't you ever do that again!"

"I'm sorry, but..."

"No *buts*. Don't you ever come out of your room in a bathrobe. You come out dressed."

"Yes, Miss Davis."

"I know you were talking to Lupe about me. Don't deny it. Don't you know that you never discuss anything with the help? Who do you think you are?"

My two transgressions were blown so far out of proportion I didn't know how to react. I just stood there speechless. This was a side of her that I hadn't yet seen. I excused myself and went to my room to get dressed.

An hour later I came into the living room timidly, still a bit shaken, ready to help her run her lines. I was scared that she would still be angry with me. She was not. While her standards were high like my father's, she would get angry but instantly let it go, whereas my father would continue to berate me for days if I had made a mistake. Miss Davis was on to the work at hand. We began.

In this movie Miss Davis was the star. The phrase she used was that she was "carrying the movie," as she was in almost every scene. *White Mama* was about a woman who takes in a black teenager because she needs the city's foster parents' fee to survive after her husband dies. The two form an unlikely bond that endures after he leaves her home. Eventually he saves her from homelessness, just as she once had saved him. This was a made-for-television movie that many in Hollywood thought was risky (even in the late 1970s) because the topic was racial integration. Miss Davis clearly relished the prospect of being in the middle of this ongoing national dialogue.

In London I'd seen how Miss Davis rewrote many of her lines, but as the main character in this film she attacked the script, taking it apart, questioning every word to determine if the line sounded true and precise. She started the session pacing as she considered the dialogue, asking me to repeat some lines several times before she decided what she wanted to change. I scribbled notes about her changes in the margins of the script. "This is so everything works as it should," she said.

Oh my gosh, she's a perfectionist, I thought. *How does anyone keep up with her?*

After three hours of work, we'd only gotten through the two scenes. I suppose she saw my slightly confused look as I rose to go to my room.

"Concentration, dedication, and homework," she repeated as I walked toward my room. "The work on this movie will be much more demanding than the way we lived in England. When you are carrying a movie, filming every day, it is like going to prison. No distractions, no socializing, complete focus. We will be leaving here at 5:45 tomorrow morning, Catherine, so plan accordingly."

I was glad that she had warned me that this film would be more demanding than *The Watcher in the Woods,* because it definitely was. We were on the set for ten hours or more every day. Instead of being filmed in the cozy atmosphere of the sound stages at Pinewood, *White Mama* was shot in a rough part of downtown Los Angeles, where there were dozens of police guarding our set at all times. While she was on the set I was responsible for her fan mail, dealing with anything that would come up at the house, and conveying the messages from her agent and her lawyer only after the day's work was done. During breaks from filming, I cared for her immediate needs. I scoped out what the caterers offered for lunch and had that list ready. When she decided what she wanted, I brought it to her, and we ate in her trailer.

As the weeks went on my responsibilities increased, particularly at home. Lupe had a family emergency and abruptly returned to Colombia uncertain when or if she would be back. Miss Davis had the agency send over a new housekeeper, Yolanda. She had good references but a difficult time remembering my instructions. She used the wrong polish on the pinewood and mahogany furniture and she used bronze polish for the silver. Miss Davis complained that the beds were not made with proper hospital corners and that she left streaks on the windows she washed. This created an unacceptable state of chaos for someone who was as much of a perfectionist as Miss Davis. When I corrected Yolanda, she scowled at me rather than apologizing or pledging to do better. This dark quality about her seeped into the atmosphere of the apartment. When we discussed whether to keep her on or not, Miss Davis described the mood around her as a black cloud, and from that moment on we referred to her as "Black Cloud." When I was addressing Black Cloud at home, I had a hard time remembering her real name.

Later that week I knew we had to fire Black Cloud, which all came down to a vacuum cleaner. Miss Davis had a fancy new vacuum that had powerful water suction but Black Cloud could not figure it out. When she vacuumed she left a pattern of her movements on the weave of the carpet, something I knew was not to Miss Davis' liking and would most certainly get her fired. The whole encounter with the clueless Black Cloud had become a joke between Miss Davis and me, and I was bursting to tell her about the vacuum cleaner episode when I went to the set that afternoon.

"Miss Davis, you'll never guess what Black Cloud did now!" I said, grinning widely. The look I got from Miss Davis collapsed that smile.

"We'll address this later, Catherine," said Miss Davis sternly.

I went to her trailer, occupying myself with the fan mail but feeling anxious and upset. This was the first big mistake I had made since the bathrobe incident. I was sure I was going to be fired along with Black Cloud.

At the end of the day Miss Davis entered the trailer without acknowledging me and went to her dressing table. She sat there taking off her makeup as my stomach flipped over with anxiety. After a few minutes she addressed me.

"Catherine, I assumed that it was clear to you that when we are on the set we focus completely on the work we do here," she said, her tone icy and exasperated. "Concentration, dedication. I do not want to hear about domestic concerns while I am on the film set. Is that understood?"

"Yes, Miss Davis."

"There is a lot of money at stake when we are making a film," she continued. "We do not waste time and the company's money on trivial matters. Furthermore, we do not discuss aspects of home life when there are strangers around. This was something I believed you already knew, Catherine."

All I could think was, *I should have known. I should have known.*

"I'm sorry, Miss Davis."

"Well, I'm sure it will not happen again."

Relief. She was not going to fire me that day.

"Now tell me," she said, suddenly with a much softer and more amused tone of voice, now ready for the joke between us. "Just what *did* Black Cloud do now?"

Shortly after that dust-up, the actors union went on strike. We thought we'd be off the set for a few weeks, but the strike lasted three whole months. At first Miss Davis was happy to have some time to catch up on the things she had neglected while she focused on the movie. Little did I realize, as the weeks became months, that the focus of her attention would become *me*.

"Catherine, I think we should discuss your work with me," she said the second week of the hiatus. "Now that I think about it, this Girl Friday position you have is not really a good description of your duties. You did an excellent job training the new housekeeper and your insight into Black Cloud was first class. I am going to promote you to my personal assistant."

She walked over to the telephone and dialed her attorney, Mr. Harold Schiff.

"Harold, I've just made Catherine my personal assistant, and I want her salary increased by fifty dollars a week starting today. Thank you, Harold," she said.

Then she turned back toward me.

"And because of that, I think we should come up with some other way for you to address me."

"I should no longer call you Miss Davis?" I asked, baffled.

"It's too formal, and not personal enough," she said. "I think it intimidates the crew that someone as close to me as you still calls me Miss Davis. Try calling me Bette."

This did not work out, as we quickly found out. I found it impossible to call her Bette. In my home and in my church we always called adults by an honorific: Mr., Mrs., Dr. I was so inhibited about calling her Bette that I had to find her in the apartment if I had something to say to her because that name would not leave my lips. It only took a few hours for Miss Davis to notice.

"You feel uncomfortable calling me Bette, don't you, Catherine?"

"Yes I do, Miss Davis."

"I totally understand," she said. "I couldn't call Jack Warner, Jack. Let's see. Try calling me Miss D for a few days and see if that feels more comfortable to you. Miss D...Miss D. You know I quite like that, Catherine. It's more familiar but it's still formal, and it's special. Miss D. And I wanted to talk to you about your name, too."

"You want to change my name?"

"No, not in the least," she said. "I want to change the *spelling* of your name. The way your parents chose to spell it is so much like everyone else in the world. If you spell it K-A-T-H-R-Y-N, it's more distinctive. People will remember that spelling."

My habit was always to respond, "Yes, Miss Davis." This was something that did not generate an automatic yes. She was changing our relationship in a positive way, but now she wanted to change my identity.

"Of course, Catherine, it is completely up to you whether or not you want to change the spelling of your name," she said. "It's a very personal matter and I don't want to impose this on you if this change is not welcome. But I want to advise you that one of the big battles in life is to stand out from the crowd."

I was turning the idea over in my head, trying to get more comfortable with it. I already had changed my name a few times as I grew up. In Catholic school it seemed as though a quarter of my peers were named Catherine. There had been so many Catherines in my grammar school that the nuns had to distinguish us from each other by calling me Catherine S while another one was Catherine M, and there was a Catherine P as well. When I got a bit older I chose Cathy. I'd changed back to Catherine in college because it seemed more mature.

Here she was calling on me to become someone different from any of those: Catherine with a *K* and a *Y*. If I did this I was distinguishing myself from the world of my childhood and my family. Perhaps I should see how it felt. I knew she had done the same when she was young. She had been named Ruth Elizabeth Davis at birth. Her family and friends called her Betty. When she chose a life in public, she wanted to stand out, and changed the spelling of her name to B-e-t-t-e inspired by Honoré de Balzac's *La Cousine Bette*. Like her, I wasn't changing my name legally, or the way it sounded. I did not have to tell my parents anything unless I wanted to make it permanent.

"I'll give it a try, Miss D," I said.

"And I will call you Kath," she said. "I like the sound of that, and like Miss D, it's not as formal, especially when we're on a set."

The smile on her face was broad, as if we had just become much closer even though all we had done was alter the way we addressed each other by a few letters.

Little did I know that this would be the start of the changes that Miss D had planned for me during the months we waited for *White Mama* to resume. Now that she had decided to keep me on with a new title, the aspects of me that annoyed her were things she believed we could work on together. As the weeks and months of that first year went by I felt as if she was conducting a homegrown version of a finishing school, one in which she tutored me in the nuances of how a well-bred young woman walked, talked, and moved through the world with a certain kind of upper-crust grace. I had always been aware that she was watching me, even when I was newly her Girl Friday. Now she was watching me in a different way.

Although I was flattered that she saw me as someone with potential, many times the attention made me crazy.

I was on the phone in the living room one evening before dinner, talking to a friend back home. When I encountered Miss D in the kitchen she had a question for me.

"Kathryn, do you know how many times you said 'okay' in that last conversation?" she asked.

"I don't," I said.

She could hear me on the phone even with the kitchen door shut, and she was listening. This was good to know.

"You were only on the phone twenty-two minutes and you said 'okay' twenty-three times," she said. "It's a bad habit, a low-class kind of diction, and I want you to break it. I came up with something to help you to stop this."

She produced a quart-sized mason jar and plunked it down on the counter.

"Every time you say 'okay' you will have to put a quarter in this jar," she said with a definitive imperiousness. "When you see the toll it takes on you, it will be easy for you to stop."

I looked at the mason jar, trying to stifle my contempt for it. A mason jar. Quarters. This was insane.

"Okay," I said defiantly, and dropped a quarter in the mason jar.

Miss D looked very pleased, both with her victory and my small act of defiance. I went to my room and blasted Rod Stewart on my stereo. I wanted out of there so bad I could scream.

The battle of "okay" was the start of her campaign to fix my voice and improve my diction. I had been raised among women who were soft spoken. My mother spoke in a low voice that had some music in it. My sisters and I adopted her sweet and modest style of speech, a contrast to the power and volume of my father's voice. As with the firm handshake, the personal assistant of Bette Davis should speak with authority, she said. The tutoring was a daily event. We'd be standing in the living room working on another matter when she would stop me mid-sentence to coach me on how to project my voice.

"Your voice comes from your diaphragm," she'd say. "Stand up so you can breathe deeper. Inhale a big gulp of air, Kath. Take it way down into the bottom of your lungs so that you have enough to project outward."

Why did I have to do this? Would the silly requirements for this job ever end? This had to be some artifact from her career on the stage. Yet when I mastered it, I could see that it did enhance my presence, and thus my ability to do my job for her.

Next on her list was fine-tuning my appearance. She was watching a morning television show that featured José Eber, then an up-and-coming hairdresser to the stars, doing a makeover on a young woman with long hair. Little did I know that she had decided that my hair needed a trim. All of the Sermak girls were proud of their long and thick hair, and most of us wore it quite long, way down our backs. Miss D wanted something more polished for her assistant, more carefully layered. She was captivated by José, who also had long hair and wore a distinctive tan cowboy hat. She called José's salon herself to ask if he would come to the Colonial House to cut my hair.

This was quite a shearing, like she was taking some of my youthful power away. Maybe she sensed that the novelty of having José set up his chair in my room would distract me from feeling that loss. As he carefully layered my hair, Miss D leaned against the doorway watching him, smoking, and reminding him not to make it too short. Once he was done my hair was shorter by nearly a foot. I appreciated how, piece by piece, Miss D was chipping away at the wild California girl. My new hair looked beautiful, and I looked ever so much more put together.

After voice and hair came posture and movement. She started with my walk.

"The foundation of a graceful walk is a graceful posture," Miss D said. "The graceful posture begins in the hips, in the tilt of the pelvis. Pull up strongly from the hips, tilt the pelvis forward, and the spine straightens on its own, the shoulders pull back. Perfect."

I'd been walking through the world for twenty-four years with barely a stumble and now I had to re-learn how to do it?

She walked over to one of the living room walls.

"Here, come stand over here, Kath," she said.

I joined her there. She turned me around so my back was facing the wall and, with gentle pressure on my shoulders from her fingertips, she pushed me against it. As I stood there fuming, her eyes scanned the places where my torso touched the wall.

"This is how you test for perfect posture," she said. "See how your derriere touches but your shoulders do not? The points of contact should be head, shoulders, and hips."

She nudged my shoulders closer to the wall. To make those points of my body touch it, I tilted my pelvis slightly to improve my alignment. I wanted out of this room immediately, so complying with these commands was the fastest way out the door.

"Now for the walk," she said brightly.

Oh no, I thought. *This is never going to end.*

"Keep your shoulders back, just as you have them now, and step forward as if you have a third leg in between your two."

Huh? Who walks pretending they have a leg between their legs? Actors, actresses, I guess, but I'm not one.

"That look on your face is not helpful," she said. "Give it a try. You'll see how different it feels."

In imagining that there was a third leg between my two I had to step wider. With wider steps, my hips swayed more than they had before. The whole motion was exaggerated and uncomfortable: the tilted pelvis, the stiff shoulders, and this liquid walk seemed like the kind of motion that would have my father calling me out as a flirt—or worse.

"This will take practice, Kath, but once you master it, you'll never want to walk any other way," she advised me.

Really? I want to walk right out the door.

"Kath, show me how you'd sit in this chair, gracefully." *No, this will never end.*

I sat down quietly.

"No, no, no...you must go like this," she said. She used her right hand to scoop the bottom of her dress forward, presenting a smooth surface to the chair so there would be no creases in her skirt. This seemed straightforward enough, and I mimicked her without her needing to correct me.

"Knees together," she said. This was also easy to do. "Depending on the situation, you pivot your knees to the side, legs at a slant, or cross them over. Never knees apart. Excellent, Kath. You're doing this one quite naturally. Bravo. Now stand and we'll walk some more."

I stood up, compliant but furious. *Do I have to completely re-invent myself to please her?* After I had waddled across the living room a few times I think she sensed my mood.

"That's all for now, Kath. Take a swim if you like. Cocktails at 4."

I went to my room, careful not to slam the door. I needed that swim. But within a short time all ideas of leaving had themselves taken foot. I had to admit that I liked what I had learned. I was learning presence from a master.

In the months of the hiatus, our afternoons had a routine. We'd work for a few hours or I'd do her errands, and then Miss D would need to be alone (and so would I). I craved movement, exercise. At the pool I was building my way up to a hundred laps, and I always had a book with me and my journal. When I was not swimming, I wrote in my journal or read my book with my sunglasses on, ignoring the other residents who were lounging around the pool.

Most of the other people who lived at the Colonial House were actors. They were very attractive people, and the men in particular had the sorts of physiques that could turn one's head. As I sat in my chaise with my book propped up on my knees, I listened to them talk and peeked at them preening in the sun. Other men reclining on their chaises had reflective fans opened under their necks to make sure their bodies tanned completely. Their talk was of body building, skin care, and movie roles, topics that did not interest me at all.

My habit was to leave the pool a little after 3:00 so that I could dress for cocktails, another tradition that entered my life during the hiatus in filming. This was something I enjoyed immediately. Despite the casual way I was raised in the hills of Southern California, my mother knew fashion and

I shared her love of it. My mother was from a well-off family and had been the New York Tri City beauty queen when she was twenty. She married a man she loved, whose family were immigrants. My parents worked hard and were successful, but my father was not the match her parents had hoped for her. I credit some of my independent streak to that same quality in my mother. My sisters and I appreciated what remained of her stylish upbringing whenever she and my father had to dress up for a formal occasion. They were stunners. We craved that style, which was foreign to the bland, suburban life we lived in San Bernardino. The Sermak girls liked nothing more than taking the train to Pasadena to shop at the big department stores with our mother, and even in the dressed-down world of my youth I'd acquired a few nice outfits. When Miss D described how we should dress for cocktails, I had several dresses to choose from.

She quickly taught me the technique of offering drinks to a guest and mixing them, and of keeping the ashtrays clear. Once she saw that her lessons in conduct and posture were taking hold, and that I fulfilled my role with a newly found grace, she allowed me to sit with the guests at cocktail hour. Her next goal was to teach me the art of conversation.

In Miss D's living room she entertained writers and directors—Sir John Gielgud, Richard Attenborough, Roddy McDowall, Vincent Price, Robert Wagner, Robert Osborne—people who liked to talk about art and the issues of the day. I studied the give and take between these strong minds while appreciating how Miss D complimented her guests, how she steered the conversation, how she distracted when someone said something inept or cruel. I was learning the art of conversation just by being in the room.

One of the regular guests whom I watched carefully was Roddy McDowall. He was a witty man, with a sharp tongue when someone offended him, but he was extremely discreet. Just by looking at him you understood that he knew much more than he was saying. His eyes reflected experienced discernment, someone who saw through pretense and recognized quality. That silence of his drew people to him, made them want to impress him, and in trying to do so they often said more than they should. Miss D had this trait too, but she was larger than life. When people met her, they were solicitous. They wanted her to favor them with her stories and her insights. If she shared something like that with them, they would have a story to tell for the rest of their lives. Roddy was not as powerful a presence as Miss D, which gave him a different kind of power. I suppose I watched him because I wanted to emulate his ability to say nothing, while speaking so clearly just in the way he held himself and took in the others in the room.

She also taught me how to host a dinner party. She started a month before the event by calculating which guests would make for a lively party. Then there was the invitation, the polishing of the silver, the careful planning of the menu, the music, and the seating chart. Next she gave me the duty of shopping for her clothes for big events. I updated her wardrobe and also brought younger people into her life. We also had silly diversions, like dressing up for George Washington's birthday or making hats out of sliced vegetables, which caused a commotion when we sported them for Easter lunch at a dear friend's home in New York. Everyone in the elevator recognized her and stared at her, but she acted completely unaware of the commotion she was causing.

When we returned to the set of *White Mama* three months later, I walked onto the set with a more confident stride and spoke with more authority to the crew. I believed that people were looking at me differently, but there was no proof that they were. Still I could sense that I was more effective in my job. I knew what my responsibilities were and did them with a cool competence that I'd never felt before, now grateful for the frustrations I had endured to acquire it. What I never could have imagined was that Miss D had still *more* that she intended to teach me.

After the movie wrapped and we were back full time at the Colonial House, Miss D told me that we would be going to New York for a month at the Lombardy Hotel. I was excited to return to New York. It had been almost a year since our first stay there, and I had learned so much in the intervening months. If walking on the set of *White Mama* after the long hiatus seemed like a triumph, what would it be like to be returning to the lobby of the Lombardy?

The weeks before we were to leave for New York were busy, but not in the way that I had expected. Again much of Miss D's focus was on me.

"In New York you'll need some new clothes," she said. "I'd like you to have a few traveling ensembles and a few more dressy dresses. I've asked Nadine, the buyer at Neiman-Marcus, to set some things aside for you. What size are you?"

"I'm a four or a six," I said.

"Really? We are almost the same size! That's marvelous. You're so much taller than I am. I have some great things you should try on to see if they fit you. Some of them would be perfect for New York! But more than the clothes we'll be focusing on something else this week. In the East people size you up at a glance, and the standards are strict and formal. Now that you work for me permanently I want you to be able to meet those standards and much is revealed by how you eat."

"How I eat?"

"Yes, how you eat," she said, taking a long puff on her cigarette as she considered how to deliver the news. "No one cuts their salad," she said with a sly grin. "So, I've hired a butler."

A butler! What do we need him for?

"In New York we may be invited to formal dinners," she said. "The array of silverware can be confusing. When I was young and was seated at a formal dinner, I didn't know what to do. My beau discreetly showed me how, but I was mortified. I never want that to happen to you. The protocol I learned is precise, and needs to be thoroughly mastered. The butler will come at 1:00 p.m. and we will be seated in the dining room with full formal dinner service and silver."

"And he will teach me what to do?"

"No I will teach you," she corrected. "He will be there so that you have the experience of being served. Dress well, Kath. I want this to be just like it would be if you were at a formal luncheon with an ambassador."

Sitting at a formally set table in the middle of the afternoon dressed in an elegant dress fresh from Neiman-Marcus seemed phony. I dreaded it. When the butler in his livery arrived at the Colonial House it took him a full hour to set our places in the dining room. I sat down before a bewildering array of glasses, multiple pieces of monogrammed silverware, and more plates than I could imagine uses for. Across from me sat Miss D, whose place was set identically to mine—with the addition of an ashtray.

"Notice the alignment of the plates, and the silver. You

work your way in from the left, the sequence of courses matches the utensil: salad fork, fish fork, dinner fork moving from the left. From the right dinner knife, fish knife, butter knife, soup spoon, tea spoon. Water goblet at the top center of the plate, then champagne flute, red wine glass, white wine glass. Dessert spoon and fork at the top of the plate facing in opposite directions, spoon angled to the left and the prongs of the fork pointed to the right. At lunch, the napkin is opened halfway on the lap."

For the first time since I took this job I just wanted to go out for fast food.

"The butler serves food on a hot plate or a cold one depending on the dish," she continued.

The butler stood to my left with a platter. He lowered it next to my plate, positioning it a few inches above to prevent me from spilling anything when I served myself. The minutiae of the way I was supposed to hold the wine glass, use the soup spoon, handle the bread and butter, all just seemed like layer after layer of ancient custom without any logic attached. When I got back into my room to dress for cocktails, I took a pillow from my bed and screamed into it until I spent some of that fury. There wasn't even any time to swim. I had to get ready for cocktails.

After cocktails Miss D expressed her approval of how well I had done that afternoon with the butler.

"Kath, you are an excellent student," she said. "It is impressive how quickly you picked up the fine points. When I came to Hollywood I didn't know any of that. I had to learn by observing others and I made some regrettable mistakes. I am trying to save you from that embarrassment. You did so well today. I know you'll do even better tomorrow."

"We're doing that again tomorrow?" I asked, incredulous.

"Yes, of course!" she said as if this was obvious. "I hired the butler for the week."

"Excuse me, Miss D," I said brightly. "I'm just worn out from everything we did today and I need to be off to bed."

In my room I put a Joni Mitchell album on my stereo and turned the volume up. I cleared a space between the shoes on the closet floor to make a place for me to sit and grabbed the phone. I dialed Helen Ann's phone number and shut the door to the closet and sat in my little clearing. There in the dark I waited for Helen Ann to pick up. *Please answer, Helen Ann, please.* At last she did on the sixth ring.

"Helen Ann, she's making me crazy! She's hired a butler to teach me how to eat!"

Helen Ann let out a long laugh at this news.

"I know it's frustrating, Kathryn," she said. "But really you are the luckiest girl in the world."

None of Miss D's sophisticated manners had come to her by birthright. She was born to an old New England family. Her parents divorced when she was seven and Miss D's mother, Ruthie, supported the family—Miss D and her sister, Bobbie—with her work as a photographer until Miss D was in her early twenties. Watching how hard her mother worked to support them, Miss D vowed one day that she would earn enough that her mother would never have to work again. This was not an upbringing that allowed time for Ruthie to teach her daughters the elegant manners of the upper class.

When Miss D came to Hollywood she was eager to learn whatever she needed to become a star. In the old Hollywood system the studios owned the actors and carefully groomed them so their appearance in public would be impeccable. She had received careful training at Warner Bros. She wanted to pass the same type of schooling on to me as her assistant and representative.

A week later we were off to the Lombardy. After all of Miss D's careful instruction, I felt much different during this visit. In New York Miss D had appointments and social engagements, some of which included me and others that did not. Among her wide range of concerns was the fact that I was not dating. She didn't want me to become bored by being so wrapped up in her life and not able to do the things that other young people did. She urged me to reach out to any friends I had on the East Coast.

I remembered that Jeff, the brother of a boy I dated in high school, was at Georgetown University in Washington DC studying to be a doctor. I got Jeff's phone number from his parents and called him. He was excited to hear from me and asked if I'd like to be his date to the Winter Ball. When I told Miss D about this invitation she was as excited as if I had been asked to be a genuine New York debutante.

"I remember once when I was a young woman I was invited to a ball and my mother insisted she knew what I should wear," Miss D said. "She made a dress for me that was completely out of fashion, a style that she liked but that made me look like a frump. I spent the whole evening standing by the wall. No one asked me to dance. This is not going to happen to you, Kath."

There was a French dressmaker, Miss Isabel, on the second floor of the Lombardy. The next day Miss D arranged for her to visit us in the suite and Miss Isabel had some fabric swatches that came from Paris. Miss D, noting that it was winter, suggested a rich brown that looked good with my coloring, accented with a subtle black satin ruffle at the neckline. I was excited about having a three-quarter-length formal dress tailored specifically for me.

"Kathryn, do you know how to dance?" Miss D asked that evening.

"Dance? Everyone knows how to dance," I said.

"No I mean ballroom dancing," she said. "Where the man holds you close and leads you around the dance floor."

"I don't. We never danced that way in high school or college," I said.

"At a formal ball you will have to!" she said.

The next day an instructor from Arthur Murray Dance Studios came to our suite with a boom box that played the kind of music my parents listened to at home—or maybe it was my grandparents. Anyway, it was music I'd only heard on my father's car radio and never would listen to on my own. Miss D and I had already cleared away the furniture in the center of the room. As the Big Band music swelled up from the boom box, I did not have any idea how I was supposed to move to it. The instructor held me by the waist with one arm and elevated my other arm as he announced the steps I had to make. It was confusing at first, and I was very self-conscious, but by the end of the hour I felt I'd made some progress. Apparently I had not made enough.

"Kath, let's keep practicing," Miss D said. I feared for a moment that she might place her hand around my waist as the instructor had, but instead she stood next to me announcing the steps as we accomplished them in parallel. I was in much better command of the steps the next afternoon when the instructor returned. This time when he took me in his arms, we were gliding around the room in graceful time to the music. At the end of the lesson Miss D and the instructor applauded me. I blushed.

Miss Isabel came to the suite to do a fitting on my gown the next afternoon. The feel of the rich velvet was intoxicating, and the subtle black satin ruffled collar perfectly framed my neckline. I stood as still as I could while Miss D observed Miss Isabel making small tucks at the waist and marking an adjustment at the shoulders so that the gown fit my body perfectly.

Miss D saw me off to Washington DC in a state of excitement, proud that she had prepared me flawlessly for this grand occasion. She even lent me her mink coat and some jewelry for the event. Our driver Robert took me to Penn Station to catch the train to DC and Jeff met me at the train station to take me to the hotel. The look on his face when he saw me in my fashionable traveling outfit was priceless! He had expected the Southern California tomboy he remembered, and here was Kathryn in her smart New York clothes and Beverly Hills haircut. He didn't quite know what to say, but obviously was glad to see me.

I got dressed in my hotel room paying special attention to my gown and makeup so that nothing would be amiss when we walked into the ball. As I came out of the elevator, the look of shock on Jeff's face was almost comical. He wasn't dressed nearly as formally as I was. He had on khakis and a blue shirt with his tie loose at the collar. It seemed as if we were going to completely different events. I did feel a little silly when he opened the door to his tiny Peugeot car that would carry us to the big event. But hey, he was a medical student and I'm sure his money was spent on more important things than cars.

Then we entered the winter formal and his stunned look suddenly made sense to me.

I was so overdressed it was horrifying. The women were in simple cotton dresses and some of the men were wearing jeans, while I looked like something out of a 1955 *Vogue* magazine. My dance lessons were not necessary either, as everyone was twirling around free-form, not gliding across the floor in elegant choreography. All the effort Miss D put into making me a standout worked: I definitely stood out in that crowd! When we decided at the end of the evening to go out with some of the other students we'd met at the dance, Jeff took me back to the hotel first so I could change into jeans.

All the way back to New York on the train I worried about what I would say to Miss D about the evening. I knew that I could not pretend the evening had been magical and glamorous. I could not lie. I would have to tell her everything.

"Oh Kathryn, I am so sorry I put you through that," she said. "I know exactly how it feels to be in that situation, only this time it was me doing that to you. You know that was never my intention."

"I know it wasn't," I said. "I know that, and I love the dress and all the preparations we made. It's too bad that none was right for this event."

Within a few days we had made this into a joke and would laugh describing me walking into the grand Winter Ball in my evening gown and dramatic hairstyle while everyone else was in corduroys and sneakers. From a distance it really was funny. And truth be known, I was actually rather proud that I had gone to the event with her standards in mind.

The sadness around it was not with me, but with her,

wrapped up in the realization that she was training me for a world that was fading from view. In the elite and elegant world of the Concorde, everyone dressed up to fly just like we did, and she was not the only woman there wearing a hat. That night at the Winter Ball I ended up exactly as embarrassed as she had been when her mother dressed her for the ball. My peers, even the upper class ones raised in society families, did not dress for cocktails and, as the Winter Ball showed, not even for formal occasions. Now she was the elderly woman coaching the younger woman into a fashion faux pas.

A few weeks later we were on our way back to Los Angeles for her appearance at the Los Angeles County Museum of Art where she would be featured in "An Evening with Bette Davis." I watched her prepare for this as if she was getting ready to play a part in a movie. The makeup artist came to the Colonial House the day of the event, and we chose a special gown for the evening. In contrast to the careful attention to the script, there was no way to prepare for what would happen that night on the stage. She would take questions from the audience, and could only try to anticipate what they would ask. I realized this would be the first time that I would see her as the focus of a public event. I had seen how her fans reacted when they were surprised to see her in public, but these fans were paying $100 or more just to be in the room with her. Miss D seemed a little nervous. I had never seen her like that. A few hours before she was about to go on stage I saw her take a Darvocet, a pain reliever. She saw I noticed.

"The day you go on stage and you are not nervous, is the day you know it is over," she said.

We arrived at the auditorium while the program already was underway, just before the audience finished watching the compilation of extended clips from her most famous films. I walked with her to the wing of the stage and saw the eager faces of the fans, hundreds of them, as they anticipated her arrival. The host announced her and they rose as one to give her a standing ovation. The outpouring of affection was so swift and genuine that I felt it too, an enormous wave of admiration that caught me at its edges. My simple Miss D, whom most of the time I saw puttering around the house cooking dinners and decorating for special holidays, was a different creature when she strode to the center of that stage. She seemed to be taller, as if the outpouring from the crowd made her larger, larger than life. After a few minutes the applause retreated, but the audience remained on its feet. Miss D stood at the center very still as her eyes scanned the audience. She brought her cigarette to her mouth, took a considered drag on it, then pulled it a few inches away and a white puff of smoke lingered around her face.

"What a dump," she said, quoting one of her most famous lines.

And the crowd applauded louder. I saw it then, and ever after I remembered the difference when a real star enters the room.

CHAPTER 4

FAMILY REUNION
July 1982

"Looking for Praise Breeds Disappointment"

MISS D HAD looked at several houses on Long Island that summer of 1982 to find the place best suited to entertain her family. The one she finally chose stood at the end of a long gravel driveway, with a patio at the back facing a private beachfront on Huntington Bay. We had come to know this part of Long Island the winter before, when Miss D and her eleven-year-old grandson, Ashley, starred in the television movie *Family Reunion*. Now she had rented a house in the same vicinity for the summer and invited her children, Michael and Bede, and their families for a reunion on the Fourth of July weekend. Separately, Miss D's other daughter, Margot, who was handicapped, would visit us later with her nurse.

Once they all said yes, little about the modest abode seemed good enough. The house was functional, but a bit neglected. A cleaning lady tidied up twice a week, but she did not clean thoroughly enough to meet Miss D's standards. Every week the gardeners mowed the lawn with a little tractor and swept the tennis and badminton courts, but they did not tackle the brush that grew around the house. The list of tasks she wanted us to finish in the two weeks before the children arrived was long, and I had a big shopping list when I drove into Huntington.

At the hardware store, I purchased her special cleaning supplies, four pairs of household gloves, and a clam rake. Clamshells lined the flowerbeds, inspiring Miss D to plan a clambake for Saturday night of the visit. Also on the list were sandpaper and paint: a gallon of black for the aging swing set. After I'd sanded off the old paint and the rust, I would give it a fresh coat of paint or two. At the garden store Miss D wanted two pairs of gardening gloves and two sets of pruning shears. As I had observed when we stayed at the Berystede, Miss D loved to prune.

I knew her habits well after three years at her side. Despite my early missteps, I was a good student and my Catholic upbringing had prepared me to follow a clear set of rules. In that way, I was a perfect assistant for a woman who lived her life precisely. What my time with Miss D had revealed to me was that I actually shared her appreciation for high standards. Growing up in a big family, life had been chaotic with a lot of demands on my parents' time and money. At this stage of Miss D's life she had more of both, the leisure time to train me in all of the finer things in life that had come to her the hard way. Had I met her at the height of her career, it would never have worked out—she would not have had the time to bring me up to speed. At moments like this, when she sent me on a complex errand to prepare for a big event, I understood how thoroughly I had mastered my job. In the stores I knew without hesitation which of the items available at the plant nursery and the hardware store would be the ones she would have picked herself.

When I returned from my errands, the front of the house was jammed with delivery trucks. Two men were unloading the patio furniture we'd picked out the day before: elegant cream and brown chaise lounges, chairs and tables, and a croquet set. In the foyer, as Miss D signed an invoice for the new dishwasher that she had just had installed, another man appeared in the doorway carrying a toolbox.

"Oh good, the carpenter!" Miss D said brightly. "Come with me."

She led us to the family room where there was a wide loft accessible by a wooden spiral staircase. This was where Bede and Jeremy and their boys, Ashley and Justin, would sleep. Miss D placed her hand on the staircase railing and gave it a shove. It shimmied and creaked.

"We cannot have those children coming up and down these rickety stairs," she said. "Can you fix it now?"

"I can."

"Good," said Miss D. "Kath, to the kitchen."

In the kitchen we spread out my purchases on the table. She grabbed the gardening gloves and the pruning shears and handed a set to me. We walked to the front of the house where a shovel Miss D had found in the garage was leaning up against a wheelbarrow. The edge of the driveway was dotted with shaggy bushes, half-dead, that annoyed Miss D every time we approached the house. At first she thought we could prune them, but in the last few days she had decided that we should take a more drastic approach.

"Kath, get the hose by the side of the house and wet the ground. That will make it so much easier for us to dig up these awful bushes," she said, placing the pruning shears on the front steps. I had a fleeting worry, *Will the owners be annoyed that we're taking the landscaping of their house into our own hands?*, that was pushed aside by the sheer strength of Miss D's determination. The bushes had to go, by golly, and we were going to remove them.

We took turns digging. While one of us had the spade in the ground, the other used water from the hose to soften the earth. Once we freed a plant, we tossed it in the wheelbarrow. When the wheelbarrow was full, I maneuvered it to the back of the house and dumped it into the pile of debris.

Mostly it was silent between us as we worked. Miss D occasionally thought up something she wanted added to one of our lists. I always carried a notepad and pen in my pants pocket. Every so often she'd exclaim how happy she was that the whole family would be in one place together or about how great this was going to look or how delicious the meals would be. She clearly was excited, and was preparing for the holiday just as she would for a movie. She reserved most of her ruminating monologues, though, for the subject of Bede's husband, Jeremy Hyman.

I had heard in bits and snippets how Bede met Jeremy in France at the Cannes Film Festival when Bede was just sixteen. Jeremy was twice that age. According to Miss D, after a short courtship Bede had demanded permission to wed, despite her youth. If her mother did not agree, she threatened, they would elope. Miss D eventually endorsed the union and celebrated it, despite her doubts. By the time she hired me, Bede and Jeremy had been married longer than Bede had lived with her mother. Miss D's continued misgivings about their marriage infuriated them. Miss D was now the outsider

in their world and, considering the intensity of her relationship with Bede, Miss D was hurt by that exclusion. When
Jeremy was around there was tension, and he tried to stay
away to avoid sparking conflict. Miss D was not shy about
describing the many qualities she loathed in her son-in-law,
which came up again and again as we worked on the garden.

"I don't mind sending Bede money," she declared as we
started on the seventh of the twelve bushes we were working
to uproot. "I would do anything, anything in the world, for my
daughter and her children. I send that money with joy. Sometimes I pay for things Bede doesn't even know about. Harold
tells me he receives bills from stores in their town, and asks
me if he should pay them. And there's the children's schooling. Of course I want them to have everything. But him! What
kind of man allows the mother-in-law to support his family?
When I think of all I've given them over all these years you
would think I would get some gratitude from him, a thank you
would be nice, but no, he *hates* me for it. Well, that's some
men for you. They have their pride and their ego."

After we were done yanking out the bushes, we grabbed
the pruning shears and started shaping the vegetation at the
sides of the house. I hated gardening. I snipped at the foliage
like a petulant teenager until I noticed Miss D at work. The
more she pruned, the more energy she had. I picked up my
pace, but I could not match Miss D. As the afternoon wore
on to early evening, she was almost giddy as she fashioned a
tidy shape out of one bush and then another. Another mono-
logue began.

"It's not just the money," she started off. "It's also the way
he treats her. She works like a slave. She does everything.
The cooking, the cleaning, and the sewing. She takes care of

those children and she runs that whole farm and what does he do? He sits in his chair and reads. I don't know how she stands it. I certainly wouldn't. He doesn't provide enough to support. You know, in a way, I blame myself for this. I never gave her a proper father. Maybe if she had a real father she wouldn't have mistaken Jeremy for a real man. Pathetic. Absolutely ridiculous. But what can a mother do?"

I said nothing. These complaints were familiar to me.

In the three years I'd worked for Miss D, whenever we visited New York she would see Bede and her family. Miss D called Bede several times a week and often sent cards, letters, and packages. She phoned Bede the moment we arrived at a hotel to tell her she had landed safely. Her son, Michael, and Miss D were respectful, attentive, and loving to each other, but they did not have the dramatic relationship Miss D had with Bede. On the phone I could hear her lavish expressions of love for her daughter. I'd heard the joy in Miss D any time Bede asked her to buy her grandchildren something as small as a pair of boots and as substantial as paying to install a large pond on their farm in Wyalusing, Pennsylvania.

From Miss D's descriptions, I imagined the Hymans living on a gentleman's farm where the mucky, smelly part of rural life was tucked away some distance from the main house. I pictured them in an elegant New England colonial mansion with a big staircase. After I had been working for her for a while, Miss D asked me to keep her company on the four-hour drive back from one of her visits.

The Hymans operated a 37-acre farm with pigs and chickens and a large stable for their horses, all of which was near the house. Their home was an 1800s farmhouse furnished with beautiful antiques Miss D had given them as a wedding present when she was closing down her house in Bel Air. Although the farmhouse was restored, it was not the grand colonial I had imagined. When I met Bede, I saw much of her mother in her. She was vigorous like Miss D, a powerful presence. She had Miss D's firm voice and striking eyes, but she was taller and blonder, with a more athletic bearing. Her long strides covered a lot of ground. Bede used the intelligence and forcefulness she had inherited from her mother to manage the farm and the family while Jeremy was away working for his long-haul trucking business.

In choosing to live on a farm in a small town in Pennsylvania, Bede had gotten about as far away as she could get from her mother and her mother's world. I knew firsthand how fraught it could get between mothers and daughters; I imagined this was even more difficult when your mother was an internationally recognized celebrity—and a personality as strong as Miss D. My first year of training by my employer was one of the toughest years of my life, and I didn't have the added complication of being her daughter. I was sure Bede had her reasons for keeping a distance, but I'd only seen them exchange quick kisses on the cheek when I picked Miss D up at the end of a three-day visit. This upcoming family reunion would give me some insight into why a visit between Miss D and Bede never lasted more than three days.

Around 6:00 p.m., when the sun was starting to set, Miss D stood up slowly from her knees, and took a step back to admire our work. We'd cleared the driveway and made a bit of progress on this side of the house.

"Oh, so much better. I'd say it was a miracle if we had not done it with our own hands," Miss D said.

Miss D made us a quick and simple dinner of hamburgers,

cucumber salad with dill, and for dessert a bowl of blueberries topped with cold heavy cream—her favorite—which we
ate at the new, round patio table overlooking our slice of the
water. The night was warm and clear and we could hear the
seagulls feasting in Huntington Bay. Miss D was content as
she always was after a day when she had checked many items
off her list. As we ate, Miss D set our schedule. The next day
she and I would spend the morning cleaning, with a mid-day
break for her while I worked on the swing set. I must have it
ready to paint no later than Thursday, as it might need more
than one coat. Every afternoon we'd spend a few hours pruning, moving steadily around the outside of the house, toward
the tangle of undergrowth near the patio.

"Think of it as a challenge," she said. "Cleaning away the
cobwebs. We'll be giving life and growth to these grounds.
Now, I want to get some window boxes to put along the side
and fill them with geraniums. Make a note. Let's go to the
nursery and buy planter boxes filled with petunias, dizzy
lizzies, forget-me-nots—we'll make an assortment. It will be
perfect."

In the beginning of the second week, when the swing set
was painted and cleaning was complete, we began what I
hoped was our last day in the garden. Miss D, for all her love
of pruning, was happy that we were about to finish. She'd
pulled her back when we uprooted those bushes and the doctor prescribed some Darvocet for her to take before we could
continue our work. Though still hale and hardy, she was, after
all, seventy-four years old. One last corner of the patio and
we were done.

She was in a great mood. We had made the world around us
so much brighter (and I think the Darvocet was helping too).

The next day two big trucks would come to haul away what we'd pruned. Plus her children would be here soon. When all was tidy, we were going grocery shopping to begin preparing all the delicious meals she had planned to serve that weekend.

We'd been working for an hour when a rustling in the bushes startled us. Miss D warned me to be on the lookout for birds' nests: "They love these bushes," she said.

As we moved closer in on the last section of the bushes we were pruning suddenly they shook again, more violently. We froze.

"That was *not* a bird," Miss D said in a voice just above a whisper.

The bushes to the left of me rustled. We looked at each other with mutual trepidation.

Then the bushes erupted as dozens of rats ran past our ankles squealing. I felt them brush against my feet and legs, a stomach-churning sensation. I screamed and so did Miss D, but we did not move as the rats continued to stream out between our legs.

That evening at dinner we laughed about how we stood like statues in the river of rats. Miss D stood up from the table with a stricken look on her face mimicking a silent scream. Then she narrated it from the view of the rodents as they cowered in the bushes while we—the noisy, smoking giants—plodded slowly toward them snipping away until they could stand it no longer. In the calm that followed our exhausting fit of laughter, Miss D savored her after-dinner cigarette. The preparations were nearly complete. Tomorrow after the exterminator visit, there would be two trucks to haul away all that we'd pruned. Then we would sweep up, order the flower boxes, and go grocery shopping. Miss D had been on the phone with Bede and Michael's wife Chou Chou almost every day to ensure that whatever anyone wanted to drink or eat or do would be provided. These were the final finishing touches before the families arrived.

"We set it right, Kath. By the time the children get here, it will be perfect. I'll make breakfast every morning. We'll have an old fashioned New England clambake on the Fourth of July. Won't that be fun? And poor Bede, how hard she works on that farm. For these three days, I won't let her lift a finger."

A year earlier, when Miss D's grandson Ashley was cast as her youthful companion in *Family Reunion*, I saw how happy she was for him, although having him on the set on Long Island that winter was a burden for her. Her work required her full concentration, making time with Ashley a distraction. She had her hairdresser Peggy Shannon to work with her on the film and assigned me to tend to Ashley.

In *Family Reunion* Miss D played a recently retired teacher, and Ashley was her favorite student. At retirement, she takes a trip around the country to visit all her relatives and uncovers a plot against her, which Ashley's character helps her unravel at a dramatic family reunion. She invites all those she has visited to join her at a house by the sea, confronts them about their scheming, then heals the rift and sets a new course for the family. The movie was mostly Miss D's, but Ashley played an important part, and played it well. He had far fewer scenes than she, though, which meant he and I had time to roam around Piping Rock Club, where we stayed from January through April working on the film.

In my travels with Miss D we'd stayed in many luxurious places, but I'd never seen anything like Piping Rock, and neither had Ashley. Piping Rock was like living in *The Great Gatsby* as styled by Ralph Lauren: chintz, early American furniture, tennis, and horses. Subdued, old-money modesty where no one ever discussed their wealth or showed off, the opposite of Hollywood. The values were understatement, good breeding as displayed in gracious manners, and courtly demeanor all in a setting that looked like the English countryside. This California girl and the Pennsylvania farm boy felt out of our depths in the world of the gentry.

We were staying in adjoining suites at the clubhouse, me with Ashley and Miss D with her hairdresser Peggy. Ashley had a lot of energy and never wanted to stay inside. The winter of 1981–82 was bitter cold, record low temperatures with abundant snow in January, the month we arrived. Forced to stay inside, Ashley would blow off steam by becoming Davy Crockett. He would don his coonskin cap with a long tail and grab his plastic rifle as he squatted behind the Windsor chair, imagining himself in the woods back home in Pennsylvania. He crawled slowly and silently over and around the prim settee, pretending he was hunting for game. Whenever there was a break in the weather, we were out the door exploring the 350 acres. Miss D's rooms faced the front of the clubhouse. As we headed out for a ramble, often when we looked back we'd see Grammas, as he called her, waving to us from her window.

Our favorite time was when the sun came out after a big snowfall. We'd walk past immaculate fields of sparkling snow spread out on the eighteen holes of Piping Rock's golf course. After being cooped up indoors with Davy Crockett it was

heaven to feel my body again in the blazing sun. We were
well insulated against the freezing temperatures. I had a
full-length down coat, heavy boots, thick gloves, and a knit
hat. Ashley was dashing in his navy pea coat and down
trousers. He was a joy to be with, appreciative of nature
and grateful for its beauty. The walks with him brought out
my athletic side, which had been muted in my years with
Miss D. As the weather improved we searched further into
the woods. Thirty Piping Rock families—Whitneys, Vander-
bilts, Rockefellers—have houses on the property, and we saw
many of those country homes. One happy day we discovered
a fort built high in the trees with a staircase leading up, and
we spent a few fun hours pretending we were in Davy Crockett's secret hideout.

Being with Ashley sixteen hours a day showed me that
something was off with him. Ashley was dreamy and I often
had to say his name more than once, louder each time, to
pull him back to earth. Sometimes Miss D and Bede got angry with Ashley when he did not respond to them, accusing
him of being defiant. I didn't see him as a brat. Ashley mostly
did what I asked and was trying very hard to please Miss D
and the director of the film. What they did not know was that
Ashley had frequent headaches. He popped aspirin all day
long.

I wondered if there was something physically the matter
with him. I knew better than to ask Miss D while she was
filming, so I called Helen Ann. When I described some of his
behavior, she suggested that he might be hard of hearing. I
wanted to pursue this but I needed something more than just
a hunch to bring this up to Miss D.

Two days later Helen Ann called. A doctor friend of hers

recommended a few simple ways to test Ashley's hearing. First test his equilibrium: ask him to walk a plank, skip rope for more than a minute, and throw a ball straight up into the air and catch it with the same hand. Next I should walk directly behind him saying his name, gradually increasing my volume until he finally heard me.

On our next walk we set out for the stables. As we hiked along beside the low fences near the horse corral, I dared Ashley to walk on the railing without falling. He did fine, his arms flailing back and forth as he gained his balance and then stepped quickly down the thin board.

At the edge of the horse barn I saw a length of rope. I grabbed it.

"Hey, how long do you think I can jump rope? I used to be pretty good. Do you want to time me?"

After I'd done about a minute I asked him to give it a try.

"Naw, I'm not very good at it," he said.

"Maybe you've gotten better. Let's see."

His first try he stumbled on the rope, and started over. After a few false starts he was able to keep it going for ten seconds. Then he put the rope down and said no more. As we started back to the clubhouse I took a tennis ball from my pocket.

"Have you ever tried to juggle?"

"No," he said.

"Do you want to learn?" I asked. "The first thing you have to master is throwing the ball up straight and catching it. Steady regular movement."

I stood looking him in the eye as I tossed the ball up to my chin level and caught it without watching it, although it was tough to grab in my gloved hand. I handed the ball to Ashley.

He took off his glove and tossed it and it strayed to the left, then to the right, then just past the top of his finger. He got frustrated and handed the ball back to me.

At the open field we came across one of our favorite sights, dozens of Canada geese feeding on the snowy green. On some of our walks we'd been there when the flock touched down, all of them landing quietly on the carpet of snow and craning their beaks to the earth to nibble. At those moments our joking and singing stopped. We didn't want to startle them, so we stayed as still as we could. This hushed field was the perfect place to test if he could hear me when I walked behind.

Ashley walked lightly on the road, careful not to disturb the birds by kicking up gravel. From a few paces behind him, I whispered his name, but he didn't twitch. Then I increased my volume to a stage whisper, then in a regular voice. No response. Then I said it sharply, with an angry edge on the first syllable of his name. The birds took to the sky *en masse*. He turned around and glowered at me.

"You don't have to shout! Kathryn, remember the geese," he said.

The geese heard me well before Ashley did.

That night when I described my test results to Helen Ann she advised me to tell Miss D, not Bede, because Miss D should be the one to speak to her daughter about Ashley's poor hearing. Miss D dismissed the news quickly.

"I don't know what you're talking about, Kath," she said. "He's fine. He's doing well in the movie. You run his lines with him. He responds on cue."

"He does, but if he's got a hearing loss he's probably learned how to compensate by reading lips," I said.

"That's ridiculous," she said. "And besides I can't do anything about this right now. I'll tell Bede after the movie is done."

The next day Ashley had a scene that required him to enter from behind a door, but he kept missing his cue. After three spoiled takes, the director stationed a crewmember behind the door to cue Ashley. When I told Miss D, she wanted his hearing tested right away, but first she called Bede. Bede was not convinced, and seemed a bit offended.

"There is nothing wrong with Ashley," she said. Her voice was so forceful I could hear her clearly through the phone even though I was standing a few feet from Miss D. "I mean seriously, Mother, if you want to just throw money away on frivolous tests, go ahead, but don't be shocked when the results show his hearing is perfect. He's just lost in his own world."

When Miss D hung up she called Harold.

"Harold, find me someone good and close by," she said. "This has to happen now."

Two days later the audiologist discovered that Ashley was 60 percent deaf in one ear and a smaller percentage in the other. In examining him, the doctor discovered a pencil eraser that was stuck way up at the top of Ashley's nasal cavity. He extracted it, estimating that it had been there for seven or more years, more than half of Ashley's life. Now that it was out, Ashley would have no more headaches.

Miss D paid a considerable sum to have the hardware of the hearing aids integrated into the arms of Ashley's glasses so the other children would not make fun of him for wearing a bulky hearing aid. The day the doctor fitted him for the glasses with his hearing aid, Ashley was seated in the car between me and Miss D when he scratched the corduroy on his pants and, for the first time, he heard the sound of his nails against the fabric.

"Grammas! Grammas! I can hear!"

After that, being with Ashley was even easier. I can only imagine how hard it had been for him to be labeled defiant and lazy, when in truth his problem was that he couldn't hear and suffered headaches from a clogged sinus.

He shot his last scene in the film at the end of March, and we all knew he would be leaving shortly after that while Miss D stayed on for a few scenes without him. He was upset that he would not be at Piping Rock for Grammas's birthday, April 5, so he decided we'd throw her a surprise party. We worked for two weeks acquiring all the items he needed to make her a thank-you/birthday card on a big piece of poster board he filled with happy images from magazines that reflected his love for her.

By the time Ashley was headed back to the farm, he was a much more cheerful young man. He had luxuriated in the affection of women who doted on him constantly. He'd proven that he was a competent actor, and it was clear that he had potential if he wanted to pursue this as a career. He also had a new appreciation of his Grammas. I imagine that at home in Wyalusing he'd not heard very much praise about Miss D from Jeremy. Here he had had a chance to see the way the world revered her, and how hard she worked. And most important of all, now he could hear clearly for the first time in his life, and his headaches were gone. This was a big three months in a young boy's life.

This new closeness with Ashley was, in part, what inspired Miss D to invite everyone to Long Island for the Fourth of July family reunion. A year after their months together she missed her grandson, whom she had helped so much and to whom she felt so much closer after the film. She was not working on another film until the end of the summer in 1982, making it a perfect moment to bring the family together.

I was not, however, so sure about her timing. When Miss D told Bede about Ashley's diagnosis, Bede called me privately to tell me that if I had any trouble with Ashley I was to go to her, not to her mother. Did I understand? I understood well enough who was paying my salary and to whom I felt loyal. It was another reminder of how important I was becoming to Miss D. More than a well-trained personal assistant who made her life easier, I had become her ally. For all the florid expressions of love between Miss D and Bede on the phone, the truth was that the territory between them was often a battlefield, and Miss D needed someone on her side. She now had someone to confide in while trying to maintain her relationship with her daughter.

These were the ingredients for the family reunion: the decades-long dispute between Miss D and Jeremy and the new rivalry between Bede and me over our relationship with Miss D. I was glad that Miss D had decided to put me up at a motel during the three days of the family reunion.

Saturday morning of the Fourth of July weekend I arrived in the kitchen at 7:00 a.m. to help Miss D prepare the family breakfast, which was set for 8:00. Miss D clearly had been up since 6:00 a.m. There was a pitcher of pancake batter in the refrigerator, bacon cooking on a rack over a sheet pan in the oven, and Miss D was cracking a dozen eggs into a big bowl to scramble.

"Good morning, Kath," she said, smiling broadly, satisfied

that everything was underway. The morning was dark with a threat of rain and the smell of coffee and bacon made the kitchen cozy. Miss D pointed to the baskets of berries and the melon she had placed next to another bowl. "After you've made the fruit salad, set the table for six. Everyone will be down for breakfast at 8:00 a.m."

The day before I'd watched Miss D revving up with worries as the morning turned to afternoon and Bede and her family still had not arrived. We'd completed the final task to get ready that morning when we moved Miss D's things into the maid's room so that Michael, his wife, Chou Chou, and their son Matthew could have the master suite when they arrived late Saturday morning. All the hours since we'd settled her in the maid's room Miss D had no place to spend her energy. She would pace and smoke, conjecturing about what route the Hymans were taking to Long Island, what kind of traffic they might be facing on the holiday weekend, whether they had stopped along the way and for how long. When had they left? Had they left early enough to make it in the same day? Would they get caught in the rain and have to stop? No, they would be here. Of course they would. But when? What should she have for them to eat when they arrived?

These thoughts cycled back for consideration every hour, along with her worry that there was something we had missed in fixing up the house. Did we have enough of everything? The second time she checked the supplies of Coke, apple juice, tonic water, and iced tea, I quickly volunteered to go to the store, relieved to be out of the house.

Not all was agitation, though. She also was anticipating a flawless and harmonious weekend filled with the special touches only she knew how to create. They would play cro-

quet on the lawn and Bede was bringing tennis and badminton rackets. Miss D and little Matthew could swing together looking out at the sea. Miss D was looking forward to
our New England clambake. She was happy describing the
children digging out clams and mussels. For these three days
her family would want for nothing and everything would be
the best.

More than that, though, as with her dinner parties in Los
Angeles, she wanted all of this perfection to appear as if it
were happening effortlessly, as it did in a movie. The meals
should appear from the kitchen as if someone had waved a
wand. The drinks would be offered at the exact moment when
someone wanted one. All the food would be delicious. And
the children and the grandchildren should never know how
much preparation she had done to make it seem this way.

When Bede had not arrived by suppertime. Miss D was
exhausted from waiting, eager to see her family, trying to con-
tain her emotions so that she could greet everyone with a big
smile. I knew she could put on that performance, but I also
knew it was important that I stay with her until the family arrived. It was nearly 8:00 p.m. when the Hymans' car finally
pulled up in the driveway, my cue to leave.

At ten minutes before 8:00 the next morning I was setting
the bacon on a platter while Miss D was making pancakes on
the griddle.

"We're going to wait for Bede and Jeremy and the children," she said. "They should be down any minute now. It's
almost 8."

After we had arranged all the platters on the dining room
table we sat chatting about how happy Miss D had been to
see Ashley and how big his brother Justin was getting. The

tone was light, but I could see Miss D looking at the dining room door, as if staring at it would make Bede appear. Then she would look at the food on the table as the steam wafting up from the platters became fainter and fainter. Miss D got up from the table to get a cigarette and started to pace.

"Whatever could be keeping Bede?" Miss D said. "Kath, could you go find out?"

"Yes, Miss D."

Outside the door to the family room I heard the sound of cartoons coming from the television there. Although it was now past 8:20, I didn't think it was right for me to tell them that breakfast was waiting for them. I thought of it from their perspective. These three days they could relax in bed, a luxury for a family that runs a farm. Let them sleep. And keep Jeremy and Miss D apart as long as possible.

Bede, though, what was she up to? She knew as well as I did how being late upset her mother. If Bede had told Miss D the night before that they intended to spend time alone as a family that morning, or that they wanted to sleep in, Miss D would have agreed and organized the breakfast for later. She hadn't done that, leaving her mother fuming at the breakfast table on the first day of her perfectly planned weekend.

I returned to the dining room. I told Miss D that I thought I heard noises like they were getting up but I didn't want to disturb them.

"No, that's good that you didn't. I want her to get some rest. But I would think the children would be up by now. Keep an eye out for them and let me know."

After some time with Miss D pacing about from waiting so long, she said, stubbing out her cigarette forcefully, "Well, then, I'll guess I'll just have to make fresh pancakes when they decide to all come down."

Her look and movement said it all. I picked up the platter of bacon and the one of scrambled eggs and followed her into the kitchen. I re-positioned the bacon on the rack so that we could heat it when the Hymans arose.

Miss D was silently furious as she dumped the platter of pancakes into the trash. She was fierce, but she was fragile. I could see she was hurt. All the effort she had made, and she was thwarted on this very first morning. I doubted, though, that Bede would see this side of her by the time she finally came down. The minutes ticked by and at around 10:00 Miss D made a request.

"Kath, make me a vodka and orange juice," she said. And I did.

Around 10:30 a.m. Bede and the family made their entrance, and it was a memorable one. Bede entered the kitchen smiling, oblivious to any disappointment she caused.

"Good morning, Mother!" she said. "This all looks *marvelous*. Look at that fruit salad, and you've got just heaps of bacon. Ashley and Justin love that. You've done such an outstanding job. Really, Mother, you do think of everything. Sit down. Sit down. Let me make the pancakes for the boys. You've done so much already."

Bede said everything her mother wanted to hear, and I saw the change in Miss D's face and posture immediately when Jeremy entered the room. I feared we might be in for a battle, but Miss D cooed back.

"No, Bede, I insist," Miss D said. "You sit down. I know how hard Jeremy has you working on that farm and with him and those boys. You never get a moment's rest. While you are here, just let me do everything."

I brought the re-heated bacon and freshly cooked scrambled eggs back to the breakfast table and sat next to Ashley, excited to see him after such a long absence.

Miss D came into the dining room with a big platter of perfectly shaped pancakes and set them at the center of the table. She sat smiling.

"Everyone dig in! Don't let them get cold," she said.

Jeremy sat silently at the far end of the table.

"When the sun comes out we'll have an old-fashioned New England–style clambake with fresh corn and lobsters. I know how you all love lobsters," she said.

"There's no clams around here," Jeremy said, finally moved to speak.

"Oh no, you are mistaken!" Miss D said. "I mean look at the flower beds. They are all rimmed with clamshells taken right from the bay here. Won't it be marvelous to have a meal that comes from clams we gathered with our own hands? I know you and the boys will have a blast digging them out of the sand. That will make the meal so much more delicious."

"That's your proof? Clamshells in the garden? I think you could buy those from a fishmonger around here if that was what you wanted."

"Why would you buy them when there are so many clams around?"

"Because there aren't any clams in Huntington Bay."

"Would anyone like more coffee?" I said.

Jeremy nodded that he would and I went into the kitchen with Miss D close on my heels. She was fuming, muttering under her breath about clams and Jeremy, about how he was going to ruin everything. She took another drink of her vodka and orange juice as if girding herself for a battle. By the time we returned to the dining room, she had mustered her smile, but I could see that she was looking uncharitably at Jeremy.

When breakfast was done and I had cleared the dishes away, Miss D and I stayed in the kitchen washing up and preparing for lunch. The tension in the house was palpable. When Miss D left the kitchen and entered the living room, Jeremy exited, going outside to the patio. At mid-day, Michael, Chou Chou, and one-year-old Matthew arrived, providing a welcome diversion.

Around 5:00 p.m., Jeremy seemed to have a change in his mood. He asked where the bucket and the clam rake were. The sun was peeking out from the clouds and it felt as though the storm was clearing. He asked his sons if they wanted to take a walk on the beach and look for clams to dig.

When they left it was as if the storm had been lifted from the house as well. Miss D was in the kitchen arranging the elements of her clambake, but she was moving stiffly.

"Kath, where did you put that Darvocet? My back is killing me right now."

I went to the kitchen cupboard and I handed her the pill bottle. She took one.

About an hour later we heard Ashley and Justin running onto the patio and into the house. Miss D came out of the kitchen quickly.

"Careful boys. Your feet are covered in sand. Take off your shoes and leave them outside."

Jeremy strode onto the patio with the bucket at his side, and a sly grin on his face. When he entered the house he presented the bucket to Miss D, smugly showing her that it was empty.

"No clams."

The look on Miss D's face was rage, but I could also see how hurt she was too. Her elaborate plans and all our hard work, and still she could not make it perfect. Jeremy would not allow her to do so.

"You must have dug in the wrong place," she said. "Maybe if I took the boys out. I mean I know how to spot them and..."

"There aren't any. I asked a man who has lived here all his life. He said that Huntington Bay has the wrong kind of sand for clams."

Miss D turned silently toward the kitchen and I followed her. She started shoving the items we had set out for the clambake back into the fridge.

"Kath, make me a scotch and water," she said.

I handed her the drink.

"He's ruined the clambake," she said. "Absolutely ruined it and the whole evening. What are we going to eat?"

"I could drive into town and pick up something. There's a good deli in Huntington," I said.

"Maybe you can call ahead and see what they have. I am out of ideas right now."

She took another drink of scotch. I watched her compose herself, breathing deeply in as she had taught me to do before I spoke. That deep breath strengthened her spine and squared her shoulders, and the second one restored a tepid smile to her face. She returned to the living room, and I followed behind her, hoping nothing more would cause conflict. But the pattern was already set. I offered everyone drinks before I headed out to Huntington to collect dinner.

When the boys asked for Coke and I said we had run out, the look on Miss D's face was defeated. Bede had said Justin drank apple juice but all he had drunk that weekend was Coke and now they had run out. Justin started crying. Ashley left the room. Jeremy exited toward the patio.

Being the outsider to the family put me in the position of seeing all sides. Miss D's need to make everyone believe that all was effortless meant that no one gave her the praise she really craved. She didn't describe the hours we put in pulling up the bushes and pruning, the afternoons painting the swing set or even the considerable money from her pocket for the dishwasher, patio furniture, the staircase repairs, and the barbecue pit for the clambake. For all the grandeur of her manner and the boldness of her personality, in the family context she seemed tentative and vulnerable. When she said she wanted everything to be perfect for her family, it really was only Miss D who needed things to be perfect. Only if she was perfect would she feel worthy of their love.

The boys asking for something that she did not have meant that things were not perfect, and neither was she. I could understand the shocked reaction on the face of Bede and the tears of Justin for upsetting his grandmother over something as routine as needing more soda, but I also felt Miss D's pain and humiliation. I left for Huntington to get a big tray of lasagna, and more bottles of soda and juice, with a heavy heart for all of them.

When I returned the mood of the house was hushed, less of a truce than a standoff. The kids were playing a board game. Bede and Jeremy were in the loft. Michael and Chou Chou had put Matthew down for a nap and were taking one themselves. Miss D was in the kitchen. She had cried, I could see, and now she was angry. The combination of the alcohol and the Darvocet had brought her emotions close to the surface.

Dinner was a grim affair, mostly silent. No one had the energy to fight. The families scattered to their rooms early. I left hoping the next day would be better for all.

And it was! The next day was sunny, perfect weather for the Fourth of July. When I arrived in the morning the boys were already up and eager to get to the beach. Miss D looked marvelous in her denim jumpsuit with a red, white, and blue neck scarf and a jaunty red beret. I admired that innate ability of families, my own included, to find a way to follow a horrible day that seemed to break the family apart forever with a cordial one. And on the next day, everyone apparently woke up with amnesia about the tensions of the previous day. As the morning slipped into afternoon the atmosphere was comfortable and even languid as Bede lounged on a chaise with Justin nearby playing with a toy truck. The children ran back and forth to the beach. Bede played tennis with Ashley, and later so did Chou Chou and Michael. The mood was harmonious as I set out the food for lunch, the plates of cold cuts and fried chicken and the salads we had made that morning.

When Jeremy was down at the beach with the boys, Miss D sat on the ground next to Bede's chaise. Soon they were deep in conversation with clasped hands. Bede and Miss D clearly loved each other. You could see it in the looks in their eyes when they had time to themselves. This was everything that Miss D had worked to provide, but it would be for a handful of minutes.

When Jeremy came back from the beach with the boys, the early fireworks began. The boys wanted to try out the croquet set, which Miss D and I had set up on a corner of the lawn. Jeremy thought it should have been set up differently and took out the diagram from the box the set came in, using it as a guide to expand the way the wickets were situated. This infuriated Miss D, who had decided to make the court smaller because she didn't want to intrude on her neighbors. The argument about this became so heated that they abandoned the game and Miss D stalked off, angry and powerless in the face of Jeremy's stubbornness.

To cool himself off, Jeremy grabbed the big metal buckets and asked the boys if they wanted to go to dig for mussels at the shoreline. The boys looked at each other confusedly, given the empty buckets of the previous day. But Jeremy was encouraging, telling them that the man he spoke with the day before told him exactly where to go to find lots of them—something he had failed to mention the day before. The boys grabbed their buckets and headed for the beach, and all was calm for a while.

Chou Chou and Matthew were seated on the bench seats on the swing, laughing as Michael pushed them faster and Matthew shrieked with joy. Miss D returned to Bede's chaise and I saw another tender moment between them. Bede had a magical influence on her mother, an ability to turn on a smile so bright and loving that the darkness around Miss D disappeared. In this second private moment they shared I saw in Miss D a hunger for her daughter, for someone who could soothe her and assure her that she was not alone in this world. I was touched by the gentleness of this interaction when the preceding days had been so rough.

I was in the kitchen when I heard the excited shouts of the boys as they came up to the patio.

"Grammas! Grammas! We've got mussels! We've got buckets of them!"

Jeremy was a few paces behind, his arms heavy with the

overflowing buckets of mussels. *Oh good*, I thought. The makings of a happy final dinner of this fractured weekend were in those buckets.

He walked directly up to Miss D and almost shoved the buckets into her face.

"Clean them," he said to Miss D. She burst into tears, but those famous eyes were raging.

"You treat me the way you treat your wife, like a servant!" she said. "Well I am not your servant and I never will be."

At that moment I knew, we all knew, that no one would remember this weekend with nostalgia. We dragged ourselves through a tense meal. The sniping between Miss D and Jeremy continued. For every caustic remark and bitter look he shot her way, she crumbled a little but would not yield. She came back at him just as hard or harder.

The Fourth of July fireworks that night were an afterthought for the adults, but I was glad for the distraction they gave the children. As the families retired for the night, all were talking about how they needed to get on the road early the next day to beat the holiday traffic home.

The next morning everyone was nearly packed by the time I arrived, loading their suitcases into their cars and making the right kinds of noises about how happy they were to have come and what a special time it had been with all of them together. There was no more amnesia about the prior days everyone was on tenterhooks. Bede was the most obsequious of all, complimenting her mother about small touches that showed she had noticed everything even as she felt Jeremy's urgency to leave.

After lunch and before they all got into their cars, I took a group photo in front of the house. I knew Miss D would want to record this rare moment in the family history. When I looked at my photographs later, I saw how their faces reflected the weekend's stress. Every person in the photo is looking in a different direction. Michael and Chou Chou had genuine smiles on their faces, but the Hymans' eyes conveyed misery. Ashley looked remote, and Jeremy seemed impatient to depart.

It was quiet in the house after they left. I went to straighten up the kitchen while Miss D sat out on one of the chaise lounges smoking a cigarette. I brought her out a fresh cup of coffee and took a seat next to her as we stared silently at the water.

"Honestly Kath," she said after a while. "I blame the rats."

CHAPTER 5

ALL FOR LOVE
April 1983

"Love Is Worth Pursuing"

LYING BY THE pool on a white chaise lounge in the desert spring sun, I relaxed. Being in Helen Ann's home in Rancho Mirage always soothed me, and on this visit I saw that it could soothe Miss D too. She knew that on my days off, I often drove the two hours east on Interstate 10 from Los Angeles to visit Helen Ann at her oasis near Joshua Tree. Helen Ann's ranch house had large windows and open spaces filled with desert light, and Miss D, like me, appreciated this contrast to her apartment at the Colonial House. At Helen Ann's, I breathed deeply and worried less. Some of the happiest hours of my life I spent talking with her in her studio as she painted.

I would sit in a chair at her desk while she walked around the studio looking at her painting from many angles as she decided what to do next. It amazed me that she could paint and talk to me at the same time because we were not just chatting about the weather. Ever since I first met Helen

Ann, when I was dating her elder son in college, she and I talked about everything. I was a young woman with big decisions to make. Helen Ann enjoyed helping me explore all my possibilities. Her advice was consistent: Be independent, confident, and open to what life might offer. Go to Europe, she said. Postpone graduate school and take the job with Miss D.

I remembered that night in her studio when Helen Ann and I talked about how a job with Miss D would change my year, and even my life. When I went to sleep in the library, where I always slept when I stayed in Rancho Mirage, Helen Ann had displayed Miss D's autobiography *The Lonely Life* on a bookstand near my daybed. I was amazed she had this book from 1962 in her library, proof of her admiration for Bette Davis. In the four years since that night, Helen Ann and Miss D had heard a considerable amount about each other but I had just introduced them a few days ago.

Helen Ann had invited us to stay with her when we came to Palm Springs for a speaking engagement. When we walked in the door, I watched Miss D as she took in the volume of Helen Ann's home, and Helen Ann herself. Miss D was Brooks Brothers, classic East Coast Yankee upper crust, while Helen Ann was California casual Bohemia. She wore loose white pants and a tunic, her waist-length hair pulled back into a thick braid. Dissimilar outwardly, they recognized that they were on the same frequency the moment they saw each other. I did not need to guide their conversations. Now, the third day of our five-day visit, Miss D was the one in the studio with Helen Ann.

Miss D was still, and silent, as she observed Helen Ann, not wanting to disturb her process. Helen Ann said that she had become so absorbed in the six-foot-by-three-foot oil painting of a goose she was starting that she forgot she had company. About an hour into her work, Helen Ann made a bold stroke on the canvas and was startled when Miss D said, "Now I see it." I was astonished that they had become close so quickly, and that Miss D deferred in some way to Helen Ann in watching her silently. I realized this was one artist's appreciation, and respect, for another.

The year I started with Miss D, my parents came to visit us in the Colonial House. They'd been up to Los Angeles for the day to attend the big annual gift show at the LA convention center and Miss D had invited them to stop by afterwards for cocktails. Although my father had been to Miss D's to drop me off or to pick me up, my mother never had. My mother seemed a little nervous at first but Miss D, fluid as a hostess, quickly made both of them feel at ease. So much so that my mother invited Miss D to visit them in San Bernardino.

I looked at my parents with pride and we were all smiling. Then I looked at Miss D, whose face had snapped from welcoming to contemptuous.

"Do you think that I am some lonely old woman who has no friends?" she said. "You think Kathryn has to provide my social life? I can assure you that is *not* the case. Kathryn works for me. She is an employee, not a friend. Her friends are not my friends. I have a family of my own. I do not need one in San Bernardino. Thank you very much."

I don't think anyone had ever spoken to my mother that way before. I wished my arms were long enough to reach out to hug my mother, who looked as though she was about to cry.

My father stood up and extended an arm to help my mother to her feet.

"Well, you know, I think we better get on the road," he said. "The traffic can be pretty thick this time of day. Thank you so much for inviting us. It really has been an honor."

He did not say it had been a pleasure.

After I escorted my shamefaced parents to the elevator, I went directly to my room. I had seen this side of Miss D, but never directed at someone I loved. I still felt the pain I had seen in my mother's face. Why would Miss D be so rude? My poor mother had been generous and kind, but Miss D had rebuked her. Her defense of her independence was so fierce and automatic that she didn't adjust it to the circumstances. I began to wonder if this was the real Miss D, the one that saw kindness as condescension. I had not seen it because I was her employee, not her peer, but it was coiled up inside her always ready to lash out at any small provocation. There must be a heart in her somewhere, I thought. If there was a heart, I would find it. If I could not find it, I would quit.

In the last three years I had, indeed, seen her heart. I saw it in the way she trained me. While she was demanding, she was also complimentary, encouraging, and grateful when I mastered something. We had become attuned to each other. When she sensed I was getting bored, she increased my duties, or taught me a new skill that might be useful out in the world. She taught me how to pack her for a trip and the dozens of miniscule decisions that had to be made to ensure that her suitcases contained everything she would need for the role she was playing, and for the rest of her itinerary. She taught me to care about the little things in life and the love of life, times you have to give up things for the greater good of others...as she did that many, many times. The specificity appealed to the Catholic schoolgirl in me, schooled in clear rules and defined expectations. Miss D certainly had those.

In the last pages of her first memoir, *The Lonely Life,* she wrote, "I have always been alone, really. I should have known enough to travel light; because no one could really come with me on my trip. I fought this knowledge for years and now I face it squarely." She wrote that her economic independence made her less likely to tolerate the boredom of marriage, and that she had sent her children off to boarding schools because she did not want to use them as crutches. "My children will never see vulnerability and sacrificing," she wrote. "I want them bound to no one, not even to me. And I am all right, I keep saying over and over. I'll be fine! I keep saying over and over!"

Miss D wrote that book more than twenty years earlier in 1962 when she was fifty-four years old—around the same age Helen Ann was the week when they met. At this point Miss D had just turned seventy-five, and her rigid self-possession now had a few cracks in it. I was witness to her vulnerability and her sacrifices. I was an employee, but I had become a collaborator in her ventures, a steady supporter who was there to help her in every aspect of her complex life—from correcting scripts for her acting roles to pulling off practical jokes. These fun times made her happy. Having an employee who understood her quirks, supported her values, and made sure that her exact standards were fulfilled had helped her to relax and opened her to new possibilities and ways of doing things.

And now, improbably enough, she and I had a common friend.

The week we spent with Helen Ann developed a rhythm quickly. Miss D made all the meals in Helen Ann's sunny kitchen, and every night we had candlelight dinners under the canopy of stars. I spent afternoons by the pool while Miss D observed Helen Ann in her studio, and there were phone calls every afternoon from Harold and Robbie keeping her up to date on work and her ongoing dispute with Aaron Spelling. Instead of a movie role or two a year, suddenly she was working all the time.

Television producer Aaron Spelling had hired Miss D to star in his series *Hotel* in which she played the owner of a grand old establishment in San Francisco. The Hollywood trade papers were filled with conjecture about how much Spelling had paid to land a movie legend for his weekly series, but what they did not know was that Miss D had not yet fully committed to the project. She'd filmed the pilot with James Brolin and Morgan Fairchild, but she hated the scripts for the episodes to come where guests and members of the staff were hopping in and out of bed in almost every scene. She told him that the name of the series should be *Brothel*. Her part, she said, was a caricature, a cardboard-cutout of a woman. Through Harold she advised Mr. Spelling to hire some better writers or she would not film more than the pilot.

We were also preparing for a trip to France, the first time I would be there since I was in college. Miss D was receiving an honor at the Cannes Film Festival in May, which was flying us first class from Los Angeles to New York, then New York to Paris to Nice. Miss D decided on the way back we'd stay for a week in Biarritz, France. I was excited that I would get to see the Cannes Film Festival, especially because I would be seeing it from the perspective of a star. Now that she was getting along so well with Helen Ann, I reasoned she would also like the Vivianos, the family I'd worked for the year before I got my job with Miss D.

I'd stayed in touch with the Vivianos over the years, and we were eager to see each other, and I was also eager to see Pierre, the handsome young man I had met when I was in France during my college year abroad. Miss D was the real instigator of my reunion with Pierre. I had described our chance meeting that day in Paris, and she knew he still wrote to me from time to time. She encouraged me to look him up when we were in France.

I'd met Pierre in 1977 when I was standing on a corner in the Left Bank with my map open, trying to figure out how to get to my hotel. Pierre came to my aid. He helped me find my hotel and was so handsome and charming with his broken English that I agreed to meet him for cocktails that evening. I said I would bring along two of my friends from America, who were arriving that evening from Spain. At the restaurant Pierre was excited to be with three women, and paid equally superficial attention to all of us. His slick charm repulsed me. One of my companions was as much of a flirt as Pierre, and they seemed to be hitting it off. After one glass of wine, I wanted to be back in my room at the hotel. Unlike all the other young men I'd met while traveling in Europe, Pierre asked me to pay for my drink. This was a man I saw no reason to flirt with, so I left him with the others, who seemed game to go on to a disco.

I suppose that Pierre did not enjoy himself that night, because the next day he came to my hotel to apologize for the way he had behaved. He invited me to dinner at his par-

ents' house and I was excited to be having a meal with a
real French family. His family was old money, way old, back
to the 13th century. Inside the family's flat, Pierre was no
longer a joking young man on the make. He dressed formally in white pants and a tie for dinner in a classic country
French dining room with a thick wooden table and upholstered chairs and walls filled with classic oil paintings, an
artful combination of formal and informal that put me at ease
quickly. In this context, his best manners were on display. I
was charmed by him then, and by his family, who offered to
do what they could to help me stay in France legally. They
said the easiest way to accomplish this was for me to take
care of a French family's children. I didn't want to be an
au pair, but I desperately did not want to go back to California. His parents recommended that I drop by the Institut
Catholique de Paris where French families advertised for
English-speaking au pairs. If I had to be an au pair just to
stay in France then an au pair I would be. Through that bulletin board I met the Vivianos, who hired me to be their au
pair for the summer in Biarritz, at the recommendation of
Pierre's mother, Geiton. I was excited to see Pierre and his
family on this trip to France, and to see how much all of us
had changed in the five years since I'd last seen them. In
truth, with all I had learned from Miss D, I was ready to show
myself off a little.

Then Miss D had changed her mind about her trip to
France. She'd come to the place in her career where people
gave her awards for, as she put it, still being alive. They were
not awards she had earned for a brilliant performance, but
ones honoring her lifetime of achievements. I knew she loved
appearing before the public, but this year had been crowded

with many of these awards, and often she would jokingly say, "With all these awards I've recently received you'd think Hollywood is bidding me farewell." After filming *Little Gloria Happy at Last, Right of Way* with Jimmy Stewart, and the pilot for *Hotel*, her energy was depleted and she didn't want to travel. She informed the Cannes Film Festival she would send me to pick up the award for her. While we were in Rancho Mirage, the festival withdrew the award. If Miss D was not coming, they'd find another star who would.

As I rested on the chaise lounge that afternoon at Helen Ann's trying to let go of my disappointment about the cancellation of our trip to France, the doorbell rang, so I went to answer it. In the driveway stood a limousine. The driver handed me an envelope that contained two scripts for a new episode of *Hotel*. He then opened the passenger door to the limo, where on the floor stood a vase with five dozen long-stemmed red roses. He handed me the flowers and envelope. I brought them to Miss D in Helen Ann's studio.

"Miss D, the scripts have arrived. Mr. Spelling sent them in a limo with five dozen roses!" I said. "Can you believe it?"

"Oh, Helen Ann you must keep these beautiful roses here in your studio for inspiration," said Miss D.

Helen Ann took the vase in her arms and inhaled the scent of the roses. As she placed them on a table next to her easel, she thanked Miss D. "Kath, take these," said Miss D as she handed me back the scripts. "Grab the cigarettes, and my glasses. Let's go read this out on the veranda."

Miss D sat down and lit a cigarette. I was always impressed by how quickly she evaluated the quality of a script. I could see by the way she snapped through the pages that she did not see much improvement at the *Hotel*.

Helen Ann came to get her cigarettes and asked if we needed anything.

"Helen Ann, may I use your phone?" Miss D asked. "I wish to make a call to Los Angeles."

"Of course," Helen Ann said.

"Kath, get me Aaron Spelling," she said.

Helen Ann handed me the portable phone. I dialed the number for Aaron Spelling's office that was on the front page of the script.

"Hello, I have Bette Davis calling for Mr. Spelling. Is he in?"

He was. Miss D took the phone from my hand.

"How dare you. How dare you send me such a script!" Miss D said. "Did you even read it?"

There was a pause.

"Well, I suggest the next time you take that money you spent on five dozen roses and a limousine and hire better writers...Good. Thank you."

Discussion over.

That night Miss D was feeling jaunty and free. We'd later know that she had decided she was not going to go any further with *Hotel*. Walking away from a project she considered beneath her always put her in a good frame of mind. As we sat after dinner enjoying the evening air, she looked content.

"Kath, I think you should go to France anyway," she suddenly said. "You deserve a break. It will be my treat. You deserve it for all the work you've just done."

I was overjoyed and she could see it from the look on my face.

"And while you are there, promise me you'll look up that young man I've heard so much about," she said, beaming my joy back to me. "Ten days in Paris, who knows what will happen? All for love, Kath, all for love."

I was excited to be on my own in Paris. From the first time I arrived in France when I was in college, it seemed familiar to me, as though a part of me had always been French. Even as a college student, I felt connected to the people, the culture, and the pace of life. The French were not as concerned about work as they were about living a good life of long meals, great food, intelligent conversation, and love, much the opposite of the more pragmatic way I had been raised. The French obsession with love, seeing it as an art rather than as the fastest route to sex, charmed me.

Miss D often said that as a younger woman she had been in love with love, and when I walked the streets of Paris again, I felt that way too. The way couples lingered on a touch, held hands as they walked, and seemed absorbed in the smallest of affectionate gestures made me crave that same kind of attention. I was not single when I was in France the first time, still pledged to my college boyfriend, who was studying at Waseda University in Japan. This trip I would be single, and I was getting encouragement from Bernadette and Miss D to embrace what romance might come my way.

When I arrived at the Vivianos', I followed Bernadette's advice not to call Pierre right away. I was tired from the trip and needed a few days to get my feet back on the ground. Also it had been many years since I had seen the Viviano children, whom I had taught to surf that summer we spent in Biarritz. Now Veronique was graduating high school just as Nicolas was entering. I had missed seeing them grow, and we all had a lot to catch up on. Those first few days flew by and I barely thought about Pierre until the moment when I decided to call him.

I was nervous when I called, uncertain what it was that I expected from him, but his voice was warm, as if he had been waiting for years to hear from me. He invited me to meet him at his parents' flat in the 5th Arrondissement. Although Bernadette gave me excellent directions via the Metro, when I walked out onto Avenue Charles de Gaulle it seemed unthinkable to waste any portion of this beautiful evening in a dark subway. I decided to walk.

Soon I was lost in the sights of Paris, a city familiar to me but which always has something new to offer, and I didn't really think about how much time it would take to get to Pierre's parents' house. I was free of concerns, of standards and responsibilities, and I was excited to feel that way. My feet found the route instinctively, down the Avenue de la Grande Armee, past the Arc de Triomphe and onto the Champs-Elysées. I crossed the Seine at Pont de la Concorde feeling light and free, unconcerned with the time as I at last found myself on the Boulevard Saint-Germain. I was thinking about what life would be like if I moved to France, if I started a career in fashion and left the United States behind. What kind of woman would I be in France now that I had received such rigorous training from Miss D? What possibilities would be open to a young woman like me? I did not realize that my nostalgic stroll had taken me nearly two hours.

When Pierre opened the door to his parents' apartment we paused at the doorway, lost in each other's gaze. He was as tall, lean, and athletic as I had remembered him, but in the five years since we'd seen each other he had become even more handsome. He had lost the young-man-on-the-make

quality that had offended me when I saw him turning this superficial charm on any attractive woman who happened to be
nearby. I remembered that night with the other women how
he had looked hungrily at one, and then at another, and then
at me, as if we were all the same to him because any woman
could give him what he was after. At the doorway, though,
his first seductive action was the most profound. He saw me.
Pierre did not give me a lascivious once-over, the kind of
male look that makes a woman feel violated. He looked me
in the eye and breathed deeply as if he was drinking me in
completely, even though his eyes did not stray from my face.
I breathed deeply too, a shock of instant attraction that left
me mute and paralyzed, except for my smile.

"Kat-ta-reen," he said softly. "Kat-ta-reen."

He placed his hand on my arm and drew me closer for the
traditional French hello of three kisses in the air around my
cheeks. He kept his hand on my arm as he escorted me into
the salon to greet his parents.

I had liked his mother and father from the first time we
met, but this time I saw more clearly what a powerful figure
his mother was. Pierre had her eyes, not the color, but the
discerning way she took the world in, a sense she gave
off that she picked up on every change in me. I did feel
changed sitting in this room. The last time I was here I was
twenty-one and unpolished, with an outfit assembled from
The Highlander Boutique, haute San Bernardino. I knew
Pierre's mother appreciated the difference.

I sat in a cream upholstered French chair with an oval
back and wide arms, while Pierre took his place on a sofa on
the other side of the room. I remembered all of my Miss D
training as I gracefully crossed my legs and reached down to

place my handbag on the floor next to the chair. I thought of Miss D. What would she do? She would not look at Pierre. I looked up from the floor and spoke to his mother.

We chatted about how I got my job and what I had learned there, about where I had traveled and dinner parties at the Colonial House. We sipped Kir Royales. As we were finishing our drinks, Pierre announced that our reservation was in fifteen minutes. We made our goodbyes and started our walk to the restaurant, only a few blocks away.

The restaurant, Le Coupe Chou, had only ten tables, an intimate atmosphere illuminated by perfectly placed lamps. The whole room glowed with warmth, the kind of light that seems to make everyone look beautiful. When the maitre d' presented us with the menus I was having a hard time deciphering the French. Pierre saw how perplexed I looked and offered to order for both of us. I was grateful for that. The first course he ordered was escargot. Escargot! I didn't know what that was but I was happy to try whatever he suggested.

"Kat-ta-reen, you are a surprise to me," he said. "I thought I remembered you fully, but I had not seen you really at all."

The escargot arrived and I saw that what I was about to eat were snails, their shells arranged in a special pewter plate with oval pockets that cradled the mollusks in garlic butter. I didn't know how to eat them, where to start. I picked up the small fork that came with the plate, my hand hovered over it not knowing if I was supposed to eat the shell or just its contents. Pierre saw my confusion and took the small fork from my hand and delicately placed it into the shell, then dipped the escargot into the garlic butter. He extended the dripping morsel on the tines of the fork and I opened my mouth to re-

ceive it. It was delicious. I appreciated his exquisite manners
and the elegant way he moved.

I noticed the ways he had changed in the five years since
we were last together. He had become a lawyer and had
started his law practice, and I liked his new seriousness and
focus, particularly because he was focusing on me.

When the meal was done, we took a walk. The night was
cool and clear as I stood close to him but he did not put his
arm around me. When he saw I was having a bit of a chill he
draped his coat over my shoulders. We walked a little while
longer and then he offered to find me a taxi. As he hailed
the taxi he asked me if he could see me again the next night.
I only had five more nights in Paris but I knew I wanted to
spend all of them with him. Yes, I said, I was free for dinner
the next night.

Back at the Vivianos', Mario was watching a soccer game
in the living room and Bernadette was in her room reading,
waiting up to hear how my evening had gone. She smiled with
approval when I mentioned we had eaten at Le Coupe Chou.
"Very thoughtful of him, Kati," she said. "It is hard to get a
table there. I suspect his father may have made the reservation for him."

The next day I was not focused on much besides my dinner with Pierre. He lived on Rue du Cherche-Midi, a quiet
and narrow street in the Latin Quarter. This was another
evening where we walked the streets, starting off with a Kir
Royale at Les Deux Magots, a café where writers and intel-
lectuals gathered on the Boulevard Saint-Germain. We sat
outside under the dark green awning and umbrellas at a
small round table and watched the people passing by. Then
we walked to Le Petit Prince de Paris, a hard-to-find hide-

away somewhere in the warren of cobblestone streets that Pierre knew so well. The place had rough charm. It had been a Roman bath and the designers who converted it into a restaurant preserved the pale stone walls and beam ceilings that stood out against the plush drapes and antiques. After dinner we walked along the banks of the Seine and through the gardens at Tuileries.

We sat on a bench in the garden. I was filled with the feeling of love. I loved everything around me: Paris at night, the food, the freedom. And I was beginning to feel I loved the man who sat next to me on the bench. That summer I had met him I was the hungry young girl, eager and restless. Now after my time with Miss D, I had lost that giddiness. I enjoyed listening, watching, and I appreciated how keeping some things about myself private helped create a kind of intimacy between Pierre and me, a sense that we were slowly revealing ourselves to each other, drawing the curtain back with care not to expose too much at once. I took everything in, but said very little because to talk too much would be to take me out of the dream I was living. I felt like Cinderella and I did not want to leave the ball. From then on we spent all our evenings together, and he unveiled the secret hideaways of Paris to me on our walks. We lingered in cafés talking, and went to the opera. Everything seemed magical on these evenings.

On my last evening in Paris, Pierre and I had agreed he would pick me up at the Vivianos'. He arrived promptly at 7:00 carrying a box of chocolates for Bernadette, a thank-you gift for allowing me to spend many of my evenings with him. Bernadette's face was animated by her contented smile. She was living her love of love through me and she could not be

happier than to observe the subtlety of the interaction between Pierre and me.

The next day I canceled the car service that I had reserved
to take me to the airport. Pierre and I wanted to spend my
last few hours in Paris together and he offered to take me to
Charles de Gaulle. We were walking on the Champs-Elysées
when I admired a white straw hat with a broad brim and
black ribbon, just like Gigi wore in the movie musical with
Leslie Caron and Maurice Chevalier. Pierre bought it for me
and when he put it on my head he said I was his Gigi, and we
kissed. As we drove to the airport it was hard to tell which
one of us was more in love.

When we were waiting at the departure lounge we did not
sit down but stood face-to-face holding each other. He told
me he felt as though he had fallen into a cloud, that his
reactions were passionate and filled with fantasy. All his ret-
icence was gone, his careful and measured self-control had
disappeared. Pierre told me to thank Miss Davis for sharing
me with him and assured me that he was already working out
how we could see each other again in California.

It was painful to break free of that moment, but I knew
that this was not the end. As the plane headed away from
Paris and back to Miss D, I knew it was time to end my work
with her. We had had a wonderful five years together, a period when we had changed each other's lives, and we would
never lose that. I had learned all I could from her and at the
age of twenty-eight I knew it was time for me to start a life of
my own with the man I loved in Paris.

CHAPTER 6

GIGI'S RETURN
June 1983

"Vigilance Is Rewarded"

ON MY WAY from Manhattan to see Miss D in Connecticut, I was reviewing everything I wanted to tell her about how I had fallen in love with Pierre. She and I had spoken often when I was at the Vivianos', but only for a few minutes at a time. Miss D had just a rough sketch of the places Pierre and I had been and what I had worn, but I hadn't had time to describe fully the walks across Paris at night, that current that ran between us. I knew she would want to hear every word of it.

Falling in love with Pierre came about in many ways because of the way Miss D had trained me. Like the young woman in the musical *Gigi*, she had educated me to be sophisticated in the way I dressed, moved, and spoke, and in the manners of the well-bred. In the process she built my confidence. My gratitude to Miss D filled my heart as I rode in the limo to Westport, where she was staying with her friend Robin. Only she and I knew how much she had done to prepare me for this life. Now she would be so happy and proud that I was about to claim it.

When Robin opened the door to her house I heard the soundtrack from *Gigi* playing on the stereo—Maurice Chevalier singing "Thank Heaven for Little Girls"—and I heard the laughter of the guests. Miss D and Robin were throwing me a surprise welcome home party! Everyone had on striped sweaters and berets. There were champagne cocktails and quiche and many questions. They called me Gigi and referred to Pierre as Gaston, the man who sweeps young Gigi off her feet in the musical. The guests mimicked the swoons of a young woman in love, and tried on the Gigi hat that Pierre bought me on our last day together in Paris. There was a real contest to get me to blurt out everything that had transpired. I refused to go too far despite their teasing. I was flattered, but I was also discreet. I was saving the details for my time alone with Miss D.

After the guests had left and we'd cleaned up, Robin went to bed. Miss D and I sat at the kitchen table to talk. After I had told her everything I could recall about falling in love, all the way through our goodbye kiss in the departure lounge, Miss D grabbed my hand.

"Kath, I'm so proud and happy for you, you know I am. Look at you, you are radiating. I cannot wait to meet him. You must be exhausted from the flight. Get a good night's rest, Gigi. There is something I need to discuss with you, but it can wait until morning. Sleep tight, and don't let the bed bugs bite."

The next morning, while I was repacking my bags, Miss D came into my room and sat on the bed.

"Kath, I have something to tell you. While you were away, just three days ago, I found a lump in my right breast. It's probably a tumor of some sort."

"Oh no!" I said, distraught.

"Harold is arranging for me to get X-rays on it. It might be nothing. I need you to change our plans, contact the Lombardy. Let them know we are coming back. Order the car for tomorrow at 10:00 a.m."

I sat down on the bed next to her and took her hand. "Miss D, I'm so sorry. Truly I am."

She took a deep breath and with that exhale moved into a different emotion.

We sat that way for a moment and then she pulled her hand away. Suddenly, there was no time to talk further; there were many things for me to arrange. I decided I would not bring up my plan to move to Paris. There would be time enough for that when we got past this.

Two days later, it was confirmed: Miss D's tumor was the size of a walnut and the doctor scheduled her for surgery.

Harold arranged for us to enter New York Hospital discreetly. We arrived at the hospital the day before the operation, dodging trucks and handcarts in the service entrance instead of the paparazzi. Miss D wore a beige suit, a blue straw hat, and the wig from *A Piano for Mrs. Cimino*, a made-for-television movie she'd starred in the year before about an elderly woman fighting to remain independent. Miss D's hospital room was on the seventeenth floor, a huge suite with windows overlooking the East River. Once we settled in, the number of people who wanted to get their eyes on her seemed excessive. When the doctors came by on rounds, there would be twelve or more crammed into the suite, and people coming in every few minutes to straighten her bed sheets, fuss over her water, and adjust her bed.

These constant interruptions were not helpful to Miss D,

who was scared. I had not seen her this frightened before and she was plainspoken about it. She told the surgeon, Dr. Shires, that if he found a malignant tumor, she wanted him to perform the mastectomy immediately. "I don't want to go through with this a second time just to tell me it's malignant and ask me what do I want to do," she said. "I want you to do whatever you need to do to rid me of it."

I could see he understood and appreciated what Miss D was going through. He was a compassionate man.

In addition to her fear that it might be cancerous, she was very concerned that we keep this surgery secret. If word got out in Hollywood that she had cancer, it was unlikely that she would work again. At her age, even if she recovered, she would be uninsurable. "The risk of financial backers investing in me again would be slim," she said. "They'd be too scared that something might happen to me on the set and the film would be lost. I would never work again."

I silently blamed the doctors the studios sent to the Colonial House to certify that she was healthy before work on a movie could begin. Their job was to give her a clean bill of health so that the underwriters would insure the movie. This lump in her breast the size of a walnut had to have been growing for some time. These doctors really never had examined her. While they took her blood pressure and listened to her heart, they chatted and Miss D told charming stories. Often she would offer them drinks and then they would leave. The studio doctors' job was to get the movie made, not actually diagnose Miss D.

Among the many tests she had the day before the surgery was a CT scan, which revealed a blockage in one of Miss D's arteries. The doctors had to decide which of her health concerns came first, the lump in her breast or the blockage in her artery. Miss D always had Harold make a thorough search for the best doctors in the field when she had a health problem, and she trusted her doctors completely. She did not question their judgment when they recommended that removing the tumor came first, but the news of more health problems intensified her anxiety. Dr. Shires gave special permission for me to hold her hand while she went under anesthetic. I had to suit up in scrubs and a mask to do this. I handed her Nerack, the small ceramic sleeping cat Bede had given her for good luck. She treasured it, and I knew she'd feel soothed by it when she woke up.

After she slipped under the anesthetic, I stood in the hallway outside the operating room watching the silhouetted movements of doctors and the nurses through the frosted glass panels in the doors. A nurse recommended that I go sit in the lounge because, she assured me, Miss D would be completely out of it when they brought her out of surgery. I stood my ground. Even though I could not see much through those opaque windows, it was as close to her as I promised her I would be. I was glad I did not leave. When they wheeled Miss D out, she opened her eyes and started talking to me, although she fell asleep shortly after she got to intensive care.

That summer of 1983, New York City nurses were on strike and the hospital was short-staffed and under siege. In the chaos, I feared the *National Enquirer*, or some other tabloid, might find a way to sneak someone in to get an unflattering photograph of her. They would not do that while I stood guard.

The doctor found that the tumor was malignant and had performed a mastectomy. Back in her hospital room, as the anesthesia wore off, Miss D was clearly in a great deal of pain. She tried not to show it, instead talking about how we ought to re-arrange the room and asking me to move "Big Bertha"—the name she'd given the IV stand—closer to her bed. Two nurses came in to take her for X-rays. *X-rays right after surgery?* What did I know, though? They were the nurses, and they weren't even sure why I was there in the first place—a twenty-eight-year-old woman who wasn't exactly family. Despite my naiveté, I was pretty sure that X-rays weren't a good idea right then. *Don't they see how much pain she's in?*

The nurses lifted Miss D wincing onto the gurney and wheeled her out. When they got her into the X-ray room and moved her on to the CT scan machine, Miss D screamed out in pain. The nurses realized that they had accidentally ripped the metal sutures from the surgery. After a flurry of nervous movement and Miss D's continued cries of agony, Dr. Shires and Dr. Rosenberg rushed in, demanding to know who took her for these X-rays.

The nurses had made a mistake—one of many to come.

That incident caused a setback. After that she was spooked by the appearance of a gurney, or the sound of its wheels as one passed in the hallway.

Miss D was determined to get out of the hospital as quickly as she could, but for the duration of her stay she adjusted to her starring role in the hospital. She had an extensive collection of bed jackets and we'd packed six of them for the stay in the hospital, assuming that would provide her with a new choice every day of her stay. In the morning, she would apply her full makeup and fix her hair. Even in the hospital she was conscious of her image. She was a trouper, up on her feet making short walks down the hallway five days after the operation, trailing Big Bertha, as she greeted the hospital staff she encountered along the way.

On our ninth day there, Miss D was out of bed, getting ready for another of her short walks. The orderlies wheeled in a gurney to take her for some more scans. When she saw the gurney she opened her mouth to speak, but only a small sound found its way out. I could tell from the fear on Miss D's face and the tremble in her voice that something was terribly wrong—that the gurney wasn't just triggering a painful memory—except no one recognized this but me. Then her face went pale.

"Now! Call the doctor!" I shouted.

The nurses turned and looked at me as though I was crazy. I ran and picked up the hospital phone and dialed Dr. Tyberg's pager. At that moment Miss D collapsed, cueing an immediate onslaught of nurses, and a flurry of hands moving to connect machines to Miss D's lifeless body. They didn't see this coming, but I had. I knew Miss D, and I'd never before seen that kind of fear in her face. It was as if she'd seen her own death.

In a way, she had. The lines on the machines that were monitoring her went flat.

"Quick! We're losing her," one of the nurses said.

Dr. Tyberg rushed in, trailing a team of doctors behind him. He grabbed the paddles to re-start her heart. Her small body jumped up a bit, but her heart did not re-start. He pulsed her again, and then again. The scene was so chaotic that they forgot to toss me out of the room. I stood in the corner praying to God that he please not let her die. She had to pull through. She must.

Dr. Tyberg pulsed her with the paddles again and again

and finally the flat fluorescent lines of the heart monitor started to dance up and down. I began to cry with relief. Then the nurses swarmed her, following the doctors' orders for drugs to be injected. When she finally opened her eyes the doctor asked her the same sequence of questions she had answered in *A Piano for Mrs. Cimino* in the scene when her character was rushed to the hospital on a gurney: "What day is today? Who is the president of the United States? What is your name?" Miss D was talking but she did not make any sense. I could not tell if she knew she was in a real hospital or thought that she was on the film set. Unlike in the movie, her words were mangled and unintelligible—even though by the look on her face, she thought she was making perfect sense. When she realized that no one understood what she was saying, her eyes became ablaze with anguish. I knew she was still in there, trying to make herself understood.

After the doctors left, I felt the absence of activity, the void left by the calamity that had just ended. Looking at Miss D made me feel helpless. There were four more bags of fluids hanging on Big Bertha and she had tubes in her hands and her arms. Her body was covered in bruises, from the accident with the staples on her wound, her fall, and the way they had to handle her to get her heart started again. I wanted to do something, even if it was just to hug her and give her some human touch but there was little for me to do except stare. The doctors said that she had had a stroke, and it was too soon to determine how debilitating it was.

The next day the newspapers and evening news quoted staff from the hospital saying that Bette Davis hadn't more than weeks to live. So the word had gotten out despite our best efforts.

I had to ignore the news from beyond the hospital room and focus on Miss D. The next few days were crucial, they said. The doctors told me that the room had to remain silent and calm. I could not turn on the television. The noise from it would disturb her, and if her medical condition ended up on the news and she heard about it, that would upset her. We had to protect her from that. I also knew that even if she was knocked out, she could hear me. I knew this from my own stay in a hospital when I was a young girl.

I was seven, and I had just made my first communion. On the way home from church, my family stopped off at a friend's house. When I saw the kids playing tetherball, I ran to join them and crashed right through a closed sliding glass door. The pane of glass shattered around me and sliced me up so badly that I was in the hospital for months while the doctors repaired the extensive damage to my legs. In the beginning of my hospital stay I was in a coma. People felt free to speak around me, to say anything they wanted, even things about how dire my condition was. They did not know I heard them. I did not understand much of what they said, but I was aware of the mood of the room. If people in my room were upset, as my parents often were, I became upset too, even though they could not see any signs of that in me.

I knew that besides staying alert for any change in Miss D, my job was to protect the atmosphere around her, to make sure that the mood was positive and loving. This might help her get better more quickly.

Because the stroke happened on the right side of Miss D's brain, it affected her left side. In the days that followed the stroke, two young doctors, Dr. Paul and Dr. Seth, came by regularly to check Miss D's toes, explaining that it took time to know how much of a person's body was affected by such a serious stroke, and that they'd be able to tell more once they found out if Miss D could move her toes. As they checked her toes, I sat on the sofa where I had been sleeping—having yet to leave Miss D alone in the hospital—willing her toes to move. There was nothing else for me to do but wait.

"I'm here," I'd say, sitting by her side. "I'm right nearby."

I'd tell her when I had to use the bathroom. Even when her eyes were closed she needed to know that I was there, since she was immensely fearful that she'd have another stroke. I realized that I had to be Miss D's voice for her. I knew what she'd want and what she wouldn't want, so I took over. I oversaw the changing of the nurses' shifts, making sure their medical charts on Miss D were updated because I had noticed inconsistencies between the information on the charts attached to Miss D's bed and those at the nurses' stations. On one occasion, Miss D suffered a terrible reaction to a new medication, so I started keeping track of when her medication was due and, specifically, what that medication was and what it looked like. Twice I questioned pills that nurses were about to give Miss D—pills I didn't recognize. I called her doctor with my concerns, and sure enough, they were the wrong pills.

After word of Miss D's stroke leaked out to the press, reporters clamored for a story about what Bette Davis had become, and about what she would never again be, but I wasn't going to let them have one. Miss D was a fighter—not only would she get better, but she'd work again. I vowed to make sure of it.

"Miss D would hate for anyone to see her like this," I said to Harold. "You and I both know that. She's afraid to even let

Michael and Bede see her yet." So we limited access to her. The edict was strict: Only the attending doctors and nurses would be allowed. No one else.

I suggested to Harold that we hire private duty nurses to try to protect Miss D's privacy and control any further leaks to the press. I also remembered from hospital fieldwork I'd done in college that the stability of having the same regular nurses brought comfort to a patient.

A week after she had the stroke, she was more alert and awake for longer periods during the day. I knew then that I was not just the guardian of her health and her safety, but also of her dignity. I took out her makeup case and, for the first time in all the years I had been working for her, I put on her makeup. I had watched her at her vanity table hundreds of times and knew the sequence of creams, powder, and eye shadow that she used on her face. I worked carefully to replicate this, but I had to stop from time to time. This face that I knew so well was now different, her left side drooping from the stroke, and in applying her makeup I was trying to bring Miss D back to the way I had always seen her. What made me stop was the fear and the sadness that this façade I was creating was nothing more than that, and that she was not coming back. Whenever that feeling overtook me, I had to walk away, to go to the bathroom and compose myself. I did not want her to get any whiff of that feeling. She did not need that from me.

Each day she got a little better, but there was some danger in her improvement. The more awake she became, the more she realized the state of her body. Her left hand was crimped in a fist and when she tried to open it and it did not cooperate, she looked at me, terrified. I could just make out from her garbled words that she was asking me what was wrong. When I told her she had had a stroke, she started to moan. "I want to die," she croaked.

From that moment I saw her slip deeper into depression. When she was awake she was not the fighter I remembered her to be. This was so unlike her as to place me further into my own despair. I didn't know what I could do for her except keep up her standards. I believed she would appreciate that even if she could not communicate that to me.

I sat there hour after hour praying, trying to stay alert and focused on what was happening with her. I kept extensive notes. Every movement she made, every expression that came across her face, went into my notebook. If she took a turn for the worse, I could provide the doctors with a chronology, helpful information perhaps. This was also for my sanity. I needed to do something to feel useful as a hedge against my despair.

Often I thought about Pierre. Only a few days earlier he and I had been holding hands in the garden at Tuileries. When my thoughts drifted in that direction I had to treat it like my hope for Miss D, not to put too much energy into creating that as my separate reality. I had no control over events anywhere, not in this room with Miss D hooked up to these machines, nor did I have any control over when I would see Pierre again. If she died... I could not think about that. If she did, though, it would take me a long time to recover, a long while before I could be the woman I was in Paris again.

Harold came often to the hospital for short visits. As I never left her room he rotated my suitcases every week with fresh clothes. I looked forward to seeing him. He kept all of Miss D's public and business life moving forward, freeing me up to concentrate on getting her better. The private duty nurses arrived according to schedule, and I knew if I called him, whatever it was I needed would arrive promptly at the hospital. Confined as I was to the hospital room and watching Miss D twenty-four hours a day, I lost track of time.

At some point, a week or maybe more after the stroke, Harold arranged for Miss D's children to visit her. I could see the joy on Miss D's face at this news, even if she couldn't communicate it well in her slurred language. I knew she would want to look her best for this. I put her hair in pin curls the night before so I could style it the morning of her children's visit. I had saved her favorite bed jacket: light blue satin covered with beige lace and trimmed with satin ribbon. I thought she looked much better than before, but there was no mistaking the looks on Michael's and Bede's faces when Harold brought them into her room. I saw their shock and then their grief, but Bede pulled it in so well. I was in awe of the way she covered her reaction and immediately said exactly what her mother wanted to hear.

"Oh Mother, don't you look marvelous in that bed jacket!" Bede said, as she walked quickly to kiss her mother on the cheeks. She pulled a chair next to Miss D's hospital bed and took her hand. "I'm so sorry you've had to go through all of this! What a terrible blow, but I know you. You're putting up a fight. I bet you get out of here in no time."

Michael just stared, trying to comprehend the change in his mother. I suspect both of us were grateful for Bede's remarkable gift of confidence and energy. She allowed me to relax a minute, momentarily to give over the emotional side of Miss D's care to her. Michael was pleasant in speaking to Miss D, talking about his children and his law practice. I was amazed by Miss D's ability to rally for this time with her children, to try to assure them that she was well and that she was not suffering too much of a setback from the stroke. To me, who had seen her struggle so hard to speak, her ability to ask questions of her son seemed like remarkable progress. Yet for Michael her thick words and wavering voice were a terrible shock. When he left the room he went out into the hallway to cry. He and Bede had a private consultation with the doctor and went off to talk, and then Dr. Tyberg came to speak with Harold and me.

He told us that he didn't think she would make it—at best she might have three weeks. Even if she was to rally, it was likely she would spend the rest of her life attended to by nurses. He even recommended that I start looking for another job.

Miss D had been so strong that day that I did not want to believe him. The next day the newspapers and evening news quoted anonymous staff from the hospital who also predicted that Bette Davis was on the verge of death. I sat in her room grieving at this news. I could not accept these grim predictions, but who was I to contradict the knowledge and experience of the doctors?

When Harold came to visit the next day the room was quiet. Miss D had rallied for the visit with her children but it had exhausted her and she had slept most of the day. I had made her up so she looked beautiful in her bed, but without her strong personality animating her, I felt sad looking at her and I could see that Harold did too. He ushered me out into the hallway to have a word with me, and to boost my spirits.

"Don't give up on her, Kath," he told me. "She'll make it. Nobody knows Bette Davis. She's the toughest woman I know. One thing I know that the doctors do not, and this is my advice to you. Never bet against Bette Davis."

CHAPTER 7

THE BATTLE BEGINS
July 1983

"There Are No Shortcuts in Life"

AFTER HAROLD LEFT, I sat at Miss D's bedside with the curtains drawn, considering what lay ahead for us. I don't remember ever feeling so sad, so weak, and so alone, even when I was a young girl. For the last five years Miss D had been the center of my world, the one who set the direction and made all the decisions. Harold took care of the details while I took care of Miss D. I had watched her fight for what was right for her and for those she worked with, as well as to bring out the potential she saw in me. In a crisis Miss D rallied and now I had to do that for her. I could not think about looking for another job. This was my chance to pay Miss D back.

After she woke up from a long nap, she didn't sleep for two days. She was on heavy doses of many medications that kept her hallucinating, but only the nurses and I saw this. When the doctors or Harold stopped by, she was focused and composed. The minute Harold left it was as if he took her sanity

Young Miss D, 1932—
Lincoln Center, New York
City. *(John Cobal Founda-
tion/Getty Images)*

On the Warner Bros. lot, 1962: Miss D, Jack Warner, and Joan Crawford
during the production of *Whatever Happened to Baby Jane*.
(Hulton Archive/Getty Images)

My diary the day of my
first meeting with Miss D.
*(Photo courtesy of
the author)*

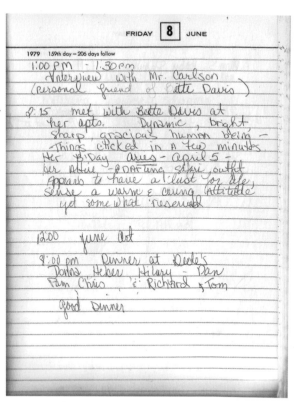

FRIDAY **8** JUNE

1979   159th day — 206 days follow

1:00 PM - 1:30 PM
Interview with Mr. Carlson
(personal friend of Bette Davis)

2:15 met with Bette Davis at
her apts. Dynamic, bright,
sharp, gracious human being —
Things clicked in a few minutes
Her B'Day Aries — April 5 —
her attire — adapting safari outfit
appears to have a lust for life,
sense a warm & caring attitude
yet somewhat reserved

12:00 june art

9:00 pm Dinner at Dede's
Donna Heber Hilary — Dan
Pam Chris & Richard & Tom

Good Dinner

Palm Springs, California
1983: Helen's Ann's home
discussing Aaron Spelling
script for *Hotel*. *(Photo
courtesy of the author)*

The Sermak residence, 1987. Celebrating one of many holidays together (like this moment in our Easter bonnets). *(Photo courtesy of the author)*

Pinewood Studios, England, 1979. Miss D and director John Hough on the set of *Watcher in the Woods*. *(Photo courtesy of John Hough)*

Biarritz, France, August 1985. Relaxing after finishing the galleys on Miss D's book, *This 'N That*. *(Photo courtesy of the author)*

The Colonial House, 1984. Miss D's 76th birthday with a surprise visit from the USC Marching Band. *(Photo courtesy of the author)*

Long Island, New York, 1982. Miss D preparing for the fractious 4th of July family reunion. (A true Yankee!) *(Photos courtesy of the author)*

Hollywood, California, 1987. Miss D's birthday celebration hosted by Roddy McDowall and Elizabeth Taylor. *(Photo courtesy of Roddy McDowall)*

Paris, France, 1987. One of many visits Miss D made to Paris. I was working for the very trendy fashion designer Patrick Kelly—he outfitted both of us in gorgeous style. *(Photos courtesy of the author)*

Los Angeles, California, 1988. After her stroke, Miss D rallied to write and promote the second edition of *This 'N That*. I was always supporting her along the way. *(Time & Life Pictures/ Getty Images)*

Niort, France 1985. Miss D making a toast to "The Mad Women of Chaillot," as she named this trip from Biarritz to Paris. *(Photos courtesy of the author)*

French Basque Country, 1985. Having lunch under the Coca-Cola umbrella: "Take a picture, Kath. If Joan could only see me now. No, Joan, no Pepsi for me." *(Photo courtesy of the author)*

Spain, September 1989. Arriving at the San Sebastian film festival where Miss D was honored with the Donostia Award. *(Photo courtesy of Isabel Azkarate)*

Spain, October 1989. The last photo ever taken of Miss D— little did we know she would pass days later. *(Photo courtesy of the author)*

with him. When I described her delusions to Harold he was sympathetic, saying how much strain I was under every day at her bedside. He seemed to believe I was exaggerating. He said I was too sensitive to Miss D.

Right after he left, Miss D woke up agitated, terrified. She pointed to the doorway, which was empty.

"No, no!" she said with as much force as she could. "That man! Get him out!"

She pointed to the sofa in terror.

"And those cats!"

Denying what she was imagining did not stop her terror. I remembered what I had learned studying psychology with Carl Rogers at USC. He taught us not to deny the delusion. Acknowledge it and invite it to leave.

I walked over to speak to the imaginary figure about his cats.

"Sir," I said in all seriousness. "You must leave and take all those cats with you or I'll call the security guard, right now."

I grabbed his arm firmly. Miss D was still sitting up in her bed watching with interest as I escorted him and his cats to the door, opened it as if to usher them out and wished them well. When I got back to her bedside, she looked at me as if to say, "Thanks, Kath." Then she fell asleep.

When I described this to Harold on the phone, he agreed that at his next visit he would just pretend to leave. The next afternoon when he said goodbye, he closed the door to her room and stood quite still, his back up against the wall. Within minutes, Miss D fell into delusions. She mumbled, wild-eyed, as she struggled to pull off her bed jacket, itching like something was biting her.

First thing the next morning, Harold brought forms for Miss D to sign to refuse these heavy medications. Harold hired round-the-clock private duty nurses, who were also another layer of security. We learned to set rules as to when the doctors and nurses would schedule their visits so the staff would not be popping in every few minutes, and she could finally get uninterrupted sleep. I hung a sign on the door that said "Please Knock." Threats came from outside the hospital too. One afternoon the security desk called to announce that Miss D's son Michael was coming up for a visit. Michael wouldn't just drop by unannounced from Boston. I told the guard to ask for identification, and the man admitted he was a photographer from the *National Enquirer*.

Once I had a team of private duty nurses I could trust, I could be away from her bedside long enough to call Pierre. I quietly carried the phone from Miss D's bedside into the bathroom so our conversation would not disturb her. I dialed him from a metal chair facing the tile wall in the bathroom.

Hearing his voice, the soft and loving way he said "Kat-ta-reen" when he recognized that it was me, was like a fall into his arms. I had called him when Miss D had the stroke, but it had gotten so hectic that we did not speak for two weeks. He said that he had called many hospitals in New York trying to find me and then remembered how Miss D always used a pseudonym. Hearing someone was thinking about me, searching for me, was a loving touch that soothed me.

I didn't really want to talk about Miss D. I wanted to hear about the world outside the hospital room, the good things that were happening with him and his family. He didn't want to talk about Miss D either. We enjoyed talking about when he could visit me in California and what we would do when he was here. He wanted to know how I was taking care of my-self. He invited me to join his family in August where they stayed in their summer home on Ile de Brehat, but I did not think I would be able to get away from Miss D for that long. He urged me to ask Harold to allow me to come, even if it was only for a few days. I said I would and hung up thinking how much I wanted to do that, but how bad I would feel ne-glecting Miss D.

Each of the drugs left Miss D's body at a different speed as we weaned her off the medication, and the changes this caused in her were intriguing to watch. Day by day, I saw her slowly regain some control over her body.

When the nurses came to change her hospital gown, they gently rolled her back and forth to take it off. As she became more conscious when some of the drugs were out of her, I could see how not being able to do something this mundane was incredibly frustrating for her. Her brain was active, but her body was not, and the amount of time spent trying to get the body to do what she wanted upset her. She often fell into a depression after they left the room. There was so much she had to re-learn that it all seemed impossible. No heartache or tragedy in her seventy-five years had ever thrown her into such hopelessness.

We had been in the hospital for more than a month when she did something that gave me a welcome sign of hope. She sat upright in bed, staring at a spot on the wall. She had no-ticed something amiss.

"Kath," she said. "That picture needs to be straightened."

"Like this?"

"No, no that's too much. Move it down a little bit. Much better," she said. "Thank you."

Miss D was looking around! And she had a strong enough voice to order me how to fix what displeased her. She started taking brief phone calls soon after that, and with each day I felt more hopeful that we would leave the hospital.

Fortunately, Miss D had not yet confirmed her decision not to participate in *Hotel*, as the scripts for future episodes gave Miss D something to get worked up about as they arrived. Even from her hospital bed, she had not lost her feistiness when it came to poor writing. In the scripts the writers had explained her absence from the *Hotel* by saying she was in a rehab clinic trying to overcome her pain pill addiction. This soap opera plot line was the final straw. Miss D told Robbie to get her out of the contract and inform Aaron Spelling that he had twenty-four hours to announce to the trade papers that she would not be returning to his series. If he did not, she threatened to call a press conference in her hospital room and denounce her character and the show. Mr. Spelling made the announcement the next day. It all invigorated her.

The better she got, the more restless she was. We were losing our minds trapped in that hospital room. Both Miss D and I needed something to focus her energies on. One night soon after the *Hotel* climax, I had a dream about Miss D writing a book. That next morning I told her about it. She loved the idea.

A short time later Robbie made a deal with the publishers for Miss D's soon-to-be new autobiography, *This 'N That*. At that point, neither of us was sure what the book would be about. I never thought it would be published. I just wanted something for us to do. For her to have work was for her to have hope. Work was always her salvation. "People will leave you, but your work will always stand by you," she'd often say.

Then Harold and Miss D agreed to give me a wonderful bonus: a week off to see Pierre. A good friend of hers agreed to take my place at the hospital so she would not be alone. I wanted Miss D to know that I was still thinking about her while I was away. I arranged with Helen Denis, the owner of Denis Flowers, to send Miss D a gardenia every day. Before I went to France I wrote notes to her, dated for each day I was away, to accompany each flower. I hoped that if she was having a rough time, all she had to do was inhale the scent of the gardenia to know how much I cared.

Miss D paid for my flight to Paris and had a car waiting at Charles de Gaulle to take me to Orly. It was her way of thanking me for standing by her through all this. I flew to Brest and then took the ferry to Ile de Brehat, one of a grouping of small islands off the coast of Brittany. When the ferry docked and I saw Pierre standing there, I wanted to fly to him—but I had too much luggage to do that. I had no idea what kind of events I would attend on this vacation so I had, Miss D style, packed four suitcases with outfits of all kinds. Some of the crew from the ferry helped me get my suitcases to the dock. The look on their faces was comical. I was definitely overdressed for this simple village life.

When I got off the boat, Pierre and I held each other for a long time. Then he looked at my pile of luggage with a grin and hailed a passing tractor and paid the driver to bring my luggage to his family's home. There were no cars or buses on the island, just two tractors and many bicycles. The tractor took off for his house and he and I walked hand-in-hand to his family's summer home on cobblestone streets along a sea wall. The pavement and the sea wall were dark terracotta, a brilliant contrast with the deep blue of the sea. The day was hot but with a cool breeze. I felt my body waking up from a dark hibernation. His hand felt so good in mine.

The family summer home was a large chateau, built in the 13th century, but with modern plumbing and electricity. Pierre's family was charmed by this young couple in love. His family let us stay in the guesthouse, a darling cottage right on the ocean. I changed my clothes there and joined the family for cocktails on the patio. The sun does not set until close to 10:00 p.m. during the French summer. We all sat outside on the terrace overlooking the ocean. Pierre's sister Marianne and her boyfriend Jones came in from sailing and other people dropped by bringing bread or wine. We spoke sometimes in French and others in English, moving easily between the two languages. I was humming inside as I took glances at Pierre or caught him looking at me.

When we went to the guesthouse, we took our time. Pierre helped me to relax, to stretch and unfurl my cares as he adored me. I fell into one of the best sleeps of my life after that and was incredibly happy that next morning to know that I had four more days with him before I had to return to the New York Hospital.

When I departed he escorted me to Paris for my flight. We agreed that it was too soon for him to commit to a date for a visit to California but that we would arrange it as soon as I knew Miss D was stable. I could not predict anything, even when she would leave the hospital, so we had to cherish the five days we had just had.

When I got back to New York, Miss D had been almost three months in the hospital. She'd definitely made progress while I was away. It was as if she had crested some kind of a wave in her recovery, past the discouragement and defeat. She noticed that I was stronger, too, and how I radiated health. She thanked me profusely for the notes and the gardenias. She was spot on and sharp as nails about everything. This was a major step for her, allowing me to leave her for a few days, and I think we all were relieved it had gone so well.

Her room no longer had the feeling of that dark time just after her stroke; the room was now full of joy. Her doctors, the same ones who had given her three weeks to live, found her recovery miraculous. She was out of her hospital bed three or four times a day making steady progress down the hallway—longer distances—and soon after my return she got rid of the walker and experimented with using a cane.

When we were finally ready to leave the hospital, I pushed Miss D out of her room in her blue leather wheelchair. She had on a chic green-and-blue-pinstriped lounging outfit and a white cap, green sandals, and blue tinted sunglasses. Harold, Dr. Paul, and one of our private duty nurses, along with the hospital security, escorted us to the limo and helped her get settled inside. When I got in alongside her and we looked out the window we both had tears of joy. To see the trees, the birds, the height of the sky was overwhelming. As the limousine pulled away from the hospital, Miss D took my hand, holding it gently until we pulled up at the back entrance to the Lombardy.

The manager of the Lombardy and four security guards stood waiting at the loading dock to guide us through the kitchen into the service elevator. In the suite Miss D wanted to look at the flower arrangements her friends had sent, read the notes, and appreciate the beauty of the presents instead of having me do it. I recognized our slower pace. How many times had we stayed at the Lombardy? More than a dozen, I was sure. The connecting scene between all of those weeks here was Miss D in her practical traveling dress deciding whom we would see and where we would dine pacing like a metronome. This return was quieter, and gentler, a side of her that few ever saw.

Once we were at the Lombardy, I was completely in charge. My datebook was filled with appointments for the doctors, physical therapists (three times a week for two hours), the manicurist (every Monday at 10:00), the hairdresser (Friday afternoon to touch up Miss D's roots), the dentist who was making her a new bridge, and the arrangements for the round-the-clock nurses. Leaving the Lombardy for all these appointments would be too much for her, so everything took place in our suite.

She continued to lose weight, which was a real concern. She could not feed herself and she hated being fed. The stroke had changed her taste for food and the medication took away her appetite. She spent a lot of money on room service as I tried to find her something she would eat. Ensure Plus now became her mainstay, as she could tolerate it and it had the nutrients she needed to sustain her. Even that got boring for her after a while, so I tried doctoring it up with fruit or ice cream, anything to get calories into her, but it was a battle I was fighting with only minimal success.

At least in the hotel she could wear clothes, but as she could not raise her left arm above her shoulder, she could not wear anything that had to be pulled over her head. I had the department stores send over chic tracksuits that zipped up the front and jaunty baseball caps, her favorites. The doctors let her keep her cigarettes as long as she switched to Vantage, a cigarette with less nicotine. And she could still have her evening cocktail, but it had to be a wine spritzer. The highlight of every evening was, once the visitors had left, sitting with her while she smoked her Vantage cigarette, her left hand in her jacket pocket and her wine spritzer at her side. She didn't like her left hand because it reminded her of the stroke, though eventually that hand did get better. This ritual was daily proof that some fundamental elements of her well-chosen life remained unchanged.

Independent of the work she did with her therapists, she and I worked in the mornings on her arm and in the afternoon with her hand. I remembered how she had described Roald Dahl's work with Patricia Neal after her stroke. He never gave up. He had therapists and companions working with her every waking minute. This was the way I helped Miss D, even when she objected that she was too tired or that she just was not in the mood.

We would stand facing each other in the living room of the suite as she instructed her arm to move.

"I am going to raise my arm and place my hand up over my head," she said to me and to her arm in a calm, firm voice. She poured all of her concentration into this movement. I could see the strain on her face, but the hand moved slowly up only to the level of her waist. She let it slump and tried again and again before she looked defeated. Then I took that hand and raised it until the look on her face showed me I should raise it no farther. Sometimes she got so frustrated by her lack of progress that she hit her left hand very hard with her right. I felt terrible for that poor hand. We kept at it and ever so, so slowly over the course of the three months that we stayed at the Lombardy, her arm edged in tiny increments up to her chin level.

The afternoon focus was trying to get her thumb and index finger to touch. This seems like a simple movement when an able-bodied person does it, but it requires every muscle in the palm of the hand to flex. For weeks, starting while we were still in the hospital, Miss D laid her limp hand on the tray table at the bed and tried to bring these two digits closer. I never detected any movement at all until we had been at it almost a month, a month of furious frustrations for her, and long massages of that hand with lotions and oils. Yet still she could not get them to touch.

These frustrations about the weakness in her left side obscured how much progress she had made in rebuilding her independence. She now entered the living room promptly at 8:00 fully made up. After we got her dressed, had breakfast (whether she ate it or not), and had a meeting or two, she took a nap. After the nap it was more appointments, and then another nap. Despite my exhaustion, I always bolted awake at 3:00 or 4:00 in the morning and could not get back asleep until I checked on Miss D.

Miss D slept with the door to her bedroom open and a private duty nurse seated in the hallway outside. Before Miss D went to sleep, the nurse gave her a sleeping pill that knocked her out until the morning. This left the nurse with not much to do, and several times when I exited my room in the middle of the night to check on Miss D, I found the nurse sleeping with a book in her hand. I'd wake her up but it happened again and again.

One night when I went to check on Miss D I smelled smoke. I ran past Victoria, the nurse asleep in her chair, and found Miss D's bed smoldering.

"Victoria! Victoria!"

Victoria rushed into the room and together we pulled Miss D onto the floor. It surprised me that despite how much weight she'd lost she was heavy to move, like dead weight. Once I got her off the bed I saw that there was a hole the size of a basketball in the smoldering mattress. Victoria filled a wastebasket with water and handed it to me. I doused the mattress again and again until I drenched it, and Victoria and I moved her into my room so we could assess if she had any injuries.

On my bed we saw that Miss D's nightgown was burnt through in the back and her back was red, the color of a bad sunburn that later blistered into second degree burns. Victoria was so distraught, of course, that this had happened on her watch. She applied ointment on Miss D's back while I called Harold. He said that I should not do anything more, he would call me back. He contacted the security guards. The guards, not housekeeping or the maids, replaced the bed and disposed of the mattress so that no one would know that Miss D had had this accident smoking in bed. Needless to say that was the end of Victoria's time with us.

Of all the physical problems Miss D had, the burns did not concern her as much as regaining her ability to move around on her own. Every day she was a little faster and faster and could move for longer and longer. Close to Thanksgiving, the doctors agreed that she was well enough to go home. It took two weeks to plan, pack, and organize everything for the return to California. I had to get recommendations for her new team of doctors, interview them, choose which ones seemed best, and make all the initial appointments for the week we got back. And Miss D wanted to see her children before she left.

Michael had come to visit her several times at the hospital, and he was a frequent visitor at the Lombardy, but I had only seen Bede visit that one time at the hospital when the doctor gave us the bleak prognosis that she had only three weeks to live. Bede had a hard time getting away from her responsibilities of her family and her farm, so Miss D sent a limo to pick her up.

The day of Bede's visit we spent extra time dressing Miss D in a cheerful pink cotton dress with flowered embroidery along the scoop of her neckline and petal sleeves that had to be lowered carefully over her head. Bede was just what her mother needed. She cooed over Miss D, told her how beautiful she looked, complimented her outfit while she cut up her food. It was as if she had sprinkled some kind of special fairy dust over the suite, a sparkle that lasted a few days, despite how disappointed Miss D was when Bede refused to stay for dinner. The very next afternoon when Miss D and I were working on getting her thumb and pinky finger to touch, she did it! Six months of effort and at last her hand could grasp. It was a great moment of triumph and a good sign for our return.

And then Drs. Paul and Seth from the hospital stopped by. Miss D had missed them, but she thought that calling them to report on her progress lacked dignity. The young doctors had missed her too. We had a lively cocktail hour as Miss D flirted with these two handsome young men. As we were about to leave for California, Miss D asked Dr. Shires if one of the young doctors could accompany us home on the plane just in case. Dr. Paul volunteered first, but Dr. Seth came to the Lombardy to see Miss D off. Harold was there, too. She had on a beautiful white skirt and white blouse, easier to put on since some range of motion was returning to her left arm. Harold told her how lovely she looked and said, "Bette, you've got your legs back."

It was true. All those hours of walking and stretching had restored the form to Miss D's shapely calves. Her legs were one of her most celebrated features when she was young.

"That's right," she said, with a bit of a coquettish smile as she looked from Harold to the handsome young doctors. "I'm back, and I am so grateful to you all."

CHAPTER 8

BACK IN CALIFORNIA
November 1983

"Reliance on Another Is Built on Trust"

MISS D DECIDED that she wanted to cook Thanksgiving dinner herself. I took out her little metal file box of recipes and we sat at the kitchen table thumbing through it as she picked out ones we'd awarded a gold star and laid them on the table to consider. As with everything, Miss D had a system. When she cooked something new, we rated it: gold for best, then silver, red, green, and yellow in descending order. For this holiday she wanted only gold star favorites. The menu she chose was squabs roasted with grapes and bacon, French-style green beans, her famous corn pudding, and pumpkin pie for dessert.

Her guest for that Thanksgiving was her dear friend, Bob Osborne. A host for the classic movie station Turner Classic Movies, he was also a historian for the Academy of Motion Picture Arts and Sciences and Miss D's confidant and frequent escort. I watched with pride as she called in her own order to Chalet Gourmet and Arrow Market, which always had the best meat and fish. When the delivery boys deposited five big bags of groceries in the kitchen, I worried Miss D was taking on too much, but she had chosen well. She ordered three squabs, really young pigeons, small birds that were easier for her to handle with her weak left arm.

On Thanksgiving morning I stayed with her in the kitchen to reach or to stir things that required some strength. After she had cleaned the squabs and patted them dry, I steadied them as she rubbed each one with melted butter and sprinkled them with salt and pepper. She halved the seedless grapes and the bacon slices. The grapes went into the cavity of the squab and she draped the bacon over the breast. I was amazed by her dexterity, no doubt partly inspired by her passion for cooking. We had holiday music playing as we cooked and reminisced about other holidays we had shared. The finished product looked like a professional chef had created it, not like something prepared by one who still was recovering from a stroke. Bob was suitably gobsmacked and visibly moved. This was a very happy day, the first feeling of the life we had had before the stroke.

We'd only been back at the Colonial House for a little more than a week. Walking in the door of her apartment had been a relief. We had been away for half a year, and those six months had been the most difficult of our lives. Seeing her favorite chaise lounge, her photos and her awards, her treasured knickknacks and mementos ended those months of yearning for the regular and the familiar. We had traveled a considerable distance together to get her back into these rooms. She moved around the house slowly in her wheelchair, assessing it, cherishing it. We went with her into her bedroom to unpack, but once we were there, exhaustion overtook her, and Lupe, who had the apartment sparkling for her return, got Miss D ready for an early night and left her to sleep.

Miss D's new team of doctors had come to visit her at the Colonial House the day after we had arrived. Dr. Paul was still with us to explain her condition in the language that doctors understand. After the holiday, Miss D was determined to accelerate her recovery. She wanted to get back to work, and she needed to be in better shape for that.

The inconvenience of the wheelchair, which was difficult to push over the carpet, was the first problem she wanted solved. We got her a walker so she could make it on her own from room to room. She was rigorous about getting out of her wheelchair to walk out of the living room and down the hallway, but it tired her out.

We started off planning our days the way we used to do, crammed with errands and activities and household projects. Quickly it was clear that we could no longer do that. She would sit in the chaise lounge reading scripts and answering fan mail, but she could only do this for an hour or two at a time before she had to take a nap. My duties kept expanding. Before the stroke, she answered the phone, made the grocery list, checked the delivery, and directed me to make phone calls or do errands. Now I did everything.

She told me often how thankful she was for all I did, but I felt the weight of the responsibility I now carried. In the beginning she had protected and taught me, but now our lives were reversed. In truth, there was no one who knew her day-to-day life as well as I did, and she became increasingly fearful that I might leave her. This concern had begun in the hospital when the doctors told her I was the one who had saved her life because I spotted the stroke the instant it struck. From the moment she knew how important those few seconds were, she was more and more certain that I was the only person who could save her life. I think this was why she soon became fixated on having Pierre visit California.

Her way of supporting me, considering how much I was taking on, was to encourage my romance with Pierre. She wanted to keep me happy, and she knew that since the stroke, most of my happiness had been my phone calls with Pierre. With Miss D's approval, Pierre and I had agreed he should come with me skiing in February, and Miss D was excited to meet him.

The principal source of joy for Miss D and me in those days was working on her book. We had developed a good working relationship when I helped her refine the dialogue on scripts, and we searched for the right word or the right piece of vernacular to express that character's point of view better than the writer had. Working on the book was different. It was an open field where we could use our imaginations, and visualize moments from her past or experiences we had shared.

We'd gotten help from her co-writer Michael Herskowitz, mostly during our stay in the Lombardy, but Miss D wanted to go further when we were back home. There was no set pattern to the way we worked or the time when we did, which was what made every day interesting. One day we might work while she sat on her chaise lounge, another we'd be at the dining room table. If she was tired, we'd set up in her bedroom where I sat on the chaise lounge while she dictated to me. I don't take dictation well. I'm not trained as a secretary, so we had to go over the notes carefully. Even if I got it wrong sometimes, we were always joyful about this project.

Indeed at times we were consumed by it. I'd wake up at 4:00

in the morning having had an insight in one of my dreams, or when Miss D and I sat down to work she'd hand me notes that she had scrawled late at night. Sometimes Miss D would hear me pacing back and forth and she would know that I was thinking about the book. She would call me in to ask what new insight I'd had. Often we'd drop everything, no matter what time of day it was, to work on the book.

I remember she once heard me pacing and called me into her room at 5:00 a.m.

"Kath, what is it? Is it about the book?"

"I had an idea about how to connect chapter four to chapter five, a great transition," I said.

She sat bolt upright in bed and commanded me.

"Get the legal pad," she said. "Turn on the coffee."

The way this kept her sharp and engaged made me think of the book as her lifesaver.

One night shortly before Christmas, I was getting ready for bed when I discovered a small lump under my left arm. The next day when I told Miss D she called Dr. Longmire, who found a growth that might or might not be malignant. He told me the worst possible scenario would be that I have lymphatic cancer, which would give me six months to live if not treated properly, and there was the possibility of a double mastectomy. When I told Miss D, our minds focused on the worst possible outcomes. Dr. Longmire scheduled me for X-rays after the New Year. In the meantime we decided to keep my health problem between just the two of us. I told only my father, and he promised he would not tell the rest of my family. I would tell Pierre if we found out that our fears were justified, because I didn't want to worry him unnecessarily.

In this period of fear, Miss D reversed our roles yet again. She became my nurse. She believed I had become sick because I was run down, exhausted, and she would not let me do anything but rest.

In the morning she came into my room just after sunrise to pull open the shutters and served me breakfast in bed. Miss D even ordered me some bed jackets so that I could rest elegantly, just as she had. Much like I had done for her in the hospital, she wanted the atmosphere of my room to be positive and hold healing energy. She sent Michael Connor, one of the doormen at the Colonial House, to the bookstore to get me the books of Edgar Cayce, the mystic Christian healer, who taught that the mind had the power to heal. This was so different from the way I had been raised with five kids in my family, where sick people were not allowed to laze away the day in bed. I had to fight my impulse to get up and do some work. Miss D liked nothing more than a challenge. Now she was rallying for me!

I was also very scared. I had been in the hospital with her for so many months, around the sick and the dying, that I was certain I was next. A double mastectomy was not the end of the world, I would tell myself. After all we had been through, though, I had the feeling it was inevitable. Influenced by the books by Edgar Cayce, I meditated every day. I would picture that lump and concentrate on it getting smaller and smaller and then disappearing.

We got through Christmas well enough. Between the two of us we had enough energy to put up the tree and decorate the house for the holiday. Once we did it helped us forget about my health problems. My sister Judy came up and helped me wrap all the presents for Miss D's fifty friends, but I felt bad that I could not talk about my illness with my sister there. New Year's was also quiet. I think we both were eager for my next doctor's visit, when I was to get the biopsy and at last we would know. We were both praying that the results would be benign.

Just after New Year's, but before my biopsy, I had entered Miss D's room and found her out on her terrace looking at the view, oddly enough with her breast prosthesis in her hand like the squeeze ball she used to build strength. I wanted to speak with her about choosing a day for Pierre to come. I asked about the first week in February—five weeks away—and there was a concerned look on her face, as if it was fine to imagine him coming, but when it came to setting a date it became too concrete for her.

On her way back into the room, she tripped over the threshold and her prosthesis shot out of her hand, hitting the television. An almost comical scene, but she didn't get up immediately. I saw she was in a lot of pain. I helped her to her feet and into bed and called Dr. Longmire, who sent a technician over with a portable X-ray machine. The film showed that Miss D had fractured her hip, a huge setback. Suddenly we were back in the hospital to have a pin inserted into her hip. I slept at the Colonial House, but I was at the hospital from dawn to past midnight. I would come home after my days at the hospital and collapse.

I still fit in my meditation, trying to shrink my tumor before the biopsy, but other thoughts crowded my mind. I was not as skillful in pushing away my conjectures that Pierre would break up with me if I had cancer. Well, that would be a good test of his true love for me, but maybe it was too early for him to be tested. And Miss D, what was she up to with that trip over the threshold? I doubted she planned to fracture her hip with that fall, but she might have staged it so that I would be too concerned about her well-being to stay away with Pierre for long. Perhaps she was hoping that because of this severe fall I would not go off with him at all, or at least delay the visit until she was stronger. *No, Miss D,* I would find myself thinking instead of meditating, *I need this visit and it's going to happen no matter what stunts you pull.*

When Miss D came back from the hospital, the mood in the apartment was the lowest I'd ever felt it. We now had to have a private duty nurse because her vital signs had to be monitored regularly, and she needed someone to monitor her medicines, too. She had to learn to walk all over again, which seemed to break her spirit. Her bedroom carpet was covered in plastic to protect the floor. She had to be helped in and out of bed. We were back in crisis mode.

Miss D hated having all these strange people around: the nurses and the new physical therapists, but worst of all a cook. Miss D did not like having just anyone in her kitchen. Despite how thoroughly she interrogated the cooks, we never found one who lasted very long; I think we went through eight of them in six weeks. Some quit after just one day. If they cooked well enough, after they left for the day Miss D would assess the condition in which they had left the kitchen. She would be furious if she found the refrigerator in disarray, or that they didn't return the pots and pans or the cutlery back in their proper places. One time she found empty boxes of frozen lasagna in the wastebasket after the cook said she had made it fresh. That one was not invited back for the next day. Another one was fired when I found two large bags of food for herself that she had charged onto Miss D's bill and stashed in the maid's closet.

The cook problems agitated Miss D, and when she got revved up she got distracted and clumsy, so she fell more. The more she fell, the more she wanted me to postpone Pierre's visit. I was frightened of her neediness. My love for her was as powerful as my loyalty, but did the fact that I had mastered my job so completely mean that I could never leave? Oh, how much I needed to see Pierre. I needed a break from the world where nothing seemed to go right.

My father drove up from San Bernardino to take me to the hospital on the morning of my biopsy. Miss D was trying to be so calm for me, but she was up at 4:00 a.m. thinking of all the what-ifs. Then a miraculous thing happened. The doctor could not find my lump. He did a thorough search of the tissue under my arm but his fingers did not discover any lumps. He consulted my previous X-rays to assure himself that he was examining in the right area, but he couldn't find it. He called in another doctor who ordered an additional set of X-rays. The second X-ray detected a spot so small they decided not to order a biopsy, but merely to wait and watch it. They ran many other tests before sending me on my way.

Either my lump had disappeared on its own, or all that meditation had caused it to slowly dissolve. In fact, it never troubled me again.

I came home to Miss D with the widest smile that had ever appeared on my face. We were ecstatic that whatever we had done to treat my illness had prevailed. The good feeling lifted the gloom over the apartment and we talked excitedly about the progress Miss D was making too. For the first time in weeks, laughter filled the fourth floor of the Colonial House—and Pierre was coming to visit in only two weeks.

CHAPTER 9

PIERRE'S VISIT
February 1984

"Loyalty Is Irreplaceable"

THE THREE WEEKS of Pierre's visit to California would be the longest time I'd ever been away from Miss D since the stroke. Miss D was trying to be upbeat about it, but I knew she was apprehensive when I was away, even though she would never be alone while I was gone. She would have round-the-clock nurses including her favorite, Gertrude, and Peggy Shannon, and Lupe, and the latest cook, of course. Also, I promised to call her every day.

Miss D insisted on booking us a suite at the Hotel Bel-Air for Pierre's first night in Los Angeles, but I drew the line when she wanted to send me in a limo to retrieve him from the airport. I wanted something less "Hollywood" as my greeting to Pierre.

I picked him up in Miss D's 1980 Ford Mustang, Black Beauty, the perfect classic American car for our trip. We pulled up to the Bel-Air around 11:00 p.m. and the concierge escorted us into The Bar—a cozy lounge with warm tan walls and dark wood chairs, like having a nightcap in a private library, jackets required. Miss D had reserved a corner table for us. As we sat down, the pianist started playing "Gigi." Miss D thought of everything! We felt like the luckiest people in the world here listening to the song he sometimes sang to me when we were on the Ile de Brehat.

It was almost midnight by the time we entered our suite. When we opened the door, there was another surprise. Smoked salmon and caviar, and a bottle of Dom Perignon champagne chilling in an ice bucket, all from Miss D. Next to the wine bucket stood more than a dozen gardenias fastened onto a form in the shape of a tree that filled the room with a phenomenal scent.

So thoughtful! We called Miss D to thank her the next morning, and when I hung up the phone I saw Pierre holding an envelope from Miss D.

"Kati, this card is addressed to 'Mr. and Mrs. Caille,'" he said.

I blushed through an uncomfortable laugh. What was she up to with this? Was she being a proper lady who did not want the hotel staff to know that Pierre and I were not married? Or was Miss D acknowledging how much she expected of Pierre? She knew I was in love and wanted to impress upon him that his intentions should be serious. Whatever her motive was, she managed to be present in the hotel room when I was trying to concentrate on Pierre. I tucked the note from Miss D into my purse in the hope that he would not think of it again.

Before we left our suite that morning, I called Miss D to thank her again and remind her that I'd be on the road for a few hours but I would call her when we arrived in the mountains for our ski trip. While I dialed her number, Pierre emerged from the bedroom with our suitcases and a subtle frown when he recognized who I was calling.

Snow Summit is a bit more than three hours east of the Bel-Air. Pierre loved riding in Black Beauty with Miss D's many cigarette burns in the wood trim on the passenger side. He rubbed his thumb over them and smiled, looking around at California with a charming face of boyish wonder. The roads were clear and it was not long before we were in the open spaces of the San Bernardino Valley, just about to climb up the road to Snow Summit for a week of skiing and being together with no one else making demands on our time.

I had arranged for the Colonial House doorman Michael to stock the refrigerator in the A-frame cabin with groceries and wine so we would not need to shop for anything. We arrived late in the afternoon as the winter sun was setting on a clear day, and the mountains sparkled. The next morning I saw Pierre examining the slopes. Snow Summit was the best skiing in Southern California, but it was not Vail or St. Moritz. Thinking of Pierre's family's homes, I understood why he was not impressed, nor was he thrilled with the slopes. These were things that should not matter to two people in love who only had a few weeks to spend together.

We rented skis and held hands in the chairlift as we ascended. We jumped off together for our first run. I thought it was glorious racing down the mountain as we got breathtaking glimpses of Big Bear Lake to the west. I hurried us onto another chairlift. Again at the bottom of the hill he didn't seem very engaged. He noted that the powder here was different from the Alps. It seemed silly to get hurt feelings from this, but I felt responsible for the snow. He should be happy, and he was not. At the end of our day on the slopes I excused myself to call Miss D from the pay phone while Pierre took back the skis.

She was overjoyed that I called. She wanted every detail. I told her our cabin was within walking distance to the slopes and how Michael had done a fantastic job stocking it with everything we needed. I thanked her again for the great idea of getting that taken care of before we arrived so that we did not have to scramble. She seemed content enough. She said Peggy and Gertrude were keeping her company and there was no need to worry. I was happy when I hung up the phone.

Not so with Pierre, however. I found him sulking in the coffee bar over an espresso. The minute I sat down with him my smile evaporated.

"I thought I'd meet you in the ski shop," I said.

"I thought so too, but you were on the phone for a long time."

"Oh, so sorry. I did not mean to be."

"You know, I am not used to skiing in California but only in the Alps," he said.

"Yes, of course," I said. "It is much different here."

"But it is not very deep powder snow, you know?" he said. "The Alps are not as close to the ocean. They are colder and it snows longer at a high elevation. Smoother slopes."

"Well, this is Southern California," I stated the obvious with a sharp edge to my voice.

"I had heard that the California mountains were steep and exciting, but this seems quite, how do you say it, quite tame?"

I had nothing to say to that.

"Is there another mountain nearby that we might try?"

You should be happy that you do not have to pay for a hotel room, I thought.

"There is Snow Valley, which we passed on the way up here, but it has even smaller slopes," I said.

"Oh no, not that one that looked like what beginners ski on in Europe," he said.

The nerve of this man!

The next night, as I was getting ready to prepare dinner, I realized I had not yet called Miss D. After dinner it would be too cold to go out. I stopped cooking to jog down to the pay phone at the clubhouse. Pierre did not look pleased about this, but I had made my promise to her and I was determined to keep it. I called and filled her in on the highlights of the day without mentioning Pierre's bad mood. When I got back Pierre had built a beautiful fire and had glasses of brandy waiting for us to sip.

He rescued the evening, but that feeling did not carry over to the next day, when again he seemed bored and restless. We had another day exactly like the one before: his uncomfortable impatience at Snow Summit, an intimate evening in the cabin, interrupted by complaints about my obligation to call Miss D. I did not know if I wanted another four days of this when Pierre's molar cracked and his filling fell out. The easy solution was to go home. San Bernardino is ninety minutes from Snow Summit and our dentist, Dr. Cannan, was also my father's closest friend. Dr. Cannan opened his schedule to fit in Pierre that afternoon, so we drove directly to his office. Our miserable ski trip was rescued by his toothache.

After he had fixed Pierre's problem, my parents invited us to dine with them that evening. He loved our home, was charming to my parents. The day was brilliant, and so clear from the patio that we could see Catalina Island nearly ninety miles away. He'd never seen a garden like my father's, and asked him questions about the plants and the landscaping, which my father was more than happy to answer in great detail.

I didn't know what to do next with Pierre. Going back to Snow Summit seemed like a very bad idea. Then it hit me— the desert. Pierre had not seen the desert yet. He could see the mountains and the desert in one trip. That's something he could brag about to his friends. I phoned Helen Ann and asked if she'd like us to come down for an overnight visit, and she said she'd be delighted to meet him.

We were about to get into the car and head for Coachella Valley when I remembered I hadn't called Miss D. I left Pierre in the car, which was a bit awkward because we'd already said our goodbyes to my parents. Pierre was left to make uncomfortable small talk with them.

"You're going where?" Miss D said, a bit alarmed at the deviation from the plan.

"We're going to Helen Ann's! Won't that be great? He can see the desert too!"

"Are you sure you are having a good time, Kath?"

"We're having the best time!"

"Well you seem to be moving around an awful lot for people who are content and in love," Miss D said.

"Oh, don't worry, Miss D. I just want him to see everything he can while he's here."

"Yes, of course that makes sense. Have a wonderful time and don't worry about me. I'm getting along just fine here. Have fun!"

The look I got from Pierre when I entered the car was not

a loving one, but as we pulled out of my parents' driveway I turned on the radio and "California Dreamin'" came on. "All the leaves are brown, and the sky is gray. I've been on a walk, on a winter's day...." The international anthem of all people who dream of California was blasting out of the radio as we made our way down the canyon. Amazing how a song can lift a mood and how that one in particular made our drive a happy one. We were in California on a winter's day, with a road open before us. Maybe being at Helen Ann's would rescue Pierre's visit.

There had been recent rains, and the desert was in bloom. The palm trees looked brighter with their fronds washed clean by the rain. Helen Ann came out of her studio to greet us when I pulled up in front and served us lunch on the patio. She suggested we enjoy the pool while she returned to her studio. We floated on air mattresses in the California sun, our hands occasionally touching as we drifted around the pool. I felt as if we'd finally broken free from the frenzy of expectations that surrounded our reunion and could at last be ourselves.

I cooked dinner that night. I thought it would be good to introduce Pierre to a traditional American dinner, rather than try to replicate the French way of dining. I made Miss D's shell steak marinated in soy sauce, garlic powder, and lemon pepper, baked potatoes filled with butter, sour cream, and chives, sautéed mushrooms from Miss D's recipe "Mushrooms Arthur Blake," and a green salad with avocados and cherry tomatoes. He loved it and it went well with the French wine he'd brought for Helen Ann. Everything seemed to be going perfectly until I excused myself to make my nightly call to Miss D.

The call was just to tell her that we had arrived and what we had for dinner. The look on Pierre's face was contempt. I can't think of any other way to describe it. I did not think I deserved contempt.

"You are so devoted to her," he said.

The way he said it, devotion was subjugation.

I kept the call brief but when I hung up the phone my fury rose quickly. We were in love, or so we said. I knew I loved him. I also loved Miss D and that was none of his business. I walked briskly to the patio, futilely trying to close the sliding glass door with a decisive movement. The frustration at being unable to close it with a snap made me want to cry. Everything seemed so terrible, and I had tried hard to make it all so perfect. And here I had this ungrateful and critical man lying by the pool on my good friend's chaise lounge with the leisure to find my efforts substandard. It was too much. Memories of a Fourth of July in New England filled my mind.

There had been so many beautiful moments during this trip, but when I told myself the story of our holiday I was more emotionally engaged with the times things had gone wrong. My feeling that I was about to cry always happened around my calls to Miss D. He saw how devoted I was to Miss D and he wanted that for himself, as he had when we were in France.

We decided to return to Los Angeles. We could rent a one-bedroom at the Oakwood Apartments in Marina del Rey, which offered fully furnished places for short-terms. I would stay with him, show him around Los Angeles, and he could finally meet Miss D. Maybe with privacy and the diversions of the city, as we had enjoyed in Paris, we could change the mood.

Pierre and I were content at the Oakwood. For those first

twenty-four hours we were living a Southern California post-card, walking along the beach in 73-degree weather in the middle of February, having (to him) exotic meals like tacos. We explored which sights of Los Angeles he wanted to see and I described some restaurants where we might eat. We had another week to fill and he wanted to see San Francisco. Why not?

The next evening I was very proud to be on Pierre's arm as we entered the Colonial House. He looked handsome in his brown cashmere sport jacket and khaki pants, and he had an armful of gardenias for Miss D, and an excellent bottle of wine. I soaked up the big smile Michael the doorman gave us as he escorted us to the elevator.

When Miss D welcomed us into her home I could tell her initial impression of me and Pierre as a couple was positive. We did look good that night. She offered us Kir Royales in the living room, but resisted Pierre's repeated invitation that she come along with us to dinner.

"No, no, but thank you so much for asking," she said. "I am anticipating a quiet evening here with great pleasure and I am very happy that it begins with the treat of meeting you, Pierre."

Pierre was charming in the way he thanked her for our stay at the Bel-Air, the gardenias, the champagne, and made a good joke about us being Mr. and Mrs. Caille. The way he described his grumpiness on the slopes was self-deprecating, and even brought a smile to my face.

"And when you return in a few months to test out moving here, what kind of a job are you planning to get?" Miss D asked.

"I had not thought that much about it," he said.

"Is there some way you could use your law degree here?"
she asked.

"Yes, I hope I can," he replied. "I think there might be
some difficulties bringing my credentials here. I am planning
to look into that when I return."

"When you return?" said Miss D. "Well, you are here now.
You could make some inquiries."

"Perhaps, yes," he said. "Or maybe I will try another pro-
fession. There are many French people in California."

"Oh, you would be a travel agent then?" she asked. One
would have to know her well to pick up the fact that she did
not consider being a travel agent a real job, or at least a job
good enough for the man who intended to take her Kathryn
away.

"No, no, but something with the French community," he
said. "I am sure it will all work out when I am here. We will
be leaving for San Francisco in a few days, Miss Davis. What
would you recommend?"

His quick change of topic did not go unnoticed by Miss
D. I watched Miss D shift gracefully to her recommendations
for San Francisco, but I could tell that the practical Yankee
would have preferred we continue to explore Pierre's future
employment.

Pierre adored Miss D. As we sat at dinner he reviewed how
it felt to be in the presence of two Oscars and their winner,
the grand style of Miss D's apartment, and the thrill of hearing her legendary voice speaking to him. He was, I might say,
star struck. When we traveled to San Francisco he was not as
cranky as he had been at Snow Summit about my daily calls
to Miss D. San Francisco had more of the feel of a European
city, and Pierre was comfortable there. We took long walks

and he enjoyed the compact feel of a more densely packed city, more like his home. I was glad that the last week of his visit ended on a high note.

Although Pierre's three-week visit was difficult, we missed each other when we were apart. On phone calls we examined why we had fought so much while he was in Los Angeles. The answer was Miss D. In Los Angeles it was impossible for me to avoid my obligation to her, and that divided my attention. Making matters worse, every way that she expressed her generosity came across to Pierre as a challenge. No, he could not afford the Bel-Air, the limo, or the gardenia tree, but we were in love. That might be enough if I were not so close to Miss D. Pierre and I decided when he got his three-month visa we'd make our start in San Francisco.

Miss D knew I was getting ready to leave her, but she did not expect that I would move so far away. We had planned that when Pierre settled here I'd spend some months picking and then training my replacement. I described our plan to move north and it shook her. Since she fell ill, I realized she had come to think of me as something of a daughter. Miss D sometimes referred to me as her adopted step-daughter, and now saw me moving away from that perspective. "All daughters leave their mothers when they fall in love," she said. "It hurt with Bede and now a second time. But I will always pray that everything in your future will live up to your hopes and dreams."

We decided the best course was for me to be in San Francisco all week with Pierre, and fly down Fridays to spend the weekends with her and check up on the conduct of my replacements. She needed a staff to replace me: besides Lupe and the round-the-clock nurses, I would have to find her an assistant and cook. I needed to start on this right away, as Pierre was coming to Los Angeles the second week in April, a few days after Miss D's seventy-sixth birthday.

I wanted to do something special for this birthday, a huge milestone after all Miss D and I had been through. Every time the subject of her big birthday came up, Miss D sang the opening bars to "Seventy-Six Trombones," the hit from the Broadway musical *The Music Man*. I realized the perfect celebration was to find a marching band to play her "Seventy-Six Trombones." Getting the USC marching band to play for her would not be cheap, so I called Harold. He thought it was such a great idea that he agreed to pay half.

The night before, I told her that I had a surprise for her and in order to receive it she had to do exactly what I asked of her on her birthday. That morning I laid out full USC gear for her: a sweatshirt, cap, scarf, all the way down to Trojan socks. Around 11:00 a.m. we heard the sound of a band in the distance. I took Miss D out to her terrace, where she saw them marching toward the building playing the famous USC fight song "Tusk," created by Fleetwood Mac. They assembled in the guest parking lot and marched up to the side of the pool.

I called Harold and dangled the receiver out Miss D's balcony hoping that it would pick up this mighty sound. After a few tunes, the band broke into "Seventy-Six Trombones" and I thought she was going to cry from joy. I dropped the receiver and ran to get my tape recorder. She applauded them, and blew them kisses. Then they started playing "Happy Birthday."

The kisses thrown from the balcony no longer seemed adequate thanks for how moved she was by this performance.

"Kath! Hang up! We've got to go down there!" she said. "I have to thank them myself."

"Of course!" I said. "Harold, I've got to go. Miss D wants to greet the band."

We made a steady, spirited walk to the elevator, then out to where the band had gathered. It took nearly ten minutes to get there, but it seemed like we were sprinting. Miss D was impatient with the elevator, and with herself, but once we got there she wanted to thank each band member individually. I saw that windows in all the floors of the Colonial House were open and residents were hanging forward applauding Miss D. I wanted to thank the band, too. They had gotten Miss D out of the apartment at last, and I hoped that it would be easier to do that from now on.

It was not, though. She remained in her apartment. As candidate after candidate came to replace me, they came through the doors eager to meet Bette Davis and then disappointed when they saw she was no longer the Hollywood star of their memories. If Miss D detected that, they were out the door quickly. In the days after the "Seventy-Six Trombones," I was in a frenzy of interviews trying to find her someone, anyone, who met her standards in looks, demeanor, and skills. This one was too bossy, or that one talked too much. At last I assembled an acceptable team the day before Pierre arrived.

I was all packed, suitcases in the foyer that morning before his plane arrived, as was our habit, but without the big red bows. It was time for me to go to the airport and get Pierre. We were taking Black Beauty up Highway 1, the coast road, and expected to take four or five days exploring California before we arrived at the apartment I had rented for us a few blocks from Union Square. Miss D and I sat on her terrace for a last cup of coffee before I left. She was excited for me.

"You have been my rock through this past year," she said. "You always said we would make it and so far we have. But we have further to go. You must not feel, now that you are going off with Pierre, that we did not make it. You have made me feel very proud and very needed all these years, and it has been especially important to me to be needed, especially by someone I love as much as I love you. Oh how I hope I'll be around to see your home and your children." I was obviously moved. "You must hurry," she insisted before we broke into tears.

I was torn. I adored this moment here on the terrace with Miss D, but I could not be late to pick up Pierre. I stood to leave and Miss D got to her feet to give me a hug.

"You are and always have been a very brave girl," Miss D whispered in my ear as we embraced. "Yes, I repeat, brave. You are starting on a wholly new chapter of your life in a very brave way. That's how I will always think of you, Kath, head high and plunging forward."

CHAPTER 10

THE BREAKDOWN IN
SAN YSIDRO
April 12, 1984

"Love Means Sometimes Having to Say You're Sorry"

Darling Kath~

You just left as I waved and waved and watched "Black Beauty" ride away.

A week ago today was my birthday and down on the terrace at this very hour were gorgeous guys playing for my 76th.

What a birthday you gave me. You looked so beautiful standing there, teasing me. How proud I felt looking at you.

Want this to greet you in San Fran.

Everywhere I look in "our" house is something beautiful you contributed to it. I ache with desperate loneliness. You have become my life. How strange that is. Without you nothing is worthwhile.

So many great moments to forget. Fear I'll always re-

member. It's hell to be the one left behind. I hope I don't
lose my mind.

Could be. At the moment you're so near. Tomorrow far-
ther away.

Will always miss you at breakfast. I'm spoiled.

Forgive crazy last remarks. You were more than gen-
erous in helping me get my life straightened out—and
giving me extra days—I am grateful for that you know
I am.

I'm grateful for so many millions of things.

Bye for now—will most likely bore you with so many
letters.

It will help me get through the days and nights.

Hugs and kisses,
Mother M.

When we arrived in our fifth floor apartment on Bush
Street there was a letter from Miss D waiting for me. I looked
at it quickly, but did not have a chance to absorb the things
she wrote. I was happy just to hear from her, a little loving
touch from home.

Immediately I was very busy setting up a life for Pierre and
me in San Francisco. Knowing that Pierre would be stymied
by idiosyncrasies of the American system, I thought there
was no need for him to try to master those. I set up the
telephone and the electricity and gas service. We bought furniture for the living room and dining room, and reserved a
corner there for my work area. I would continue to handle
Miss D's fan mail and some of her other business.

After a few days of rushing around, I was very happy

with my new workspace. Pierre came into the dining area to assess the arrangements. Then he asked where his desk was.

What a terrible mistake I had made, but it was an innocent one. The men in my family worked outside the house. Wouldn't Pierre soon be working at his office? That's what men did.

He was busy, in fact, and mostly outside our apartment. He contacted all the friends of friends from France and soon he was going out to lunch and we went out for dinners with French people he looked up. Life was very social and exciting, but none of this resulted in job interviews. I was too busy with Miss D to monitor his progress.

Fridays when I flew down for the weekend, I had a full agenda of duties. Almost every week included screening more job candidates. People rarely lasted a week on the fourth floor of the Colonial House. Every week I arrived to domestic chaos, and I know how this upset Miss D. She told me she could not invite people over to visit until her problems with the help were straightened out. She said she was too embarrassed to entertain friends when everything was in this disarray.

In between visits, she had begun to write me the most extraordinary letters, full of emotions that I'd only witnessed her expressing to Bede. Often she started them when she was waiting for me to call or at the minute I left for San Francisco. "You've just left and I have that same goddamned sinking feeling—what a chum-friend-daughter you are to get me out of here—so many thanks—thanks is such an inadequate word sometimes. 'Life can be a lonely thing' and it is without you."

Other letters would start with a memory or a yearning: "The place I miss you most is in the kitchen and sitting on the terrace after dark (as we so often did) and using your address books and anything else in your writing. It's all done so well. My brain goes on and on about you and our life here. Bede warned me once, 'Don't put all your eggs in one basket' when I was talking about how great you were. I should have listened. In spite of my 'present hell' I wouldn't have missed any of it. You're cute, interesting, fun and beautiful! You're out to dinner tonight. Wish I'd asked you to call me and tell me about it like you always have. I've always been so flattered you talked to me about your evenings out!!"

I wrote to her too, and spoke with her several times a day. I loved opening the mailbox and seeing a letter from her. Her affection for me was in every word on the page, but I did not feel such unconditional love from Pierre, who continued to be very busy, but still did not have a job. We were beginning to quarrel, but I was not having any apparent troubles with Miss D, except in finding my replacement.

More than a month into our new routine I flew down in a pretty good mood because on this particular Friday I did not have to hire someone new. The latest replacement had lasted two weeks! She was very different from the rest—a quiet older woman with dark hair and owlish glasses who hardly spoke. She dressed like a secretary from the 1950s. This modesty might have been what pleased Miss D, as they seemed to be getting along well.

On the way to the Colonial House from the airport, I stopped off to pick up some flowers for Miss D. Her new assistant was out on an errand, and Miss D wanted me to sur-

prise her by placing some of the fresh flowers on her desk.
Right on her desk, laid out for anyone to see, was a writing
tablet filled with notes about Miss D's condition and behavior, and quotes of things she'd said, ready for the tabloids. I
called Harold, who instructed me to destroy the notepad and
fire her the minute she returned.

The next week during my daily phone calls with Miss D, I
could tell that she was in a bad state of mind. I told Harold
that I was worried, and he agreed. He, too, had heard the
sorrow in her voice. I asked him what he thought of me sur-
prising her by taking her away for a few days. He thought it
would be a great break for her and that I should set it up. I
called to warn her that I was flying down a few days early.
She should have a bag packed because I was whisking her
away. Her mood was so low that instead of being intrigued,
she simply said, "Okay."

When I got to Colonial House, I saw Miss D's Christian
Dior duffle bag in the hallway, her makeup kit, and a hanging
bag with her dresses. She sat in the living room tying the
bow on her white shirt, muttering something to herself. She
looked ready to go, but her words said that she would not.

"I'm not going," she said. "You wasted your time and your
money coming here."

"Oh Miss D! Don't be like this!" I said. "You don't know
what I have in store for you. Aren't you even a little curious?"

"I'm not. I'm staying right here," she said.

"No, you can't do that!" I said. "You haven't left the house
since your birthday when the band came. The weather is
beautiful, the best part of the spring. Come on! It's going to
be so much fun."

"I'm not going."

"You certainly are going."

"Why? Why do you care? You don't care about me any-more."

"That's not true and you know it. Why do you think I flew all the way here and planned to take you away? I certainly didn't have to."

"No, no, go back to SF, I'm amazed Pierre allowed you to come. He probably can't stand me either."

"That's not true and you know it."

This was starting to get ridiculous. I had to call her bluff.

"You are going," I said.

"No."

"Get up."

"I don't want to."

I walked over to her chair and placed my hands on each armrest so that I could look her in the eyes.

"You are going because if you do not get in the car with me right now I will leave and you will never see me again."

I stood back. She met my stare. Then slowly she got to her feet, steadied herself on her cane and walked toward the door. I could see from the look on her face that her mood had not changed, but she was compliant, which was all that I wanted at that moment.

We got into the back of the limo silently and I asked the driver to raise the dark glass between us so that he could not see us or hear our conversation. We remained silent as he drove down Sunset Boulevard and got on the Pacific Coast Highway north. Just south of Santa Barbara was San Ysidro Ranch, an exclusive resort we had visited before, where I hoped Miss D could get some energy back.

I could see she was getting agitated, uncomfortable being

out of her apartment. My heart was aching for her. She turned toward me, furious.

"And where are we going?"

"On an adventure," I said brightly. "It's a surprise."

"Don't treat me like an infant! Tell me where we are going."

"No, you're just going to have to wait. Guess! I'll tell you if you're right."

"Oh you'll tell me, will you? You'll play your game? I'm not playing games. I'm not."

She raised her right hand up to the top of her head, yanked off her wig and threw it to the floor of the limo. I tensed. She fidgeted with fury. I feared she might open the passenger door and throw herself out onto the freeway. We sat facing forward, her wig splayed out on the hump on the floor. I bent down to pick it up and put it on the seat between us. After a while she stopped fidgeting and put her wig back on before the limo pulled into the portico at San Ysidro, which she refused to even acknowledge as familiar.

San Ysidro Ranch is built into a hillside of the Santa Ynez Mountains with a clear view of the Pacific. Creeks and waterfalls rush through the grounds and out toward the sea. I reserved us a light-filled two-bedroom cottage with beamed ceilings, a fireplace, and a cheerful terrace surrounded by flowering plants. We didn't pause to look at the view of the ocean when we arrived there, but went directly to our rooms, agreeing we would meet for cocktails at 5:00 and then go to dinner. Even if she was not happy, we did need to eat, but I was expecting we'd make it an early night.

When we met for cocktails, I thought she looked very sharp. They seated us pleasantly at a prominent table by the

big fireplace in the Stonehouse, the hotel's small, rustic dining room. It was a chilly night and being so near the fire
made our table inviting. The warm colors of the room and the
soft murmur of conversation helped me relax but not for long.
When the waiter came and I ordered Miss D a wine spritzer,
she said sharply, "Don't treat me like a child!"

A hush fell over the dining room. People had been sneak-
ing glances at Miss D, and I heard some whispering, "Is that
Bette Davis?" Now that her voice rang through the room, she
had their complete attention. She had mine too, but there
was nothing I could do. She was furious, muttering to herself,
seemingly unaware that we were in public. I had never seen
her like this. She was in a world of her own and I didn't know
where that was. I could not hustle her out the door to save us
from further embarrassment. I had to let this play out no matter where she took it. She fell silent, pouting like a little girl
not getting her way.

She saw the look on my face of disbelief. I looked around
self-consciously, and she saw it.

"I have a notion to just rip this tablecloth off. Oh, wouldn't
you love to see that?" she said. "Bette Davis has gone crazy.
Yes, she's gone mad."

Our food arrived and she had no more outbursts. Back
at our cottage, we went to our rooms. I sat on my bed,
stunned. What was I to do? I had been sure her attitude
would change the moment I got her out, but it only seemed
to have gotten worse. This was the situation we were in and
I did not know how to make it better. I felt lonely too. I
thought of calling Pierre, but he was no longer supportive
when it came to Miss D. All I could do was hope that things
would be better tomorrow.

The next morning when I came out of my room Miss D was sitting in the living room fully dressed and repentant.

"Please sit down, Kath," she said. "I want to apologize to you."

I sat on the sofa opposite her chair.

"You have done so much for me, Kath, you have stood by me like no one else, and you do not deserve to be treated the way I treated you last night," she said. "I am very sorry."

We had breakfast on the terrace with no cross words or mumbling, and I saw her relax. We took a short walk along the pathway to collect some flowers for the table on the terrace, and went down to the dining room for lunch. That afternoon, after a nap, we decided we'd luxuriate in the Jacuzzi hot tub. There was a breeze coming from the ocean that created a light coolness across our shoulders. The water was good for her left side, and I watched her let her legs float freely in the water.

I wanted to talk about how far she had come in the last year, but she did not want to look backwards. She wanted to talk about Pierre, a subject that was off limits for us. She sometimes asked about him, but only as a courtesy, out of respect for our relationship. In the Jacuzzi, she wanted to talk about the future because she was impatient for me to come back to LA.

"So what does Pierre do now? How are his job prospects coming in San Francisco?" she asked.

"He's met many people," I said. "The French community welcomed him."

"But he doesn't have any way yet to practice law?" she asked.

"He found out that if he wants to get a law license, he

would have to go back to school for a year," I said. "He doesn't find that appealing at all."

"So what's his second choice?"

"He wants to be a creative director at an advertising agency," I said.

"There are many creative agencies in San Francisco," she said. "That is a good place to start."

"Well, he doesn't want to start too low at his age," I said.

"He must do something," she said. "I don't know how you're getting through all the complications in San Francisco. Isn't it twice the problem thinking about Pierre and his future? I want to tell you to forge ahead just for you. You're so tired. You stay awake every night planning and worrying. Doesn't he see that?"

"He hasn't mentioned it to me," I said.

"He does not tell you how gorgeous you are?" she said, disgusted. "Two months up there without a job. Why you've kept respect for this man during his stay here in the U.S.A. is a wonder to me. He's used you. He's used both of us! Plus you're taking all the blame on yourself. If he's going to do nothing, I think he should do it here. At least here you can do your job without so much back and forth every week."

"That would wound him, if I told him we were moving back here before he could get a job," I said, thinking about what a difficult conversation that would be.

"Well, he really doesn't have much to say about it once you make up your mind, does he?" she said. "He doesn't pay the rent. Isn't there anything he wants to do, something he could do better down here than up there?"

"Lately he's started to talk about going into real estate,"

I said. "He thinks it would be easy to get qualified as an agent."

"Oh, that's perfect!" said Miss D, delighted. "I know Jon Douglas. He's a friend of mine, and one of the most success-ful agents in Los Angeles. He's got offices everywhere. Tell Pierre I can make an introduction for him."

"You would?"

"Of course, I'd do anything to help you two get along," she said. "He comes back here, gets a job, and there will be a lot less stress at home. You two have a good chance once he can contribute to the household."

By the next day it was all decided. When I returned to San Francisco I would explain to Pierre that there was a great opportunity in real estate for him in Los Angeles and we were packing up the house and returning to LA so he could launch his new career. Perhaps he would be upset by this, but with a job, that would fade quickly, Miss D firmly believed. Once I got used to the idea, it seemed so obviously right for everyone concerned. Pierre and I could be together in our own place and Miss D would no longer be so lonely. Harmony everywhere as soon as we got back to Los Angeles.

When I walked into our apartment in San Francisco after that weekend and saw Pierre, he was overjoyed to see me. More so than ever before. He even had a gift waiting for me on the table: a beautiful set of earrings. I was deeply touched and couldn't understand why he had done something so thought-ful when he didn't have any money, but I was happy he had. It was a loving touch and I appreciated him even more so for thinking about me.

Pierre had a meeting the next day. Normally I would be in LA on a Friday afternoon with Miss D but since I had just spent the week with her, I was in San Francisco for the first time since we moved there.

The phone rang and the caller was a woman asking for Pierre. I said he was out but I could take a message, thinking this was a business call. No, no, she said. She was Natalie just calling to thank him for the other night.

The other night?

When he returned I told him Natalie had called and he was upset with me, as if this was my fault. I thought of the gift. Every time he was guilty of something suddenly a gift arrives. The gift was his confession.

I confronted him, but he insisted this was not his fault. This was nothing, and besides this woman came on to him. He reminded me how much he loved me. It was just a simple flirtation and that was all it was.

I was less receptive to his present now. I had decided San Francisco was not meant to be and he had a better chance of getting a job in Los Angeles. Miss D was willing to help him and introduce him to prominent people in real estate there. We had to act quickly because his visa was running out in a few weeks. If we wanted to stay, he needed to have a job before then.

We moved back to the Oakwood apartments a week later. Miss D had arranged for him to meet with Jon Douglas. He was encouraging, but he advised Pierre that in order to be hired he would have to study for his real estate license. Pierre did not welcome the idea of going back to school, even for a few months, and he wasn't even sure he wanted real estate. A few weeks later his visa expired, and he had to return to Paris. The decision was forced on him, but by his own inaction.

I was relieved he was gone. We had had some great times, as we always did, and remained very attracted to each other, but without him working I began not to respect him. Neither did Miss D. I wasn't asking for the Bel-Air, but I was not willing to support a playboy. I wondered if there was any future for him and me. I hoped there was, but it was not now. Once again I reaffirmed my commitment to Miss D.

CHAPTER 11

ON THE BEACH IN MALIBU
July 1984

"Beauty Always Shines Through"

MISS D AND I decided that she could focus more clearly on
finishing her book if we rented her a house by the ocean. I
knew she always felt calmer there, and the Colonial House
seemed so dreary after all that had gone wrong since we returned from New York. Our lives could not be the same as
they were before, and she needed a new environment. It was
mid-July, almost exactly a year since the stroke, when she
moved into a beautiful little house that I found her in Malibu.
The house was right on the water; waves swept up beneath
the deck at high tide. At low tide she only had to take a few
steps down to feel her toes in the sand.

I rented an apartment nearby, the first place I'd ever lived
on my own, just north of Geoffrey's restaurant on Pacific
Coast Highway. It was small, but perfect for one person, and
its swimming pool catapulted out from the hillside and offered a spectacular view of the Pacific. I rarely swam in it,
though, because of my many daily duties with Miss D.

I came to her house early every morning for our walk on the beach. Placing her foot on the uneven sand helped stimulate the nerves on her left side. Sometimes she paused to shift her foot around in it to work on her balance. We walked on the beach at least twice a day. We counted her steps, going a step farther each time.

In the evenings at sunset we'd have cocktails on the deck. Miss D loved to watch the surfers sprinting toward the water, beautiful young men with broad shoulders and trim torsos highlighted by their bright neoprene wetsuits. Miss D remembered that I had surfed when I was in high school, and she was full of questions about how you pick a wave, how you ride inside its curl, how you know to position yourself at the right angle to skim across its glassy undersurface. After one of these discussions she announced our agenda for the next day.

"Kath, tomorrow I want to buy you a surfboard."

I couldn't argue with that. All our talk of surfing made me want to be back in the water. The next day we drove to a surf shop where Miss D was as excited as a curious little girl as she handled the wetsuits and admired their colors. We stood in front of the rack of surfboards for a long while as the salesman explained the advantages of their different lengths and weights.

I ended up with a long board—ten feet long—in a royal blue color that delighted Miss D. She was amazed at the size, which was too long to fit into Black Beauty, so the two men who owned the surf shop delivered it to her house after they closed up shop.

Miss D could not wait for me to get out into the water. The next day when the tides were favorable, she took a seat on the deck as I dashed down the stairs with my long board tucked under my arm and jogged out alongside all the other surfers. I was self-conscious. My skills were rusty and I feared I'd lost my touch. Miss D was sitting on the deck with her eyes trained on me. I would be embarrassed if after all these hours of reminiscing about my agility, I fell off my board on the first run.

My fears were unjustified. That feel of the water on my skin, the joy of paddling toward the waves and ducking through them again and again until I found one that I liked, none of it had dissipated in the eight years since I'd surfed with the Viviano children at Biarritz. Time evaporated in the water, and with the encouragement of Miss D waving at me from her deck. I finally came back in when the sun started to set. Miss D told me I'd been out there for nearly three hours. This house in Malibu was good for both of us.

In Malibu, as her health improved, I observed a further softening in Miss D, a gradual lowering of the barriers between her and the rest of the world that often comes to people who have escaped death. All those years before, when she had sharply rejected my mother's offer that she come to our house for dinner, were forgotten. She had become more willing to invite life in, and that life now happily included my family and my family's friends. My family now called her Auntie B.

Miss D had met Dr. and Mrs. Cannan, my parents' best friends, at their Christmas Eve party a year earlier, one of the early cracks in her previous demeanor toward my family. Now for Mrs. Cannan's upcoming fifty-eighth birthday, she thought it would be wonderful to invite my parents and the Cannans for dinner in Malibu.

She sent a limo to San Bernardino to make the guests feel special. In those days one rarely saw a limo in that city unless it was for a funeral. They came first for cocktails at my apartment, which I had decorated with dozens of colorful birthday balloons. The ladies were in dresses and the men in jackets and ties, a semi-formal approach to a summer dinner at the beach. They were giddy from the limo ride, something that made me grin. I guess I'd gotten used to the easy availability of limousines in my years with Miss D. After admiring my view of the sea, and the cute way Miss D and I had decorated, we hopped in the limo and drove three quarters of a mile to Miss D's. As we entered the house we were greeted by a big banner saying "Happy 13th Birthday." Miss D explained that, as far as she was concerned, once you pass fifty years of age you get to create your own number by adding the two digits of your age together so that you remain forever young. And to this day, they all remember the magical gift she gave them.

While we were in Malibu, Miss D signed the contract for her first acting job since the stroke as a supporting cast member in a television movie called *Murder with Mirrors*. This was a joint British and American production, filmed in England, starring Helen Hayes as the Agatha Christie character Miss Marple and Miss D as her American friend. This was a small part for Miss D, but one perfectly suited for a post-stroke comeback. She played Carrie Louise Serrocold, who had fallen ill and suspected foul play was the cause. Miss Marple came to visit her at her estate in rural England to investigate this mystery, but found a murder in addition to that. The press coverage of the pairing of Helen Hayes and Bette

Davis in this British classic was all praise, and our whole household was buoyed by Miss D getting back to work. From the moment she signed the contract, she was determined to be at her best.

But she also was frightened that the effects of the stroke would not allow her to be in top form. After all, she had not worked in two years. In some sense taking this part was a test for her. She wanted to work and although the doctors told the film company Miss D was fully recovered, she feared she might not live up to the expectations everyone had of Bette Davis.

Late in July, as soon as the negotiations were final, Miss D increased the length of her walks on the beach. Before, I had been the one who was urging her to go a little farther, but now she was keen to go on and wanted more. She wanted to use my pool to build strength in her legs. Years ago she had been to the spa at La Costa to get in shape for a film and there she learned water exercises. She had from July to October, when *Murder with Mirrors* would start principal photography, to get stronger. This meant daily sessions at the pool.

At La Costa she had learned to steady herself by placing volleyballs under each arm as she kicked to strengthen her legs. To maintain balance in the water, she had to strengthen her abdominal muscles. She loved this exercise because it was so hard to get right. She could feel it making her stronger.

I brought her back to my apartment to test out how she would do in the pool. I had all of the equipment she would need waiting for her by the side of the pool: volleyballs and floats, towels, Ensure Plus, and a pitcher of water. She entered the pool slowly from the children's steps, gradually getting used to the water around her. Very carefully she placed her foot on the bottom of the pool to steady herself. She hesitated at every step that took her deeper until she started to float a little off the floor of the pool. I shoved a volleyball toward her and she positioned it under her right arm, then one under her left. She paused for a while as she adjusted the balls in the hollows of her underarms. She pushed off from the slope at the floor of the pool and was free floating in the deep end.

Floating upright, she fussed with the volleyballs until she felt them firmly underneath her arms and she stabilized. I was holding my breath. I feared the balls would shoot out from under her arms and she would sink to the bottom of the pool. I stood anxiously at the side of the pool hoping I could rescue her if she started to falter, but she did not. She kicked her right leg, and then a fainter kick from her left, sending her trajectory on a curve. She adjusted the force, trying harder with the left leg and not as hard with the right. Her concentration was fierce as she got steadier and stronger in her kicks. By the time she reached the edge of the deep end I was crying and so was she. A year ago they had given her three weeks to live and here she was swimming in a pool overlooking the sea. When I helped her out of the water, we hugged each other firmly.

"We're going to make it," I whispered in her ear.

"Yes, Kath," Miss D said. "We are."

The next few weeks, as we took our daily walks on the beach, the clear California light illuminated the return of her health, energy coursing through her once again. Her circulation was stronger and I saw more color in her cheeks. As this became the norm instead of a new phenomenon, we started to talk about how I would leave her after she made this film

in London, a perfect end to our time together. We had started
our relationship on the set in England, and we would end it
there as I went off to Paris to live. Whether or not it worked
out with Pierre, I would find out that winter when I kicked off
my move to France by having Christmas with his family. Ever
since I was a little girl in San Bernardino I had wanted to
work in fashion, and since Miss D had opened my eyes to the
bigger world, my dream was to do this in Paris. If everything
continued as it was going on this glorious upward swing, I'd
fulfill my dream that next year.

Suddenly we went from having very few things to fill our
days to having too many, the kind of pace we had before her
stroke. Every day we worked on the script, as Miss D wanted
to make sure that she had fully memorized her part before we
left for England. Also, I was searching for my replacement,
and training her.

As Miss D felt more and more confident in her walk and
at the pool, she wanted to entertain her friends. Now that she
felt like she was back, and Hollywood agreed, she could see
her friends again too. She wanted to throw a dinner party for
her closest friends.

The guests would be RJ Wagner and his wife Jill St. John,
Roddy McDowall, José Eber, and Marion Rosenberg. The
sun on the deck was too strong in the early evening, so Miss
D decided we'd have cocktails on the patio, which was warm
like a tropical rainforest, shielded by palm and banana trees.
We were planning a grand menu, but then Miss D decided
she should not add stress to her recovery. I reserved a table
for us at a renowned French restaurant in Malibu, called the
Beaurivage.

All of this was bobbing along joyfully, like a surfer waiting to catch that perfect wave, until the morning Harold called me at my apartment before I was scheduled to arrive at Miss D's. Harold's voice was unsettling. He told me he was flying out to California and wanted to see me alone.

"I have not said a word to Miss Davis yet, but rumor has it Mrs. Hyman has written a book about her mother—and I hear it's not a pretty one," he said.

"Oh no!" I said. "That's impossible. Bede would never do such a thing. They have been discussing passages in Miss D's book on the phone daily, and Bede never said a thing about her book."

"I want you to meet me at the Colonial House at noon tomorrow," he said. "We will call Mrs. Hyman together and speak with her about this. Perhaps she has not thought of the effect this will have on her mother."

"I can't believe this. Are you sure? If she publishes it, it will kill Miss D," I said. "She will want to die all over again."

I struggled through my hours with Miss D. I met Harold at the Colonial House the following day. We phoned Mrs. Hyman together from Miss D's bedroom so that Lupe would not overhear. "Bede, I am asking you please to think of your mother and what she has been through this past year," Harold said. "This book can wait. You do not have to publish it now."

Bede remained firm that her book was a homage to her mother, and that she doubted Miss D would find anything in it that was objectionable.

"Then why does the publisher have it under lock and key?" Harold asked. "I could not get a copy of it to review before I called you. Anyone who is allowed to read it must do so at the publisher's office."

"If it's such a nice book, then why is it such a secret?" I asked. "If you told your mother you were writing a book about her, she would not stand in your way. She'd want to read it first, of course, for accuracy, just like she is doing with you on *This 'N That*. Please don't publish this book. If your mother finds out you did this behind her back, the shock of it all might kill her."

Bede explained that the publication date was set, and she intended to surprise her mother with it on Mother's Day. If we told her before then, Bede warned, any harm that came to Miss D would be our responsibility, not hers. She insisted that it was a book that her mother would grow to love.

After she hung up, Harold and I sat speechless, not certain what we should do next.

Should we tell her about the book now? Emotionally, I certainly favored that. I felt terrible keeping a secret from Miss D. But if I told her and she died, that would forever be on my conscience. I was not willing to risk that guilt.

Harold suggested we call Dr. Tyberg and Dr. Shires. Without hesitation, both of them advised us not to tell her. Her recent progress had been strong, but she was still weak. A blow like this could set her back weeks or months, and even cause her to have another stroke, which she likely could not survive. More than the physical danger, Harold believed that she would withdraw from the film and might never work again. That surely would kill her if news of the book did not.

I continued my steady support of Miss D, working to get her stronger and finalizing the details for the dinner party. We were also working daily on her book. I placed frequent calls to Bede when we were working on the chapter called "Sons And Daughters." Miss D wanted to check that what she wrote did not misrepresent the facts or hurt Bede's feelings. Every time I placed one of these calls to Wyalusing, I was suppressing my fury. I wondered if that day at the hospital, when the doctors said Miss D had three weeks to live, was when Bede had decided to sell her story. The next time they saw each other was when Bede visited her at the Lombardy, charming and complimentary, the light of her mother's life as always. I wondered if even as Bede was cutting up her mother's food, complimenting her and feeding her, she held the secret of her book inside and the coming betrayal to be experienced by her mother.

We spent hours getting her ready for the dinner at Beaurivage. She had selected a red and white silk dress that clung to her elegant form and showed off her now firmer and stronger legs. I did her hair, which looked full, lustrous, and shiny. She also hired a makeup artist. When she was completely put together, and looking great, she asked me for something she had not asked in the year since the stroke.

"Kath, bring me the full-length mirror," she said.

When she was in the hospital, I had never brought her a mirror. I decided I would wait until she asked, and she never did. In fact, she avoided them. We did not use a mirror when I put on makeup. When she started to do it herself, I was amazed that she did it by instinct and by feel so that she would not have to look at her face. I appreciated her instinct to protect herself from that, particularly when she saw shock in the faces of others when they saw her for the first time after the hospital. I often wondered when she would be ready, and it came just a few minutes before she was going to be seen by her dear friends.

I carried the mirror to the wall and placed it so that she

would have to walk over from her chair to face it. She sat for a moment and glanced at it leaning against the wall, then stood tall and paused, her eyes shut as she straightened her spine and took in a breath. She walked over to the mirror and stood before it. I was focused on the Bette Davis eyes.

I saw that same critical eye that had examined her face on the big screen when we were filming *The Watcher in the Woods*, our first movie together. I watched her gaze widen to take in her full physique. She gave herself a thorough once-over, starting at her feet, which were planted solidly on the floor, no wavering. Her legs looked great and her figure filled out her dress well. As her gaze ascended past her level shoulders to look herself in the eye, a smile started to take over her mouth, opening to a full grin. All in all, it seemed, she liked what she saw.

"Not bad," she said, shaking her head slightly in agreement. "Not bad for an old broad."

Cocktails were set for 5:00 p.m. at Miss D's with dinner at 7:00 p.m. All of Miss D's friends knew that when you were invited to her home, you should arrive promptly. None of her guests would be late.

She was triumphant and proud, as she had every right to be. Her adoring friends lavished her with praise and she was able to announce that we would be leaving soon to shoot a movie in England. At the Beaurivage, ours was the liveliest table, full of laughter and storytelling, and continual toasts to Miss D. Of all the nights I had lived and all the nights to come, I will always think of this one as one of my happiest.

That night, after the guests left, we sat on the deck listening to the sea as Miss D smoked and we talked about this wonderful evening. We were departing in a few days for the

Lombardy, but we would only be staying one night in New York before we flew to England. Miss D had one more detail for me to arrange.

"Kath, we'll only be in New York for a short while," she said. "Make a note for me to call Bede tomorrow. I want to see her that evening when we get in to New York before we leave for England. I'll ask her to the Lombardy for dinner. It's been too long since I've seen her."

CHAPTER 12

A FAREWELL FROM BEDE
October 22, 1984

"Chaos Can Breed Clarity"

BEDE WALKED INTO her mother's suite at the Lombardy carrying a large black Bible. She placed the handsome, leatherbound book with gilt-edged pages on the coffee table in front of her mother.

"Mother, I have a bon voyage gift for you," she said.

Miss D looked at the Bible, and up at Bede, then back. She reached forward from her chair to pick it up.

"What a surprise," Miss D said. She placed the book on her lap and paged through it. "Thank you very much. I will treasure it." I was at the edge of the living room getting drinks for everyone. Miss D reached over to the pewter cup on the side table and chose a cigarette. She picked up her lighter and brought the flame to the tip. After she had taken a drag on her cigarette and exhaled, she placed the Bible back on the coffee table.

"Have you taken up religion in a more serious way?" Miss D asked.

"Jeremy and I have allowed the Holy Spirit to reveal Himself to us, and our lives are richer now that we walk with God," Bede replied.

"When did this happen?"

"Oh, a few years ago now. A man came round to the farm distributing pamphlets about the word of God and we invited him in," Bede said. "At first Jeremy was toying with him, teasing him about his beliefs. Then we started to listen and when we heard the power of what he had to say, well, that was a day that changed our lives forever."

"That is quite a transformation from the way the two of you were when you met," Miss D said.

"That was decades ago, Mother. We renounce that past," she said firmly.

"Renounce the past," Miss D said. "I think as you get older the work is to accept it. Your past is part of you."

I recall how Bede's demeanor changed when she began to speak about the powerful force of the Devil in the world. She explained that she saw the Devil as real and too powerful for us to combat on our own. Bede felt strongly that we could only fight him with the help of the Lord. I could see the shock in Miss D's face at these words coming from her daughter, particularly when Bede offered her mother a route to salvation.

I brought everyone their drinks and an assortment of hors d'oeuvres that had been delivered by room service. Miss D was looking at Bede absolutely mystified, speechless.

"The foul spirits are definitely the Devil's turf," Bede continued. "They have led you astray. The divorces, the drinking, the smoking, all of that is against God's laws."

"Bede, don't you think that's a narrow-minded way to look

at the world?" Miss D asked. "Many good people I love and respect have those habits."

"Go ahead, call me narrow-minded," Bede said. She took up the Bible. "My mind is as wide as the pages of this book. Mother, please, repent these sins, denounce the lures of Satan, or I fear your soul will be doomed to hell. I am begging you, Mother. This is why I brought you this gift."

"Thank you, Bede, for your love and concern for me. I see religion has made you happy," Miss D said. "You are positively glowing with robust health." Then a slight pause. "Are the boys as well?" I marveled at Miss D's control. This was Miss D's deft way of switching subjects.

Bede relented for a while. She filled her mother in on the progress of the boys and the farm, but the topic continuously returned to the state of Miss D's soul. I was moving quietly at the edge of the room, making sure that the ashtray was emptied, and that Bede and Miss D had enough to drink. Harold arrived, and he sat calmly, never saying a word, watching these two strong women parry and thrust, Bede always trying to direct the conversation back to God, quoting scripture from memory, as Miss D steered her back toward her grandsons. Although I was not a part of the conversation, I was hyper-alert, waiting for Bede to raise the topic of her book.

But in the several hours of Bede's visit, she never brought it up. When she was gathering her things to go back to Pennsylvania, she and Miss D embraced and I heard Miss D thank her again for the Bible and tell Bede that she had given her much to think about.

Miss D was gracious but troubled by this sudden change in her daughter. She sat in the living room after Bede left, looking at Harold in disbelief.

"Whatever has gotten into this girl? Can you believe everything she just said? This is my Bede, my beloved daughter who now has become 'born again' and feels the need to lecture me."

I watched her pick up the Bible and open it, then close it and place it back on the coffee table. I knew that book well from my decades in the Catholic church, but Bede's brand of Christianity was very different from the teachings of my church. I did not dwell on that but rather on how Bede spent her time with her mother talking about sins and sinners without the courage to discuss the writing of her book in the context of the Fifth Commandment—to "honor thy father and thy mother."

The next day we were off to London on the Concorde, and in the Savoy Hotel by 8:00 p.m. When we arrived at the hotel, Miss D asked me to dial Bede so she could let her know we had arrived safely. Miss D started to unpack while I placed the call.

"Miss D, the call is not going through."

"Try again."

"I will, but the recording said that the number has been disconnected."

"Disconnected? How could that be?"

I tried to place the call again.

"Miss D, I'm getting the same recording."

"Let me hear that recording."

I passed the phone to her.

"What? Did they forget to pay their bill? Or maybe there's a storm? That's not like Bede. Have the operator keep trying."

After a few hours had passed, Miss D began to get very concerned. She started to pace the room, taking short puffs on her cigarette.

"I fear something horrible has happened to them."

She paced and turned.

"Kath, call the police department in Wyalusing. Tell them we want them to check on the Hymans. Find out when you should call them back so they don't have to place a long distance call."

Two hours later when I called the desk sergeant he said his deputy had discovered a FOR SALE sign in front of the vacant farm.

"Where have they gone?" said Miss D, on the verge of tears. "And why wouldn't she tell me? I only saw her two days ago. Kath, get Harold on the phone."

Harold hired a private detective who tracked the Hymans down in the Bahamas. When Harold got Bede on the phone, he insisted she call her mother.

Miss D had dozens of questions about how they had decided to leave, and when, but Bede was unruffled by her mother's alarm, acting as if she had done precisely the right thing by not letting her mother know. Bede said she didn't want to bother her mother because she was working so hard writing *This 'N That* and was about to start a movie, her first since the stroke. Something big like this would just be a distraction to Miss D. She was only thinking of her, she said, never wanting to cause her any pain.

I didn't know if Miss D was convinced, but work on the movie was about to start. She did what she always did. She put her personal troubles to the side so she could concentrate on her work.

I was seething. Finding that her daughter and her family had fled the country without telling her caused Miss D considerable pain, and she did not even know about the forthcoming book.

Normally on the set of a movie in which Miss D has a supporting role I was not very busy, but I was on this film. Miss D and Helen Hayes had never worked together before, and they did not become good friends. They were cordial, and Miss D was thoughtful. She saw that unlike her, Helen Hayes did not have an assistant. Every day she urged me to ask Miss Hayes if there was anything she needed and to bring whatever it was to her, or arrange for the crew to do the same.

After the initial shock of the Hymans' move wore off, Bede invited her mother for the holidays. Miss D was excited about Christmas in the Caribbean. She kept urging me to come with her. She was so looking forward to seeing Bede and her new home, but I had to decline the invitation. I had longstanding plans to spend Christmas in Paris with Pierre and his family.

Pierre and I still missed each other. I had not seen him in five months, and whenever I felt sad or isolated, I thought of him as my answer. There had been good and bad between us, much of it around his disinterest in finding work in California. He had a good job in France. He was a litigator in a respected law firm. With him fully employed and me pursuing a career in fashion, we would be free to try one more time to make this work, on his turf. After the movie had wrapped, I would return to California to close down my apartment and the house in Malibu before I flew to Paris for Christmas. After tying up a few more loose ends for Miss D in the New Year, I would move to France permanently. It was long enough away that Miss D had agreed without much fuss. She was still concentrating on the movie.

Meanwhile, it was agony for me to keep word about Bede's book from her. I had never lied to her, and this news would devastate her beyond anything we had faced since the stroke. All of her doctors had agreed about that, but still I ached every day in dread of the moment she received the news.

Harold said he would tell her as soon as she finished filming. I kept checking the shooting schedule until I could be certain that Miss D had filmed her last scene. I called Harold the night before and told him it was time. When we got back to the hotel, the phone was ringing in the suite. It was Harold. I stood in the doorway as I watched this news destroy Miss D.

I could not hear what Harold was saying, but I knew he would speak plainly. Miss D took in a big gasp of air and sat down, staring at the floor in disbelief.

"What, what are you saying? My Bede has written a book about me? Impossible, she would never do that. I don't believe a word of what you are saying.... How long have you known about this?" she asked.

He told her and she looked at me. She could tell Harold had already told me because I was crying.

When she hung up the phone she could not look at me. When she did I was the focus of all of her rage.

"How could you not have told me? You! You're the one that I have trusted with my life! This is such a betrayal. I can't bear to look at you. You have robbed me of my joy in making this film."

I felt her anguish as if it were mine, but I couldn't find anything to say. Maybe someday she would appreciate why I had to keep this from her.

"How could you do this to me? You're just like her...a betrayer...After everything we've been through. Why? You kept saying 'we'll make it. We'll make it.' For what? For this? To have both my beloved daughters betray me?"

I stood there crying.

"I should have just died."

"I am truly so sorry," I finally said as the tears streamed down my face. I had no other words.

I heard the familiar sound of a manila envelope shoved under the door into the hotel suite, a message from the production company. I opened it to find that Miss D was not in fact done working on this film. They needed her to re-do a scene.

With all the composure I could muster in the moment, I said, "Miss D, the director wants to re-shoot one of the scenes," I said.

"Oh my God, no!" she said. "I can't. No, I can't. I cannot do this, not after what just has transpired."

She put her hands over her face to shut it all out for a moment. When her hands came down I saw the pain in her face. The energy she summoned to present a brave face to the world had deserted her. Her left side drooped ever so slightly because she couldn't maintain that posture.

Then slowly but surely I saw the transformation I had seen a dozen times in the nearly seven years I had worked for Miss D. She began to sit up in her chair and shifted her weight to rest more firmly against it. She reached out for a cigarette and lit it. She inhaled and exhaled and shifted again, becoming more settled in the chair. Each element of this familiar act restored confidence and her mastery over her mood. After three long puffs, she spoke.

"What scene do they want to re-shoot, Kath?" she said. "Is there some dialogue we need to go over?"

I handed her the re-written scene and we simply went to work. She did the re-shoot the next day in three takes. We left London together as usual, and she spent Christmas with Michael and his family while I went to Paris. We did not speak of Bede's book or my role in its cover-up for many months. I knew Miss D, though. We had not gotten past this yet.

CHAPTER 13

ROAD TRIP: DAY ONE
~BIARRITZ TO BORDEAUX~
August 3, 1985

"Sometimes You Have to Get Lost to Find Your Way"

EIGHT MONTHS AFTER we parted in London, I met Miss D at
Charles de Gaulle airport, and we flew southwest for our ten
days by the sea in Biarritz. By the time we left the Hotel du
Palais on our motor trip to Paris, Miss D seemed invigorated
by the sea and by my company.

At the age of seventy-seven, she had decided this trip
would be different. We would wander where the road took us.
I wanted at least to make hotel reservations so that we did not
end up in some questionable lodging, but Miss D insisted. If
we found a village or a winery we wanted to explore, she explained, we should not be forced to interrupt our time just to
make it to our hotel for the night. There would be rules, of
course. Miss D couldn't live without some structure, but they
would be few. As she put it, "Even spontaneity requires a bit
of planning."

We decided on five:

1. We would depart every day by 10:00 a.m.
2. No freeways or motorways, only country roads.
3. We would take the coast as far as we could before turning inland to Paris.
4. Wherever we happened to be between 12:00 or 1:00 p.m., we would stop for lunch.
5. By 4:00 p.m. we would register in the first hotel or country inn we found.

Merely the fact that she was willing to free our schedule in this way showed me that she had regained most, if not all, of her Yankee strength. And that she had regained a measure of her independence from me.

We pulled away slowly from the hotel, in our rented black BMW we named Beaute Noire, French for Black Beauty, our name for the black Mustang we drove in LA. I positioned a small tape recorder between us on the console, another acknowledgment of how different this trip would be. We had decided to record our conversations as we drove and, if we could remember to do it, at the hotel. When I was traveling Europe as a young woman, I had my tape recorder along and narrated my journey. Those tapes meant the world to me and my family, and Miss D loved the idea that we would have a record of our rambling.

I had a general sense of direction, but I was not experienced driving in France. I missed U.S. road signs that announced destinations and distances in big letters. French road signs were a jumble of symbols and shapes that were hard to figure out as we zipped past. I feared I'd get us hopelessly lost, but that did not appear to disturb Miss D.

I was glancing at Miss D in the passenger seat with a cigarette in her right hand, a map of France spread out on her lap, and the Michelin Guide in her left, but she was ignoring those. She stared out the window, not at the map.

"Kath, we shall head in the general direction of Bayonne," she said, waving her cigarette forward with a graceful twist of her wrist.

But where was Bayonne? Or rather, seeing as Bayonne was east, at the edge of the Adour River, which way was east? I knew Bayonne was not along the coast but, in the spirit of the trip, I decided to see where fate directed Beaute Noire.

We drove past several golf courses, with Miss D lost in her thoughts, scanning the green expanses and glancing at the sea. As we approached our first roundabout, I tested to see if my navigator had a plan.

"Okay, Miss D, which direction?"

She quickly looked down at the map.

"Oh, Kath, I'm so sorry."

I heard her rattling the map frantically as she scanned to pinpoint where we were.

"Actually I'm pretty sure I know how to get us out of here," I said. "It's the next roundabout where I'll need help."

Before we knew it we were at the next roundabout.

"Miss D, hurry. Which exit do I take?"

I circled the roundabout.

"Right? Left? Or straight ahead?"

Miss D quickly stubbed the cigarette out in the ashtray so that she could use both hands to study the map as we circled the roundabout again.

"I don't know!"

"Well, what does your hunch say?" I asked. "I think if we want to head north, we should try going right."

We made another circle of the roundabout.

"That sounds like an excellent idea," Miss D said brightly. "If you say right takes us north, then right it is."

We motored along the coast, and Miss D sighed at the beauty of the green hills and the brilliant blue of the Bay of Biscay. I didn't have time to take in the scenery because I was trying to figure out where we were. I saw a sign for Bidart, a small Pays Basque town near the border with Spain, not in the general direction of Bayonne.

"Miss D, check the map," I said, as we passed through Bidart. "No, no, no. This is the wrong direction."

"What do you mean?" she said. "It's perfect! There's the water and we're following the coastline."

"Yes, but the coast is on the wrong side of the car!" I said. "We're going south."

I continued forward looking for a place to turn around. I saw a sign for Saint-Jean-de-Luz.

"Saint-Jean-de-Luz! Mario and Bernadette's daughter, Veronique, was married in Saint-Jean-de-Luz. I attended the wedding. It's practically at the border with Spain!"

"Really Kath, it doesn't matter," said Miss D, not in the least bit interested in making it right. "Let's stop here. We'll figure it out later."

We pulled over at Saint-Jean-de-Luz, a little town with whitewashed buildings and vivid red tile roofs. The modest marina was filled with fishing boats painted in deep, bright blues, reds, and greens and decorated with flags and banners. When we exited the car, Miss D's face displayed a child's joy of the new. She walked the cobblestone streets with a light step, pausing at the railing overlooking the harbor to admire the boats and breathe in the sea air. We turned away from the harbor and toward the town to get some coffee, unmolested by passersby. On the stroll back to the car, she stopped at every little shop that caught her eye.

I was so pleased I could bring her to this. She was free, thousands of miles away from the scandal of Bede's book. In the ten days since I had met her at Paris, it seemed all but forgotten again.

"Kath, look at these gorgeous fresh vegetables," she said as we walked past a fruit and vegetable stand. "Let's buy some fruit for the road. Let's get a few of these beautiful apples. What's the French word for apple?"

"Pomme. S'il vous plait, madame je veut bien deux pommes," I said to the woman tending the store.

"Oui madame," she said. *"C'est cinq francs."*

"Ah bonne," I replied. *"Merci madame, et bonne journée."*

I gave her five francs, and we took our apples with us to the car. We headed north, coast on the left, and passed Anglet.

"I think we're lost," I said with an edge of fear in my voice.

"No, no," Miss D said. "We can't be lost because I navigated us here. That means it's meant to be and for us to see."

A little after 1:00 in the afternoon we were on a country road somewhere between Anglet and Capbreton, and getting hungry. I had Miss D's medicine in a cooler in the trunk of Beaute Noire with bottles of Ensure Plus so that she could take her pills on schedule no matter where we were, but we really wanted a proper lunch. Miss D spied a large hand-drawn sign at the entrance to a farm announcing *Déjeuner*. Lunch!

"Let's stop here, Kath," she said.

I parked the car in a dirt clearing where a farmhouse was visible in the distance. There was no one in sight, just roosters and chickens roaming through a lot decorated with wheelbarrows filled with red and white geraniums. In front of the barn, a few patio tables with metal chairs were shaded by red and white Coca-Cola umbrellas. Miss D sat down at one of the tables with a big grin on her face.

"Take a picture, Kath," she said. "Ah, if Joan Crawford could see me she'd be so angry at me sitting under a Coke umbrella. No, Joan, no Pepsi for me."

We settled in at the table in the fresh French country air, admiring the sheep grazing on the hill and the chicken roaming about our feet. A young waiter came and handed us the menu du jour. It was simple, whatever was grown fresh or caught that day was the plat du jour.

"You know Caroline, the girl I was trying out to replace you, told me a story about Joan," Miss D said. She pulled out another cigarette and a farmer seated at the table next to us took a lighter out of his overalls and leaned over to light it for her. I was flabbergasted that she did not wave him away. They exchanged big smiles, and he returned to his seat still smiling. I couldn't tell if he was just being gentlemanly or he recognized her.

"Caroline said that she was at a movie theater where Joan tried to sneak in unnoticed, but everyone made such a fuss that she ended up signing dozens of autographs."

A waiter came to the table carrying the plat du jour, a platter of roast chicken served on a bed of new potatoes with branches of thyme, rosemary, and slices of broiled lemons. The smell was heavenly.

"Well, I can tell you that Joan never wanted to *sneak* into anything in her life!" Miss D laughed. "You know how I keep my identity camouflaged?"

"Like we did when you checked into the hospital: dark

glasses, regular clothing, a wig to disguise you, and a hat," I said.

"Yes, of course," she said. "Joan came to the movie theater all made up and wearing fur and diamonds, the very opposite of incognito. Caroline said she can't even remember the film they watched. That had to be Joan's intent."

"The opposite of you," I said, with a grin.

"Oh, wouldn't Joan Crawford be thrilled if she could see what I'm going through, ohhhh boy," she said. "I think she'd quite enjoy my misery. That I have to go through this heartbreak with Bede"—she took a puff—"that I have to, is just, well it's just terrible. Fortunately she's not around to see me."

"Maybe she would be kind to you," I offered. "After all, if she were alive she would have lived through the same humiliation when her daughter published *Mommie Dearest*."

"No, her daughter waited until she had passed to write her book. Do you think that's what Bede expected?" she asked, taking another inhale of her cigarette. "Do you think she signed the contract with the publisher when the doctor said in the hospital that I only had a week to live?"

I did think that, but I didn't want to say it. Bede was a subject I did not want to encourage.

"Oh, what do I care now?" she said. "I don't want to talk about that. Look where we are! We're in this gorgeous place. We're having fun again, and I've missed it. Nobody seems to understand me and what I'm going through. But you do! We will have a fine meal and we won't talk about that."

A *mere* temporary reprieve, I thought. Bede's book was sure to come up again.

After lunch, she said we should head toward Cap Ferrat and we believed the signs were pointing us to Cap Ferrat,

which I knew was on the coast, but I'm glad we didn't try
to make it. Later I learned it was nearly 400 miles away.
I'll never know where we missed the turnoff or how long we
continued in the wrong direction. Those little roads we were
traveling on were not always on Miss D's map, even if she
were reading it correctly. Instead, we ambled through the
countryside. She enjoyed the sheep and the cattle, the stone
farmhouses. At one point she called our improvised route
"the Yellow Brick Road," a road of happiness.

By 4:00 p.m. we found ourselves near Bordeaux, and reg-
istered in a little hotel we picked out of the Michelin Guide.
As soon as the bellhop had put down her suitcases, I took out
my Polaroid camera, my recent innovation for our hotel trips.
Before Miss D and I re-arranged the furniture, I snapped a
few pictures of the room. That way we could leave it exactly
as we found it when we checked out the next day.

Once we had set up her room, I went to mine, agreeing we
would meet in her room at 7:00 and go to dinner. We got out of
our road trousers and into dresses, accented with jewelry and
makeup, a big transformation from the road. Cocktails first.

*"Monsieur, s'il vous plait, elle voudrait un vin blanc et un
bouteille d'eau avec gaseous,"* I said, asking for sparkling water and a glass of white wine.

"Avec glaçon," added Miss D, remembering that you had
to be specific if you wanted ice in your drink in Europe.

"Oui, madame," answered the waiter.

*"Ah, merci. Je te donne?...Merci. S'il vous plait, le vin
blanc...Oh, pardon."* I ordered us glasses of white wine and
bottles of Perrier.

"Hmmm, I can't decide, Kath," Miss D said. "I'm not sure
what's on this menu."

"There's a Saint-Jacques sauce *gingembre et citron vert*, which is pan-seared sea scallops in a ginger-lime sauce, or you love salmon, what about Salmon Sauce Endive." Trying to pronounce it in French. It's a salmon sautéed with Belgian endive, shallots, and white wine with lemon and butter.

"What is *Le Raie* with wheat and baby onions and a cream sauce?" The waiter saw I was trying to figure this out when he said with his French accent, "Madame, it's a skate fish with a mild sweet taste. It's sometimes compared to the taste of scallops or that of white fish."

"Jesus," Miss D said. "Look at what those people next to us are eating. I think we should just get that and stop looking at this menu. I'm looking at that *panache de poisson*. And then I will have some kind of dessert."

"All right, we will ask the waiter."

"*A les deux, a les deux, le* two, is that right?" she asked me.

"Pardon?"

"*A les deux,*" we said at the same time, and laughed.

The waiter had delivered Miss D's glass of white wine, which sat before her on the table awaiting my attention.

"What?" Miss D asked, picking up on my discomfort.

"I'm scared to pour wine in with the Perrier," I said. "This is France and they will find it a crime to mix wine and club soda together. I'll do it when the waiter is not looking."

"Yes, of course, we don't want to offend people here," she said. I looked around the restaurant to see if anyone was watching and poured the Perrier into her glass. This was the moment when she always missed her nightly scotch.

"There are so many things I can no longer do. I spent hours training this new girl, but she does not seem to get it. It was so much different with you."

"Not at first! For months every day I thought that you were just about to fire me."

"Well, honestly Kath, that's because I was," she said. "I thought when I hired you that you were much older and you had traveled the world with that Princess. I thought you knew how things were done. When I found out how young you were, I called Harold immediately. When I sent you down to your aunt's in DC, I interviewed many people for your position, women who were older and had served aristocratic families. They were so old and stuffy they exhausted me. That's when I knew my hunch about you was right, even if you had no idea what you were getting yourself into."

"Why did you ever keep me on after that? What did you see in me?"

"Poise. Discretion," she said. "There were two moments when I knew."

"In London?"

"Yes. When I told you to make me that three-minute egg," she said. We both smiled at the memory of how she went to her room and left me to figure out how to cook an egg in a hotel suite that had no kitchen, or even a hot plate. "When you came to my room to ask me how to do it, there was fire in your eyes because I'd tricked you, but you never said a word. I liked that."

"What was the second time?" I asked.

"At that disastrous dinner at Roald Dahl and Patricia Neal's house," Miss D said. I remembered it well. I pictured that dining room, Miss D before the stroke, the three open bottles of wine on the credenza, and the eyes of Miss Neal as she started to pick me apart. "She attacked you. There's really no other word for it. And you remained composed, and held it elegantly, until we were back at the hotel. Very mature. I was impressed."

"I didn't know what to say."

"That doesn't keep most people from talking."

The waiter delivered our fish, so Miss D paused for a moment. The stew was served in a thick-rimmed shallow bowl with artfully arranged bright pink shrimp, a few scallops scattered around a few pieces of cod and salmon, all accented with a bright yellow saffron cream sauce. We breathed in the scent of the delicious sauce before choosing which piece of fish to sample first.

"And beauty," Miss D said. "It is important that you are well put together."

"Oh, Miss D." I blushed.

"It's true, Kath," she said. "I know it now that I've hired and fired so many people to replace you who were not pleasant to look at. None of them lasted very long. They came to work for the Bette Davis they knew from the screen. They expected a glamorous life and not to have to work too hard. You know how to work, like I did all those years. Very little of that is the image most have of life with a star. When you appeared at the Colonial House, I didn't know what I wanted. I didn't think I needed anyone and I certainly didn't want anyone to live with me. Now I feel that loss of you every day. Not that I'm trying to make you come back. I know you have to live your life. I want you to do so.

"I do miss you though," she added.

"I miss you too, Miss D," I said. "It's funny. I recognize since I moved here that when I think of home, I think of my room at the Colonial House, not my room in San Bernardino."

"That room will always be there for you, Kath," she said. "Always, as long as I'm alive."

"You are my rock, Miss D," I said, and reached out to hold her hand for a few seconds.

I missed our collaboration, our secret language. We had been together for so many years, and she had shaped my sense of what was right and proper, that I knew the moment that something was amiss. I knew her almost as well as I knew myself, but she was the one who gave me the language to describe it, the manner to endure it, and the grace to leave at the exact moment before it all went too far. We could only bear to touch lightly on the subject of death.

"Oh this fish!" I said. "Isn't it delicious? They must get it directly from those fishing villages we passed along the way."

"Yes, it is marvelous," she said.

"And those apples! How did you pick them? They were perfect," I said. "How did you know those particular apples would be the most fragrant and flavorful? Are they a type they grow in New England? I was so glad you had them because we really needed a snack when we were trying to find this hotel."

"They were perfect, but I'd never seen them before," she said. "They must be a unique French variety."

"How did you like this first day? I mean, I know we got a bit lost, but you looked so happy in Saint-Jean-de-Luz. You never get to walk through the streets of any American city like you did there."

"It's fun to have you with me," she said. As close as we had been in so many ways, at this moment I felt for the first time like we were just two friends sharing a nice time.

She signed the bill for dinner and we went up to her

suite and returned to our more comfortable roles of employer/employee. I already had unpacked her suitcases when we re-arranged the furniture before dinner. I laid out Miss D's clothes for the next morning. Miss D offered me a wine spritzer.

"Kath, let's make a pact, you and I," she said when we had our wine spritzers in hand.

"Okay. What kind of pact?"

"Whichever of us dies first, the other will see to it that we look beautiful at the last," she said.

"Oh, Miss D!" I said. "I don't want to talk about that!"

"Why not? It's not maudlin," she said. "It's practical. You never know when it will happen or how, so it's best to be clear on these things."

"I don't want to think about it."

"That's how things go wrong. Lack of planning. That's what I don't want to think about."

I was so emotional being forced to think about this, I did not have anything to say.

"Kath, you have seen me in ways that no one has seen me, not even my family," Miss D said. "You are the one I can trust to make sure my wishes are fulfilled. Can't we agree?"

"We can."

"I want to be properly made up and looking dignified," she said. "Don't let them dress me any which way. Please. And I want you to make sure that my face is made up exactly as I would do for you."

"Of course," I said. "And if I go before you do, you will do the same for me."

There was still a little wine left, so to make it light, I raised my glass.

"To whomever goes first."

Miss D did not raise her glass to meet mine.

"No, no...I need you to hear this," she said. "I want to be buried very early in the morning, 4:00 a.m."

I got out my datebook and started to make notes.

"Before sunrise. Everyone knows my sarcophagus is at Hollywood Hills Forest Lawn up on that hill overlooking Warner Brothers, at the Court of Remembrance. I don't want any press swarming around. I want this to be private, just family, cousins, Robin, Harold, and you. If you do this early in the morning they will not be able to photograph. That would be a horror! If something like that ended up in the press, I would be so upset."

"How would you know?"

We laughed.

"We've talked about this," she said, still smiling. "We don't know what waits for us on the other side, do we?"

"We've made some guesses about heaven," I said. "The nuns and the priests have painted me a vivid picture, but no one really knows."

"All right, promise me part of the pact is whomever goes first will leave the other a sign of some kind."

"A sign?"

"Something only you or I would notice, but something that is explicit."

"It's a way to show the spirit lives on, it's just the body that dies. That's what Carl Rogers, the psychologist I studied with at USC, always said. It's a way to say we are safe, and that there is somewhere beyond this life."

We stayed up until 2:00 a.m. talking about Pierre, and I shared some stories about my new job. As we parted for the

night, Miss D was feeling wise and warm. As uncomfortable
as the discussion of death had made me, for her it was a relief
that we had discussed it.

"So we have a pact," she said, as we said our good nights
at the door to her suite. "I know you will never let me down,
and I would do the same for you."

Back in my room I sat on my bed thinking what an odd
day this had been, unlike any other I'd had with her in all
these years. Driving without direction, happily being lost, de-
tached from a sense of urgency about anything, including
death. This was a Miss D who was letting go of the old ways,
the old arrangements, and encouraging me to do the same.

CHAPTER 14

ROAD TRIP: DAY TWO
~BORDEAUX TO POITIERS~
August 4, 1985

"True Friendship Is Forever"

WHEN I ENTERED Miss D's room to escort her down to break-fast I could see this day on the road would be different. Miss D was all in leather. She had on a pair of black leather pants that looked great on her slim figure, a leather jacket and a leather cap, as if she were a tiny senior citizen version of Marlon Brando in *The Wild One*. I could not help but greet her with a big smile, and it was clear that she understood why I was looking at her with such amusement. My Miss D, the formal and precise Hollywood star, was ready to rumble, black leather in Beaute Noire.

After a quick breakfast, we sat in the car for a moment to examine the map and pick a direction. Miss D wanted to travel along the coast, but she also wanted us to drive through the Loire Valley, one of the world's great wine regions, and pick up a few bottles for our time in Paris. When I looked at the map, it seemed to me that accomplishing both of those goals was impossible. If we were to hug the coastline, we would have to travel west, but to reach the valley, we needed to take a north and easterly direction.

After some discussion, we decided that we should take A10 out of Bordeaux and veer off on a side road when we wanted to see some of the coast. As we began, we played a game to test our French, re-arranging the letters we saw on the signs we passed to make other French words. Trying to speak only in French was fun for me, but it limited what Miss D could say as she had learned her French a long while ago and it was not as fresh in her mind. She was game, though. She seemed game for anything.

I sped along playing our game, and the minutes passed quickly. We had gone a distance, all the time I was waiting for an indication from her as to what exit I should take for us to reach the coast.

"Qu'est-ce que c'est sortie, S-O-R-T-I-E?" Miss D asked.

"Exit," I said.

"Ohhh, mon Dieu!" Miss D exclaimed. *"Sortie! Sortie!"*

I took the next exit I could, heading for Rochefort. Miss D was not at all rattled by the fact that we had no idea where we were, or that we did not have a definite idea of when we would arrive.

"Enormous, mon Dieu, mon Dieu! An enormous flock of sheep, *ag—ncau,"* she said, correctly retrieving the French word for sheep as we passed a field dotted with a grazing herd, but we did not seem to be nearing the ocean. I pulled over to the side of the road so that we could both take a look at the map.

"Pourquoi ici, enorme?" Miss D asked what we were doing when I exited the car. She got out too, and we stood leaning over it with the map spread out on the hood.

"Maybe this route," I said. "We are on N10 and if we got back onto A10 which would continue...maybe this is the route we want."

"To Poitiers," she said.

"I know, but we were on this route and I want to get on the red line and we were on the red and yellow, see we were on A10," I tried to explain.

"I know, and from Poitiers there is a crossroad."

"There is? Where?"

"I saw it," she said, "Out of Poitiers, you go to Chateau-briand."

"Chateau—ou?" I said. "That isn't right."

"This little road, it runs right along the sides of this, the red one," she said.

The confusion between where we were, where we wanted to go, and the fact that Chateaubriand was a cut of meat and not a destination was causing a bit of confused tension between us as we stood beside Beaute Noire, assessing the ominous dark clouds that were gathering on the horizon. I was a little concerned. We were having a hard enough time navigating as it was. The rain would only make it worse. We needed to have a destination before the deluge began.

As we stood by the road with our flashers blinking, moving the big map around on the hood, a farmer came by on his tractor and stopped just ahead of us on the road. He was sympathetic to these two damsels in distress, and hopped down from the metal seat to advise us. He was in his work clothes: well-worn dungarees, a tattered sweater over his striped shirt, and a gray tweed porkpie cap angled sharply from the right side of his head so that it nearly rested on his left ear. You could see from the look on his face he was equally amused and concerned by these two befuddled Americans. What could I do but ask him for directions?

"Ou est aller dans le rue N Dix, qu'est que je fait?"

"National Dix?"

"Oui, National Dix."

"On Angouleme ou no, ou vous allez?"

"Non, pas Angouleme, je suis allez Chatellerault."

"Chatellerault!"

"Oui."

"You speak English?" he asked, frustrated that we might not be communicating clearly.

"Oui."

Everyone laughed.

"Come," he said. "Follow me."

I thought he was bringing us to the N10, which doesn't in fact exist. Instead he brought us to the A10 and waved to us as we merged onto the road that we thought would take us in the proper direction, but very soon Miss D had other ideas. The road was too smooth, too wide, had too many cars and therefore was not ideal for adventure. We had only been on A10 a short time when I heard Miss D fussing with the map.

"Well, there is a sign to Chateaubriand isn't there?"

"Chateau..."

"It looks like that on that map, anyway. That you will see."

"No Chatellerault and then to Tours," I said.

"What?"

"There is no Chateaubriand," I said. "It is Chatellerault."

"Well I could use some Chateaubriand right now," Miss D said. "It's past noon, is it not? Aren't you getting a little hungry? And this route that we are on...this big road. Don't you think it's a little depressing?"

We had forgotten our rules, and Miss D was reminding me in the gentlest of ways that we needed to get back to our plan, minimal as it was.

"I'll take the next exit and we'll find a place for lunch," I said.

Somewhere in the countryside between Villers-en-Bois and Celles-sur-Belles we saw another handmade sign on a piece of wood leaning up against a wheelbarrow announcing *Déjeuner.* I pulled into the parking area between several well-used trucks and a few dusty motorcycles. This had to be a place that only locals knew about, something that delighted Miss D.

"This is perfect, Kath!" she said. "There is no way anyone would recognize me here."

Inside the converted barn, the space was rough and the ceilings high, with carefully placed windows that let in just the right amount of light on the tables. We got a table in the corner next to a window that looked out on the farm and ate our simple and delicious meal of chicken pot au feu, an endive salad with goat cheese and walnuts, and a freshly baked baguette to accompany a cheese platter for dessert. As we ate the wait staff started to get a little restless, and I saw them speaking to each other behind their hands as if passing a confidence. I feared that the older waiter had recognized Miss D. Finally he could not stand it anymore. He came up to our table and, in the most charming and halting broken English, asked Miss D if she was Bette Davis.

No one had spotted Miss D for two days. When he saw that his hunch was correct Miss D was so gracious. He asked her if she would sign the tablecloth for him so he could have it as a keepsake of the day such a famous person ended up at this farm.

Word truly travels quickly in a small village. By the time we had paid the check quite a crowd had formed in the kitchen. Miss D signed the tablecloth for the waiter and blew her fans in the kitchen a kiss. When we exited the barn, we found even more people were waiting in the parking area to see Miss D. To our surprise, she had an audience of nearly thirty as we made our way to the car followed by her fans.

I was a little ahead of her with the keys in my hand when I sensed that she was no longer at my side. I turned around to see that she had paused at a Harley-Davidson motorcycle that was parked a few feet from Beaute Noire. Miss D stood there for a moment, hand on cocked hip, and nudged her leather cap so it was at a strong angle, appearing almost as jaunty as the farmer who had rescued us by the side of the road that afternoon. The crowd applauded and several of the men whistled at her striking pose. I was impressed. I had not seen that sassy attitude coming from her in some time.

Miss D had enjoyed her brief performance and the response she had received for it. We drove for a while in a contented silence, savoring that lovely ending to the meal. I noticed that for all this time we had been driving, Miss D was so distracted, or perhaps so satisfied, that she had not lit a cigarette.

"Would you like a cigarette?" I asked.

"Oh, I was just about to pass you one," she said. "I don't want to keep bothering you if you don't want one."

"No, I've got one," I said, lighting it. "Oh, look at that hill up there. It's so pretty."

"Yes."

"I guess that is Poitiers," I said. "And we have not found a winery in all the time we've been on these little country roads. How can that be?"

"Honestly I do not know," said Miss D, taking out the map again as she tried to determine where precisely we were. "We have not yet entered the Loire Valley!"

"You're joking!"

"No!" she said, now fully engaged in her cigarette as she examined the map. "Poitiers is right on the edge of the valley, if I'm reading this map right, and there has been no sign so far that I can do that!"

We both had a good laugh at that truth.

"The Loire Valley, it is mostly east of Poitiers," she said. "I think tomorrow's drive is the one where we will see the chateau and be able to buy our wine."

Miss D was sharp and in command of herself, if not of the map. We made our way to Poitiers, glimpsing the Clain River as we drove. Poitiers is a city from the 13th century next to the Clain, but the most beautiful part of it is on a hilltop that allows a view of the Boivre and the Clain valleys. We could see that hilltop coming closer and closer.

"You know, Kath, this trip has been very good for me and I want to thank you for that," said Miss D in a voice that was decisive but also affectionate. "You are bringing me into the world in a way I have not had the freedom to experience in a long time. Of course we have so many beautiful memories, you and I. All the years we have had together. I will always cherish the birthdays, and the presents, all the things you used to do for me. I will always love those but you must know that I can make it without you now. That's why on this trip we travel as friends."

Despite all the time I had spent speaking to Miss D's doctors about how we must make her more independent of me, at this moment the truth of what she said hit me very hard. The years of care I had devoted to bring her back to some semblance of self-sufficiency had paid off, and I understood that that was positive. It was something I had hoped would happen. Yet when I felt her pulling away from me, I was hurt. It seemed so abrupt, this declaration she made. How could it be true that she did not need me?

"Of course, Miss D," I said. "And we are having such a good time. We will always cherish these weeks."

I hoped my voice was strong and steady and that I was masking well how many feelings were rushing through me as I considered this different way of losing Miss D. She did need me. I knew it. I needed her too. I did not know what shape our new arrangement would take now that neither of us was the one in control.

CHAPTER 15

ROAD TRIP: DAY THREE ~POITIERS TO ORLEANS~
August 5, 1985

"Only a Real Friend Can Tell You the Truth"

THE NEXT MORNING both of us were eager to get on the road. This day would take us alongside the Cher River heading north and east toward Paris, past the many chateaux of the Loire Valley, beauty around every turn. We wanted plenty of time to stop along the way. We passed Chateau de Chenonceau, a grand old place from the 16th century whose gallery stretches the width of the Cher. As we continued, and the Cher merged with the Loire River, we fantasized about what it would be like to live in one of these grand places with the huge tall rooms and the handcrafted windows.

"I would love to live in France," Miss D said.

"I saw those houses on the river and they're absolutely beautiful," I said. "I want a house on the river."

"Rivers are divine to live by."

"I know," I said. "You had one."

"Yes, I had a damn good river," she said. "I loved it."

We drove on for a while more.

"A house by the river," she said. "I would like to have that again."

"I remember you showed it to me that time we visited with Robin. I loved seeing the river. Didn't you call it 'Twin Bridges'?"

"I was so glad to have a home available for Michael once more, for holidays and vacations from college," she said. "I was deliriously happy to be back in my New England in a house with classic proportions. Here you would want something different."

"Yes, limestone from this valley, a traditional French house. Pierre's great-grandfather had a house with fifty-two rooms, and twelve rooms for guest quarters. And they still have it."

"And if I were to move here I would want the garden by the river, as I had in Connecticut," she said. "I do not think I could set up a place here unless I had you to handle the details and deal with the French."

"Of course I would help you."

"I would only want to move to be closer to you, and your life is on a different path now, Kath," she said. "I am not trying to trick you into our old working relationship. I keep going over and over recent behavior of mine. I am so afraid I have robbed you of your feelings for me."

"Oh Miss D, no!"

"Yes, but I had my reasons."

I let that remark stand without an answer.

"Why didn't you tell me, Kath?"

"Tell you what?"

"Why didn't you tell me about Bede's book?"

"We've discussed this! You had to concentrate on your

work. We have never kept secrets from each other and doing that felt terrible, but Harold agreed."

"Yes, you agreed and Harold agreed. Everyone was treating me like a child who had to be handled, like a goddamned baby who couldn't take it."

"Oh Miss D, don't...I," I said. "I admit it was a mistake to keep this from you, and again I apologize."

"I could have stopped that book, you know I could have," she said. "When a publisher gets a call from Bette Davis he pays attention."

"Harold tried."

"Harold is not Bette Davis."

"True."

We did not need to argue about whether or not the name Bette Davis still had enough power to stop the publication of the book.

"If I called Bede, I know I could have talked her out of this embarrassment," she continued. "But you and Harold, you did not give me a chance."

"I'm not going to apologize for this anymore, Miss D," I said. "It was not just Harold and me. The doctors insisted we keep it from you also."

"That's ridiculous."

"They said if we told you, it might cause you to have another stroke, or a heart attack. You were still weak back then. Either of those could have killed you."

Miss D lit another cigarette as she considered the news that it was the doctors, not me or Harold, who saw her as too weak to recover from another setback. She took another drag on her cigarette, staring out the window at the vineyards we passed and the green hills in the distance, and then another drag.

"But it didn't kill me," she said. "I shot a scene the next day."

I turned to smile at her. She was amazing. I knew we would never have this argument again. Miss D had won because she defied everyone's expectations. That was the victory she needed to finally settle this once and for all.

After that exchange the mood in the car was brighter. We stopped at a vineyard in Amboise to buy a few bottles of wine and at a nearby restaurant to have lunch. Just south of Orleans we found the perfect hotel, the Hotel Le Rivage in Olivet. Our rooms faced the Loiret River, overlooking the gardens, the very view we had imagined in the car. We settled in our room and decided to have cocktails there before dinner at the hotel restaurant.

"Tomorrow, we're going to take the motor route into Paris. Don't you think?" Miss D asked.

"Well, I'm going to look at the map," I said.

"Kathryn is some navigator," Miss D said, as if I had been the one in charge of our route. "She goes on little side roads and things, and ends up smelling like a lily. Everybody gives her directions and they're wrong, and she changes them, and then she figures it out."

"Oh, that sounds absolutely charming the way you are describing it, but you are describing how we were constantly lost," I said.

"No, it's true. It is part of our trip."

"You flabbergast me."

"It is the truth. It is the truth. I dread to have this trip over. The pleasure of your company," she said. "Gawd. Maybe you do know, cuz maybe you miss me as much as I miss you."

"Of course I miss you. I miss you every day. I will take you to some little places in Paris," I said. "But Pierre won't be there. Gawd damn Pierre. He had to go on that last minute trip to London or he'd be with us right now."

"Yes. Gawd damn. I am really sorry."

"So is he because he really wanted to show you his hometown."

"No I'm sorry, sorry I said to you all those years ago that when you were in France you should look up that young man you met in Paris. It is nice, just me and you. I am telling you I will look back on these days many, many times."

We went downstairs to dinner. The food was not spectacular, although we had been spoiled by the delicious lunch we had in Olivet. It did not matter because the atmosphere was sublime. Our table was right on the river and there was a piano player in the bar, just enough distance away that his music was a gentle presence at our meal. He favored jazz standards, a favorite of Miss D's.

I brought up the subject of Pierre again, trying to describe some of the places we might go with him when he could finally join us in Paris. I could see that this topic annoyed Miss D.

"Well I think it's not to spend too much time making plans when it comes to Pierre," she said. "His schedule is not under his control, and besides we can have fun on our own, at your apartment, seeing your friends."

"We always have fun, but we can have more in Paris with Pierre, I think."

"I want so much for you to be happy, Kath. I don't want to say all this but hopefully you'll think about it and have it worry you a bit. I don't approve of Pierre as a permanent part of your life. I will despair of your future if you marry him."

"Really Miss D, I think this is something that is best left to me," I said, bristling. "We are in love. We have given up so much for each other."

"What did he sacrifice for you?" she snapped. "He's here at home and he has a job. You basically were giving up two loves at the same time. A job you loved and a woman you met through this job. Not easy."

I took a sip from my glass of wine as I considered how to answer her. I love Miss D like I love my parents and best friend, no question about it. My love for Pierre was different. She knew this but what was she trying to force me to see?

"Kath, it is your life to live but I want to save you from heartache," she said. "I suppose no one can if you are determined to have it broken by this man. He is weak. Why can't you see it? Plus you take all the blame on yourself. Consider all this carefully, promise me you will."

"I promise you I will consider carefully," I said, although I did not want to see Pierre the way that Miss D described him. I also knew, after the life she had lived and the men she had known, I would be foolish not to consider what she had to say. Her wisdom came from the heart, and from hard experience.

She looked at me coolly.

"You're making the same mistake I made with men. I now know what a fool I was. Guess you'll have to wait a long time to know what I know about supporting men," she continued.

"I'm not supporting him."

"Hasn't he moved into your apartment?"

"It made sense," I said. "I had the nicer flat."

"That's not the only way a woman supports a man, Kath," Miss D said. "Of course you support each other emotionally or this would not be love. You have a job and he has a job, and you do all the housework, correct?"

"Well, yes, I do," I said. "But you know men. They cannot be bothered and soon the place is impossible to live in and you're quarreling all the time."

"I understand that," said Miss D with emphasis. "It has always struck me as an essential imbalance that can break up a love affair. You do the work, but you resent it, and he seems not to notice when you do but he notices when you do not. And if he complains, that's one less bit of love between you."

"I never thought of it that way, Miss D," I said. "When you say it, I can feel a little anger rising in me, though. Am I angry at Pierre?"

"If you are in love, you feel all the emotions," Miss D said. "You feel your emotions as well as his and all of it is powerful. That is love, and I confess even at my age I do miss it. I am ever the optimist, though. Who says I will not fall in love again?"

"I would never count that out, Miss D!"

After a good meal and a fine bottle of wine, we started to go back to both our rooms with a sense of an ending that neither of us wanted to acknowledge. We had had the best time during our days on the road and we had covered a lot of ground, physically and emotionally. The place we started was dark and tumultuous, as if we were still trying to disentangle the many strands that kept us bound. We had been employer and employee, mentor and protégé, mother and daughter, and now, we had all but left those roles and structures far behind us on this road. Now we were truly the best of friends.

I knew we had days ahead to explore Paris together, but we would be among my friends and eventually Pierre. I wanted to hold on to these last hours because I had begun to appreciate how precious our times together were now that we lived so far apart for much of the year. No one understood my dreams the way she did. She had been with me as I matured from a young girl to a young woman, and she had witnessed me imagine the future I was claiming now. She wanted all of it for me, even more than I could imagine.

"You know, Kath, I have been thinking about your domestic predicament," Miss D said, her face momentarily obscured behind an exhalation of smoke. "This is a question of value, is it not?"

"What do you mean?"

"Most men are raised by their mothers to be princes, and that is how they expect their women to treat them as well," she said. "You have a job, and so does he, but his job is the more important one. He cannot be bothered with the cleaning or the laundry. This means that even if you have the better flat and the better job, you have the lesser value. This was always a problem for me with men."

"It seems to be a problem for the ages," I said. "A problem without a solution."

"Can I make a suggestion then?"

"Please."

"When you want to remind someone of your value, you go on strike. You show them what happens when you do not do the things you normally do. Let things go," she said. "Put his clothes in a pile in the corner, not in the hamper, and do not do the dishes. Leave them all in the sink."

"Ew, I don't want to live like that," I said. "I couldn't live with things all over the place."

"That's what he's depending on," she said. "And if you do

it and leave, you do not have to live with it that way. He does."

She was grinning, very amused by the notion of leaving behind chaos, rather than being forced to live in it. After a moment, I was grinning too.

She was still helping me imagine my future.

CHAPTER 16

ROAD TRIP: DAY FOUR
~ORLEANS TO PARIS~
August 6, 1985

"Friends Make Each Other Stronger"

THE NEXT MORNING, a glorious summer day, I came out of my room to find Miss D seated at the dining room table with her wig box in front of her, smiling.

"I'm going to wear my wig today," she said. "*A Paris, c'est magnifique*. To say that I'm excited about getting into Paris is the understatement of the year."

"And we're going out to dinner in Paris!" I said.

"We're not going to tell people we have arrived."

"We will tell no one," I said. "I'll take you to a cute little restaurant near my house where maybe no one will recognize you."

"I'd love that. Without telling anybody, so we can do as we please at first," she said. "It's not very far from here. If we take the motor route."

"I don't worry once we get closer to Paris," I said. "I figure it will take forty-five minutes to find my way. I tell you driving here can be crazy."

"I want to see it all. I want to see Paris at night, to walk down those streets. I cannot wait to see your apartment. I know just what it looks like from all the times you have described it. And your little window where you planted geraniums in the window boxes, the tiny kitchen, I can picture it all."

"We'll have dinner in my apartment one night, too. You and I can go shopping together. I know you will love all the little shops, the cheese shop, the *boulangerie*, the charcuterie. You can meet my friends, and Olivia De Havilland has invited us to dine on the Sunday before you leave. Maggie Nolan, head of *Celebrity News*, has a list of invites for you to go over after you've settled in. It will be fun! Oh, and my apartment, did I tell you, there's no elevator, five flights of stairs. Do you think you can do it?"

"Of course."

We found the motor route easily and were speeding along much faster than we had traveled on the country roads. I missed that slower pace, and when we saw Paris ahead I felt sad that our adventure was coming to an end. We had traveled a great distance together, but I wanted a day or two more. I did not know what it was, but something felt unsettled between us. Then Miss D spoke.

"Kath, I have written a poem for our trip. Do you want to hear it?"

"Of course!"

The Mad Women of Chaillot

From Biarritz to Paris
We were never harassed

or embarrassed
As from town to town
With nary a frown
We had a ball
the two of us
And everyday with no fuss
We drove and drove
Until Paris became a must.

"I love it! We shall write it on your map, and both of us will sign it as a memento of this trip."

"What a great idea. Thank you. We have had a good trip haven't we, Kath? A true chum you are to me, a dear friend."

"Yes, Miss D."

"There is so much I want to live for. I want to live for your future. If I live a lot longer, it will be because of you."

"I want you to live forever."

"And about last night, I want to say one thing more," she said. "You are quite right not to take advice about love from a woman who has been married four times. I have often been the loser at love, so why should you listen to me? I promised myself when I was young that when I was old and gray I would have no regrets in the romance area, and I have kept my promise. I did not ignore my desires. You should follow your own."

"Thank you for that, but I heard everything you said, Miss D, and I understand you were not talking really about Pierre, but about understanding my value."

"Value? I know I said that word to you last night but this morning it did not sit so well with me. It's such a commercial word. We're talking about love, Kath. I want you to understand how eager I am for you to find a man who can love you in the way you deserve and give you everything in life that you dream of."

"That's asking a lot, Miss D," I said.

"Is it? Or is it asking just enough? Never forget, Kath, you are a much stronger person than you think."

I looked in the rearview mirror and saw that the car behind us was a little too close for safety. There were two men in the front and the one in the passenger seat had a camera with a long lens. We were still a few miles from Paris, but the paparazzi had already spotted us.

"Miss D! The car behind us has a photographer!"

"Speed up, Kath! I'm not ready to be photographed!"

Miss D took out her compact and began to smooth her hair as I accelerated, dodging around a few cars to try to lose the car behind us. I did not like driving this fast and was terrified I'd get us into a crash. The car pursuing us swerved into the left lane, then sped up to pull alongside us. I floored it and moved to the right. The car in front of me was puttering along in the slow lane, so I took evasive action and cut across two lanes of traffic to get to the fast lane again. I heard the squealing tires of the other cars as our pursuers maneuvered to catch us.

Miss D was gripping the door rest and had her other hand braced on the dashboard. A glance over at her only increased my anxiety, so I kept my eyes flittering between the road and the rearview mirror. The paparazzi pulled up next to Miss D on the right and I floored it again, speeding quickly up behind a truck before I pulled to the middle lane and accelerated. I had no idea how fast we were going.

A policeman on a motorcycle pulled up alongside me gesturing for me to pull off the road. Oh no, I was not going to allow the paparazzi to get a photograph of a rattled Miss D stopped by the police. I pointed to Miss D. He seemed not to understand why I was gesticulating so dramatically.

"Miss D! Lean over and wave at the officer. We need help!"

Miss D leaned forward and waved at the officer. He immediately recognized who she was. Out of the corner of my eye I saw him pick up his two-way radio. He must have called for back-up because within a few minutes another motorcycle officer, and then another and another, pulled up alongside us on the road. They formed a V in front of us with lights flashing and sirens on, we drove into Paris protected by a phalanx of officers and no paparazzi on our tail.

As we pulled up to my apartment at the Rue Robert Fleury, Miss D reached over and placed her hand on mine.

"We did it, Kath," she said. "We made it."

DENOUEMENT IN
SAN SEBASTIAN

IN THE YEARS since our motor trip through France, my relationship with Miss D continued as the best friends we had become. What Miss D said to me that last day on the road about understanding my value and not settling for something less caused me to look at Pierre with different eyes. We quarreled more after I returned from the road trip. Neither of us was happy, so we recognized that we should end our relationship. I stayed in France and pursued my dream of work in the fashion industry.

Although Miss D and I were separated by an ocean and then a continent, we saw each other several times a year. I only took jobs that offered me the flexibility to go to her when she needed me to prepare her for a movie role or other projects. We toured the United States and Europe when she was promoting *This'N That*, and later for her film *The Whales of August*.

While I was in France, we spoke by phone twice a week,

continued to exchange letters, and communicated in the form of cassette tapes. In these we would ramble freely, describing our surroundings and the pressures and joys of our days. The more specific and insignificant the topic was, the more entertaining the tape would be. In one, I described my apartment and everything I saw on my walk to the Metro, then realized I'd forgotten something at home. I kept recording as I made my way back to the apartment, retrieved the document, and returned to catch the subway. That was one of Miss D's favorite tapes because, she said, she felt like she was right there with me in Paris. For her part, she couldn't figure out how to work the cassette player. Dozens of times her recording would begin with her exclaiming, "Oh no! I think I just taped over a whole side of this." Almost every cassette I received had some version of her sighing, pacing, smoking, and finally saying, "This new girl, Kath,"—*puff*—"well…she's just not working out."—*puff*—"I think I will have to let her go tomorrow." Listening to these cassettes made us feel like we were in the room together, or back on the road from Biarritz to Paris.

For four years we were very busy as she received many awards that celebrated her body of work. After the stroke, she was less dismissive of these ceremonies than she had been years before in Palm Springs when she refused to travel to the Cannes Film Festival. Miss D visited me when she was honored at the Cesars (the French Oscars) and the Deauville Film Festival, and when she received the French Legion d'Honor. She believed she deserved the Kennedy Center award and had been passed over because of her outspoken Democratic politics. But in 1987 the Kennedy Center nominating committee wrote to her asking whom she thought deserved the award and she sent back her own name. They honored her that very year, showing that politics had not been a factor. Ronald Reagan, or "Little Ronny" as she called him from when they had worked together in *Dark Victory*, was the president who placed that medal around her neck.

In January 1989, Miss D and I were in New York when she discovered she had a rash. Her doctor assured us it was nothing. Applying ointment regularly would heal it, he said, but it did not. In April when we were in New York to accept the Lincoln Center Award, I got concerned when we realized that in those four months she had not healed much at all. Miss D's cancer had been in remission for five years, so we did not see it as a sign that it had returned. Back in Los Angeles Dr. Guiliano examined her at the Colonial House and ordered six weeks of radiation.

I closed up my apartment in Paris and moved back into my room at the Colonial House. I stayed with her in her hospital room that first week and was the only one allowed to wheel her into her radiation treatments. We tried to keep her condition a secret by telling the staff that she was being treated for malnutrition, and she did look gaunt. Sure enough during those six weeks the *National Enquirer* published a story headlined: BETTE DAVIS STARVES HERSELF TO DEATH.

After a week, they released her and I took her to the hospital Mondays and Thursdays for the next five weeks for treatment. The radiation wiped her out, of course, but after a day of rest she was up and out of bed, going out to dinner with friends. I kept her spirits up telling her that as soon as she was well we'd be on our way to Spain to accept a lifetime achievement award at the San Sebastian Film Festival. We were even planning another road trip: to Lourdes, which was only two hours from San Sebastian.

As a young Catholic girl, I had been fascinated by the story of Saint Bernadette and the fifteen visions she had of the Blessed Virgin in the caverns at Lourdes. With her bare hands Bernadette dug into the dirt at the place where the Virgin Mary had directed her, and from that place a spring emerged that had miraculous healing qualities. I'd always wanted to visit, and I was happy that Miss D did too.

Miss D was not conventionally religious. She did not attend weekly worship services, but she kept her mother's Bible close at hand on her night table. Raised in the Baptist tradition, she believed in God. To her God showed he was watching over her by giving her signs and portents. She was convinced something greater than she was directing the course of her life. She believed "God helps those who help themselves." Both of us were fascinated by the miracles at Lourdes and wanted to visit to feel the unique energy of the place. As a child when Miss D had measles she dreamed she had been cured at Lourdes, but despite all her world travels it was one place she'd never visited.

Lourdes had touched my life as well. When I crashed through that sliding glass door at the age of seven, a woman who returned from Lourdes brought me a medal that the priests there had blessed because she thought it would help me with my healing. I healed. Although the recuperation was lengthy, I kept that medal nearby. I had shared this story with Miss D and we discussed how much both of us wanted to visit that healing grotto, if Dr. Guiliano would allow her to travel.

To show her doctors her vigor, she went to their office for her appointment instead of receiving them at home. I must say she was brilliant pleading her case. This Oscar-worthy performance persuaded them that she felt great and that seeing her fans would make her feel even better. To our amazement, they agreed. They said the treatment appeared to have killed off any cancer, so she was cleared to go.

Back at the Colonial House our spirits were flying high. She set up her command center in her bed, but soon was up on her feet making lists miles long and directing me whom to call. My datebook shows daily calls to Harold, to the festival director, and to arrange to have her makeup and hair done while we were in Europe, plus dozens of other details prior to our September 13 departure to New York, Paris, Biarritz, and then to San Sebastian.

The day we left, after the doormen took down our thirteen suitcases, each tied with a big red bow, Miss D paused at the doorway. With her hand on the doorknob, she scanned the apartment and then paused to take a long look at her Banjo Clock. "I wonder when I'll see this place again," she said.

I was on red alert from before we left Los Angeles. I had sent ahead a month's supply of her medications and cases of Ensure Plus in case we wanted to, or had to, stay on. We flew from LAX to New York and then to Paris where I had arranged for the famous Michel Deruelle to do her makeup before we arrived in San Sebastian. He was a genius, the best in the business, and knew how to emphasize those Bette Davis Eyes. She looked gorgeous when we boarded the plane to Biarritz.

What a thrill it was to step off the plane when we finally made it to Biarritz and have the Pays Basque Marching Band there to greet us before driving into San Sebastian. The plaza in front of the hotel was jammed with thousands of fans who

had waited hours in the sweltering 90-degree heat, held back
by police at the barricades. When Miss D stepped out of the
limo and onto the red carpet the crowd began to cheer. She
leaned on my arm for a second, positioned herself with her
left hand on the pillar so she could wave to the crowds with
the other. After the darkness of those weeks in the hospital, Miss D was showered with love and light, just what she
needed.

"*Buenos tardes,*" she said, and the crowd roared.

She wanted to greet them and thank them, so we walked
slowly and deliberately to each corner of the courtyard. She
looked better than I had seen her look in years. They say
when someone dies they blossom like a flower. Little did we
know this would be her final wave goodbye to us all.

Each interaction took a lot out of her. When we got to the
hotel suite she met with the director and Pilar Olascoaga, the
general-secretary of the festival, and the person responsible
for inviting Miss D. We unpacked and went over her many responsibilities as the honored guest: private interviews, press
conferences, private luncheons, the presentation of the best
film award, and the gala dinner afterwards.

After the others had left, Miss D took a walk around the
suite, scrutinizing the furniture to determine how we would re-
arrange it. Something caught her eye outside and she walked
to the window to see a banner for the new *Batman* movie with
Michael Keaton and Jack Nicholson that was so huge it took
up most of the front of the building. She chuckled to herself as
she regarded this cartoon figure with his face obscured and his
body swallowed by a floor-length black cape.

"Would you look at that, Kath?" she said. "My era of
Hollywood is over. I've come here to pass the torch."

She may have felt that way, but the fans did not, and they were plentiful everywhere we went. One of her duties was to attend a press conference that was supposed to last an hour. The room was packed with more than two hundred journalists, the most they've ever had to this day. Their knowledge of her life, both professionally and personally, was astounding.

She enjoyed it so much that she gave them two hours. She answered questions about her movie roles and her personal life, including whether or not she was similar to perhaps her most famous character Margo Channing from *All About Eve*. Miss D said she was not because she'd never been obsessed about her age. One reporter asked her what it was like in her era of Hollywood. I think her answer reflected her feeling about seeing Batman outside her window.

"I have no era. I was acting back then and I am still acting," she said. "My era will end the day they put me in my grave."

After a long rest, that evening she received her award, the Donostia. This was a glorious triumph and she looked spectacular standing on the stage bowing to her fans, who had lined the streets for blocks in the pouring rain just to catch a glimpse of her. When the mayor presented her with the prestigious award she stood for a moment, took a long inhale from her cigarette and, looking out at the mass of people, and with a wave of her hand, said, *"Buenas noches"* as the smoke ascended into the audience. The crowd gave her a lengthy standing ovation over ten minutes long for her sixty years spent entertaining them.

The next morning, when Michel arrived to do her makeup, I could tell he was a bit under the weather. There was a flu bug starting to fly around San Sebastian, and I was hyperaware of every sniffle and runny nose, remembering what Miss D had just been through.

Miss D started to sniffle that afternoon and I phoned Dr. Guiliano and Harold. Miss D told me not to worry.

Her final duty was to present the award for the best film, a tie between the film from Bolivia, *La Nacion Clandestina*, and the film from the United States, *Homer and Eddie*. The director, Andrei Konchalovsky, dropped to his feet and knelt before Miss D before taking his award. The crowd burst into enthusiastic applause, a great ending to the ceremonial part of her trip to the festival. She had been a genuine star throughout.

I knew we were in trouble when she told me backstage that she was too tired to go to the gala dinner, something she never would have missed. I just didn't know the depth of the trouble.

The following day, after she'd slept in and felt a little better, she insisted that I go to Lourdes without her. "I need rest and my energy back," she said. "Kath, you always wanted to visit Our Lady of Lourdes. Why not go tomorrow for both of us? We can use all her prayers."

That night we each wrote down our wishes and folded them into tight one-inch squares. In my note I pleaded for her to spare Miss D's life, and both of us asked for blessings on her book.

In the car to Lourdes that next morning, I was somber. I had thought of this as a road trip for us, just like our journey from Biarritz to Paris, but a shorter one because of her health. Sitting in the back of a hired car I thought about the power Lourdes had to heal the sick who came from all over the world. Miss D would get better, I believed. She already looked a bit better, didn't she? She knew her body and her energy level, she was just being cautious. Yet it was undeniable that she was weak and exhausted in a way that sleep did not replenish. All we needed was to get her an IV that had worked so many times before when she was depleted. I was sure if I prayed to the Blessed Virgin at Lourdes, she would help me with Miss D. I even tried bargaining with her: if Miss D pulled through, we'd put her in the updated edition of Miss D's book *The Lonely Life*.

I say with all due reverence that Lourdes is a tourist trap, like an amusement park the size of Disneyland. I didn't expect it to be so big, which was a shock to my system. I had imagined a quiet and reverent place rather than one with every street lined with gift shops selling "holy water" in small plastic bottles with crosses on their fronts.

I had the driver wait as I found my way to the grotto where hundreds of people were lined up. With all these people, how will she ever hear our prayers? I wanted a private place to be alone in, not herded through like cattle. This was a dilemma I didn't expect.

Our Lady must have heard my prayers. When I threw our wishes, they landed right at her feet. A priest gently tapped me on the shoulder. I was so focused and the grotto was so quiet that I thought I jumped ten feet with that unexpected touch. He seemed to know my heart's feeling. He invited me to stay with him in the special place in the grotto where the clergy prays.

I prayed to Our Lady of Lourdes with all my heart. I don't know how long I stayed praying and hoping she'd hear me. As I stood to leave, I asked for a sign to know she heard my prayers. As I turned to exit the grotto, the sky, which had been filled with gray clouds, opened up to bright sunlight and everyone around me exclaimed in reverence. The clouds quickly closed back again, but I felt truly Our Lady had heard me.

On the trip back to San Sebastian, I continued praying as I looked out the window at the countryside. I was staring into the sky and was awestruck when I saw the figure of the Virgin Mary made out in the clouds. I turned away thinking I was delirious, and then looked back. She was still there, and then she was gone. I was now convinced the Blessed Virgin had heard our prayers.

When I returned to the hotel and gave Miss D the holy water and medals of the saints that the priest had kindly blessed, I couldn't believe she had something for me, too. Even though my birthday wasn't until much later in October she had a present for me: a beautiful brown cape with fur trimming that I had admired in one of the shops in the lobby. Exchanging these gifts brought tears to both our eyes, particularly when she had me try on the cape. I felt a pit in my stomach. We had always waited for the actual birthday date to give a gift but I had received my birthday gift two weeks ahead of time.

As the day went on she continued to weaken. I spoke with Dr. Guiliano and Harold every hour. I did not sleep. I tried to remain calm so as not to worry her. After two days when she did not improve, Harold arranged for a medical jet to take her to the American Hospital in Neuilly, a suburb of Paris.

When I was trying to get her dressed for the early morning flight, I found that I could not zip her skirt. Her stomach had expanded within hours like she was having twins. We camouflaged this under her coat just in case we were discovered. There was no time to think about it. Deal with the "Now" of emergency.

We left Spain on Tuesday, October 3. Miss D, despite the illness, was excited about her first flight on a private Learjet. Although the crew brought out a stretcher, Miss D had no intention of using it, and she didn't. She wanted to know about the plane and asked the crew all sorts of questions including their previous destination: Switzerland. She looked at me and said with a droll voice, "Don't tell me what this is costing."

At the American Hospital, as soon as the doctors completed their first round of tests, we asked for a cot for me and set about trying to make the room as homey as possible, uncertain how long we would be there before she was well enough to go home.

The second day the doctor told us she was improving and I could start to make the travel arrangements for us to go home. I was booking a direct flight to Los Angeles when her white cell count went haywire. Her cancer had simply exploded.

The doctor asked me to come out into the hallway for a moment. There he told me that the cancer had rapidly spread and Miss D would not make it. He did not know how long she had: a few hours, a day at most. For all my denials and assurances, I knew deep down that this was so. We agreed that I would tell her first, and a few minutes later he would come in to speak with her more about it.

At times like this, we did not need to speak in words; she knew by the look on my face. Tears welled up in my eyes no matter how hard I tried to hold them back.

"Kath, come here, give me your hand," she said.

I sat on the bed next to her and took her hand. She was growing weak.

"You know, I've had a wonderful life and am so grateful for these last few years. You've given me so much joy and you must always remember that," she said.

I was wiping my tears back and trying not to sniffle.

"Now, you must be strong and you will be. You're my step-daughter and I'm so very proud of you," she continued.

"Miss D, I'm so, so very sorry."

Her inner peace showed on her face, and in the tone of her voice. Miss D had accepted it. She did not have any questions for the doctor, only an apology.

"I'm so sorry to do this to you," she said. "I apologize for the terrible calamity that will ensue when the press finds out that I died here in your hospital."

I will never forget the astonished look on the doctor's face. He was prepared to offer her sympathy but she was offering it to him.

"Please do not put me on any kind of life support," she said. "I want no nurses hovering around, only Kath. You will promise me?"

"Yes, I promise," he said. He started to cry and then he excused himself.

After he left, Miss D told me to call Michael and then Harold. She did not ask me to reach out to Bede. She had her quiet moments with them over the phone, comforting those she loved so deeply. She told me she did not want them to come because she did not want "this bedraggled body and the look of death" to be their last memory of her. She was not worried that I would have the same trouble with my memory of her.

"They don't see me every day like you do, Kath," she said.

"In a few months, you will forget how I look when I pass over and it will fade from your memory. One day you will find the right moment to explain this to them. I'm so proud of Michael and his family. And his boys, I'm only sorry I won't be around to see them grow up to be fine young men."

And she was absolutely right.

I thought I must be strong for her as I had been in the hospital after the stroke, but she wanted to tell stories. We talked about the fire drill at the Berystede, and remembered how grand the staff looked in those yellow fire hats I found in London. We laughed about me going down to the Winter Ball at Georgetown University dressed in my evening gown among all those students who were casually dressed, and the butler and the dancing lessons. We relived how lost we got on our road trip from Biarritz to Paris and how we thought we were going to Cap Ferrat but we ended up in Bordeaux.

Miss D had me laughing so hard my sides were splitting when she said again in that low, droll voice, "Honestly, Kath, I blame the rats."

As she began to weaken, we became more serious. As she came in and out of consciousness for a few moments at a time, I barely spoke. I wanted only to hear her words and her wishes.

Miss D thanked me again for standing by her during the stroke and for bringing her to San Sebastian.

"From the moment I accepted the offer to appear in *Murder with Mirrors*, I dreamed of the day Kath and I would celebrate the completion of the film. There was no celebration. I was denied a final victory because of the news I received by phone from New York two days be-

fore the end of the picture. I was told that my daughter
B.D. had written a book about me and not, rumor had it,
a kind book. My beloved B.D., whom sometimes I loved
over and beyond my love of my work. It was impossible
for me to believe. Even now, having read it, it is just as
impossible for me to believe.

Though robbed of our celebration by this news, the
fact that I had successfully finished my first film after
having all those illnesses was a celebration in itself. As
Kath so often assured me we would, we did "make it."
Once more I had been given proof that one's work is always what one can rely on."

Moments when she woke she was lucid, which gave me
hope that she was still fighting to stay alive. Then I recognized she was fighting to say everything she wanted to say to
me before she died. One of the last times she was alert she
asked me to promise her something.

"Someday you will write about the time you spent with me,
Kath," she said. "And when you do, I want you to start in
Biarritz."

Writing was the farthest thing from my mind then, but I
promised her I would. I spent nearly thirty years trying to
keep that promise.

Friday, October 6, I wore Miss D's necklace with all her good
luck charms, because we needed luck. It was a quiet day
as Miss D was sedated with morphine to help her with her
pain. Around 11:00 p.m. it started to pour buckets. This was
a good sign, I thought, because she loved the rain and said it
always brought good luck. I was praying when I noticed that

her breathing was getting heavy. I squeezed her hand, hoping she would squeeze back as she had those days in the hospital after the stroke, but I got no response. At 11:35 p.m. she no longer inhabited her body but her spirit was all around me. I called for the nurse, who phoned the doctor who came immediately to officially pronounce Miss D's passing. I asked to have an hour alone with her.

I pleaded for Miss D to help me get through all this. My mind was racing about all the tasks I had to complete to get her home. I would need to call so many people, arrange for how her body would be transported and also handle the press. I felt overwhelmed and I did not want to make a single mistake. My panic overcame any fears.

Then I heard her.

"Kath, I'm with you every foot of the way," I heard her say unconsciously in my head. "You're strong. I've taught you well and we'll get through this..."

I felt it was like she was there with me. Whether this was my adrenaline kicking in—or that I was a bit delirious—it worked. The next day I chose the most elegant and most expensive mahogany casket, called the Empress, for her. She was dressed in an elegant black evening dress and matching black fur hat designed especially for her by Patrick Kelly. Harold told me not to do her makeup because he thought it would be too painful for me. But I had made a pact with her and that was all that mattered to me then.

As I worked applying her makeup, I was numb. I did not feel her spirit. The moment I finished, the mood of the room lightened. I felt gratitude, her thanking me. Then my tears came at last. When the morticians came to seal her casket, it suddenly seemed all too real.

We flew back to California on the morning of October 10; the Air France VIP staff protected us. I was allowed on the tarmac to watch the ground crew gingerly load her casket in. They reserved first class seats for Miss D and one for me. We'd taken this flight dozens of times together and I had a sense of her seated next to me, which made me smile, imagining her on this particular flight. Our flight to France from the U.S. was one of the last ones on which passengers were allowed to smoke. What would she have done if they told her she could not smoke on the return trip? Ah well, they always made exceptions for Miss D.

Michael, his wife Chou Chou, Harold, and Miss D's good friend Robin were waiting on the tarmac to greet us when we landed in California. After they paid their respects, I returned to Colonial House to enter it alone for the first time.

In the elevator to the fourth floor, I opened the door and turned off the burglar alarm. It was a cold feeling when I walked in at first. Lupe had not been there that week to make the house cheerful with flowers. I was beyond exhausted, feeling numb and so alone, yet relieved to be back at the Colonial House where I felt protected. Then, I reverently paused before I walked into Miss D's bedroom to turn on a light as if she was there. I looked around her room, and felt despair.

I slowly walked into my own room and collapsed on the bed, trying to comprehend these past few weeks. I quietly in my head started talking to her, wondering if what I heard in France was make believe, or me just trying to get through it the best I could. When suddenly, it was like I heard her again.

"Kath, I'm here with you." I sat up on the bed, and it was like I felt her presence right there in the room with me.

It was the most bizarre yet comforting feeling. Then, I heard her.

"Kath, remember what we had said whoever went first would leave a sign. Go look at the Banjo Clock and see at what time it stopped."

I walked out into the hallway, thinking I'd gone mad and there stood the Banjo Clock stopped at the exact time of her passing in France minus the eight hour time difference.

I stared at the clock for the longest time before touching it. I ran my hands over the smooth wood and traced the engraving with my fingertips, thinking about the last few days in San Sebastian and all the promises fulfilled since then. I felt peace at being home, a feeling of being protected by her, and I knew I could not tell a soul about this clock. It was better to keep this between me and Miss D.

I do not profess to know what happens when we die. I do know I still feel her protecting me. People often ask me if I miss her, and I say that I still feel her presence around me. Especially while writing this book. It's so much a part of her. In the end this book is an account of Miss D's final wishes, her final say, and even in her own words, setting the record straight. It is the story she made me promise to tell in the inscription she wrote in her 1959 American College Dictionary, which I discovered that she had left for me after she passed.

Thank you Miss D for your beautiful gift, "you did stand me in good stead while writing 'The Legend.'"
    Love, G.G.

And to her fans, this book is her gift to you with love.

ACKNOWLEDGMENTS

The writing of every book is a story of its own, and mine began nearly thirty years ago, when Miss D made me promise that I would tell "our story"—and that when I did, I should start it in Biarritz, France. After all that we had been through in the ten years I had been her employee, protégé, and friend, that seemed like a peculiar place to begin our tale. I spent decades writing this story—in my apartment, taking leave from jobs to work on it, hiding away at friends' vacation homes, pretending to write directly to Miss D, and yet I could not get it right until I started it, as she had recommended, in Biarritz. Thank you, Miss D! Perhaps our journey would have been told much sooner if I'd followed her suggestion from the beginning.

At last I am at the culmination of fulfilling that promise, and I find myself with so many people to thank. First and foremost: Michael Gornall, a very dear friend who twenty-eight years ago encouraged me to start it, at no matter the cost, and has stood by me through thick and thin—to the very end. My incredible literary agent and friend, Joy Tutela, who stuck by me all these years, always believing in this book and never giving up on it. Danelle Morton, an amazing and talented writer, who helped me find the heart and the love that was in our story.

To my supportive team at Hachette Books: Michelle Howry, my editor, who has been so enthusiastic from the beginning and who went the extra mile for this book; the publishing team of Betsy Hulsebosch, Michael Barrs, Joanne Pinsker, and Lauren Hummel, for helping me plan a great launch; and the production crew consisting of Melanie Gold, Marie Mundaca, and Jennifer Runty, who worked incredibly hard to meet all the deadlines. To Amanda Kain, for the brilliant and captivating cover that uses one of my favorite images of Miss D, one that was also made into a painting (that I treasure) by J. Elneth. And to my publisher, Mauro DiPreta, and his associate publisher, Michelle Aielli, for giving *Miss D & Me* a place on the Hachette Books list.

Heartfelt thanks, too, to my social media gurus, for your expertise and creative genius. Nikki Lazos, who operates the Bette Davis and Miss D and Me Facebook pages, Instagram, Twitter, etc.; the team at CMG and Ryan Pluckebaum, who represent the Bette Davis Estate; Tony Zawinul at Zawinul Media, for his work on my promo video; and Matt Hanover at The Hanover Group. Thank you.

I would like to thank R.J. Wagner who, when he asked me if I had an attorney and I told him I didn't, said, "Stay right there, don't make a move; I'm calling you right back." And he did. In minutes, I had the most brilliant lawyer, Jeffrey Briggs, who has become one of my dearest and loyal friends. I do not make a move without his wise counsel. Through thick and thin, he never gave up on me or this book. Inch by inch he stood steadfast and never wavered, always telling me, "It's going to be great, Kath." You made this book possible, Jeff, for without you, I'm not sure it would have happened. It might have taken another twenty-eight years. From my heart and Miss D's, thank you.

And to Miss D's friends who knew her and reached out to me in support of this book, I'm forever grateful: José Eber,

Greg Gorman, George Hamilton, Olivia de Havilland, John Hough, Carol Kane, R.J. Wagner and Jill St. John, Ann-Margret, Roddy McDowall, Robert Osborne, Stefanie Powers, and Geena Davis and her Institute on Gender in Media.

Every writer needs support outside the professional realm, and I had a mighty army of supporters from my team of friends: Helen Ann de Werd, Mario and Bernadette Viviano, Veronique and Nicolas, Dr. and Mrs. Donald Cannan and family, Emma Baksi, Sandra Becker, Ronee Bernes, Christie Burton, Heidi Crane, Robert Crivell, John Downey III, Steve Forest, Dottie Galliano, Danny McCall, Gor Megaera, Sheila Mitchell, Marc Nuno, James Radiches, Doug Troland, and David Ybarra.

Specific thanks to Cyrus Copeland and Lori Nelson for their astute comments on the drafts. As writers, your insights were so valuable, and they helped me make some important decisions. Jane Scovell, who many years ago came up with the title *Miss D & Me*.

Special thanks to Michael Merrill, Miss D's son, who has been a steady friend to me for the past twenty-eight years. He has been generous in support of the book, granting me complete freedom to tell this story as I saw it. He knows, as only someone who knew Miss D well does, that she would not hesitate to describe the good along with the bad. I know he believes that ultimately I was doing this also for her fans, who have encouraged me to write this book. Thank you so much for your patience.

And to Stephanie Longmire Lazic, one of my best friends, like a sister to me. You're a fabulous editor; you relentlessly read, reread, edited, and made heartfelt changes. I'm forever grateful to you.

A very special thanks to my family, who have been listening to me talk about this book forever. They held their tongues as I took part-time jobs to write (and then I still couldn't get it done!). They did not criticize me when I put the book on the back burner, only to start it once again. I'm sure they were worried about me, but they only offered me love and support. Thank you to Pam, Coleen, Cas, Judy, and your other halves for remaining by my side.

In recent years my parents passed on. My father died, at the age of ninety-five, just as I was finishing the manuscript. He stayed with me to the end, to the moment when I sent the final pages off, and I am so grateful to him for that. We as a family celebrated his life, and I can do that wholeheartedly now that I see more clearly, through writing this book, exactly how important he and my mother were to me. And to the rest of the Sermak Clan. You all know who you are, and that I love you.

In 1997, Michael Merrill and I decided to create the Bette Davis Foundation to continue Miss D's legacy in the arts. This nonprofit and tax-exempt institution awards scholarships to outstanding college students who show promise in the craft that Miss Davis was, for many, the epitome of excellence. In conjunction with the scholarships, a Bette Davis Lifetime Achievement Award is presented to an actor or actress whose work exemplifies the high standards Miss Davis set forth.

For more information about the Bette Davis Foundation, or to make a contribution in honor of this remarkable woman, please contact:

The Bette Davis Foundation, Inc.

c/o Michael Merrill

100 State Street

Boston, MA 02109

BetteDavis.com/foundation/